Navigating California Statutory Laws, Codes, and Regulations for LPCCs

A Practical Desk Reference for LPCCs, Associates, and Trainees

BY: DANIEL STEWART, PHD

DISCLAIMER: This book is intended for informational purposes only and does not constitute legal or ethical advice. The information contained herein is based on publicly available sources and is believed to be accurate at the time of publication. However, ethics, laws, and regulations are subject to change, and the information presented may not reflect the most current legal or ethical developments. This book is not a substitute for professional legal advice. Readers are strongly advised to consult with a qualified attorney licensed in their jurisdiction for legal advice regarding their specific circumstances. The author and publisher of this book disclaim any and all liability for any actions taken or not taken based on the information contained herein. Any reference to individuals by name or case scenarios provided are fictitious and do not represent a real individual or actual client data.

The information provided in this book should not be relied upon as a definitive statement of the law or ethics. It is essential to refer to the official ethical standards, statutes, regulations, and case law for complete and accurate information. Specifically, this book is not intended to provide guidance on clinical decision-making, specific ethical, legal cases or situations, the application of the law to individual circumstances, the interpretation of specific legal terms or provisions, or any legal strategy or course of action. Readers are solely responsible for their own ethical decisions, legal decisions, and actions. The author and publisher make no representations or warranties, express or implied, regarding the accuracy, completeness, or suitability of the information contained in this book. The views expressed herein are those of the author and do not necessarily reflect the views of any organizations or institutions. By reading this book, you acknowledge and agree to this disclaimer.

Copyright © 2025 Daniel Stewart

All rights reserved.

No part of this publication may be reproduced, distributed, or transmitted in any form or by any means, including photocopying, recording, or other electronic or mechanical methods, without the prior written permission of the author, except in the case of brief quotations embodied in critical reviews and certain other noncommercial uses permitted by copyright law.

ISBN-13: 979-8-9929732-1-1

TABLE OF CONTENTS

INTRODUCTION vii
CHAPTER 1: EDUCATION AND LICENSURE REQUIREMENTS 1
   EDUCATIONAL PATHWAYS AND DEGREE REQUIREMENTS 1
   OUT-OF-STATE EDUCATION EVALUATION 4
   INTERNATIONAL CREDENTIALS ASSESSMENT PROCESS 7
   EXAMINATION PROCESS AND REQUIREMENTS 11
   PRACTICUM REQUIREMENTS AND GUIDELINES 16
   POST DGREE SUPERVISED PROFESSIONAL EXPERIENCE 21
   HOUR TRACKING AND DOCUMENTATION 25
   LICENSE APPLICATION PROCESS 30
CHAPTER 2: SCOPE OF PROFESSIONAL COUNSELING 35
   DEFINING PROFESSIONAL CLINICAL COUNSELING 35
   PSYCHOLOGICAL TESTING PARAMETERS 39
   TREATMENT PLANNING AND ASSESSMENT 44
   CRISIS INTERVENTION BOUNDARIES 50
   BOUNDARIES WITH OTHER PROFESSIONS 55
   EMERGING PR ACTICE AREAS 58
CHAPTER 3: PROFESSIONAL PRACTICE STANDARDS 65
   CREATING COMPLIANT INFORMED CONSENT DOCUMENTS 65
   ETHICAL FEE SETTING AND BILLING 70
   ADVERTISING AND MARKETING LEGAL BOUNDARIES 76
   DOCUMENTATION AND LEGAL COMPLIANCE 80
   PROFESSIONAL COMMUNICATIONS PROTOCOL 85
   PRACTICE POLICIES AND PROCEDURES 91
CHAPTER 4: MANDATED REPORTING FOR MINORS 97

UNDERSTANDING REASONABLE SUSPICION STANDARDS 97
IMMEDIATE RESPONSE PROTOCOL 102
CONSENSUAL SEXUAL ACTIVITY GUIDELINES 107
PENALTIES, LEGAL PROTECTIONS AND IMMUNITY 112
CHAPTER 5: ADULT MANDATED REPORTING 117
UNDERSTANDING ADULT ABUSE CATEGORIES 117
REASONABLE SUSPICION STANDARDS 121
GATHERING REQUIRED REPORT INFORMATION 124
INTERACTING WITH ADULT PROTECTIVE SERVICES 125
PENALTIES, LEGAL PROTECTIONS FOR REPORTERS 128
CHAPTER 6: CONFIDENTIALITY AND LEGAL DUTIES 133
FOUNDATIONS OF CLIENT CONFIDENTIALITY 133
LEGAL EXCEPTIONS TO CONFIDENTIALITY 140
MORE ON DUTY TO WARN REQUIREMENTS 146
MANAGING SUICIDAL IDEATION DISCLOSURE 150
ELECTRONIC COMMUNICATION PRIVACY 154
MULTI-PARTY CONFIDENTIALITY CHALLENGES 158
PROFESSIONAL CONSULTATION PROTOCOL 161
CHAPTER 7: RECORD KEEPING REQUIREMENTS 165
LEGAL REQUIREMENTS FOR CLINICAL RECORDS 165
CLIENT ACCESS RIGHTS MANAGEMENT 167
ESSENTIAL DOCUMENTATION COMPONENTS 172
RECORDS STORAGE AND ACCESS PROTOCOL 173
THIRD-PARTY RECORD REQUESTS 177
CHAPTER 8: HIPAA COMPLIANCE 181
UNDERSTANDING HIPAA'S CORE COMPONENTS 181
PROTECTED HEALTH INFORMATION GUIDELINES 185

ELECTRONIC SECURITY MEASURES	188
CLIENT RIGHTS AND ACCESS	194
SPECIAL CIRCUMSTANCES AND EXCEPTIONS	198
BUSINESS ASSOCIATE AGREEMENTS	203
BREACH NOTIFICATION PROTOCOLS	206
CHAPTER 9: PROFESSIONAL CONDUCT AND ETHICS	211
DEFINING UNPROFESSIONAL CONDUCT	211
SEXUAL MISCONDUCT AND BOUNDARY VIOLATIONS	217
MANAGING DUAL RELATIONSHIPS	221
MAINTAINING PROFESSIONAL BOUNDARIES	225
INVESTIGATION AND ENFORCEMENT PROCEDURES	229
CHAPTER 10: MENTAL HEALTH HOLDS	235
UNDERSTANDING 5150 HOLD CRITERIA	235
EMERGENCY RESPONSE PROTOCOLS	240
CULTURAL CONSIDERATIONS IN CRISIS	241
CHAPTER 11: WORKING WITH MINOR CLIENTS	247
LEGAL FOUNDATIONS OF MINOR CONSENT	247
DIVORCED PARENTS AND TREATMENT DECISIONS	250
FOSTER CARE CLIENT PROTOCOLS	254
EMANCIPATED MINOR TREATMENT GUIDELINES	256
CAREGIVER AUTHORIZATION PROCEDURES	257
RECORDS MANAGEMENT FOR MINOR CLIENTS	260
CRISIS INTERVENTION WITH MINORS	264
MULTI-STAKEHOLDER COMMUNICATION PROTOCOLS	265
CHAPTER 12: TELEHEALTH PRACTICE REQUIREMENTS	269
TELEHEALTH FOR THE PROFESSIONAL COUNSELOR	269
VIRTUAL SESSION SECURITY PROTOCOLS	271

REMOTE CRISIS MANAGEMENT PROCEDURES 276
  VIRTUAL SESSION BEST PRACTICES 279
  INTERSTATE PRACTICE REGULATIONS 283
CHAPTER 13: LEGAL PROCEEDINGS 287
  UNDERSTANDING LEGAL DOCUMENT TYPES 287
  MANAGING ATTORNEY COMMUNICATIONS 291
  SPECIAL CIRCUMSTANCES AND EXCEPTIONS 295
  NAVIGATING DEPOSITIONS 296
  PREPARING FOR COURT TESTIMONY AS FACT WITNESS 299
  EXPERT WITNESS GUIDELINES 304
Subject Index 309
Laws, Codes & Regulations References 311

INTRODUCTION

Professional clinical counseling stands at the intersection of mental health care, legal obligations, and ethical responsibilities. This book aims to guide counselors through the complex web of laws and regulations that govern their practice. Whether you're a student preparing for licensure, a newly licensed professional, or an experienced counselor seeking clarity on specific regulations, this resource provides the essential knowledge needed to practice legally and ethically.

The field of professional clinical counseling has evolved substantially over the past several years. What began as a profession with limited recognition has developed into a well established mental health discipline with specific legal definitions, educational requirements, and practice parameters. As the profession has grown, so too have the laws and regulations that define and govern it.

For many counselors, navigating these legal requirements can feel overwhelming. The rules are numerous, sometimes ambiguous, and frequently changing. A misstep can have serious consequences, from licensing board complaints to civil liability, or even criminal charges in extreme cases. Yet most counseling programs provide only basic coverage of these critical legal issues, leaving many practitioners feeling uncertain about their legal obligations.

This uncertainty can lead to two problematic responses. Some counselors practice defensively, restricting their services unnecessarily out of fear of legal repercussions. Others may inadvertently violate regulations simply because they aren't aware of specific requirements. Neither approach serves clients well or allows counselors to practice with confidence.

My own journey into this topic began during my early years as a clinical counselor. Despite excellent training in therapeutic techniques and ethical principles, I found myself repeatedly searching for clear answers to practical questions: What exactly falls within my scope of practice? When must I break confidentiality? How should I respond to a subpoena? What documentation am I legally required to maintain?

These questions led me to dive deeply into the laws and regulations governing our profession. I discovered that while the information existed, it was scattered across numerous sources, licensing board publications, state codes, federal regulations, case law, and professional association guidelines. Assembling this information into a coherent framework required years of research, consultation with attorneys, and practical application.

This book represents the resource I wish I'd had when beginning my practice. It brings together the essential legal knowledge that every professional clinical counselor needs, presented in accessible language with practical examples. Rather than simply listing regulations, each chapter explains the reasoning behind the requirements and offers concrete strategies for implementation.

The laws and regulations covered in this book serve several important purposes. First, they protect clients by establishing minimum standards of care and ethical practice. Second, they define the boundaries of our profession, distinguishing clinical counseling from other mental health disciplines. Third, they provide a framework for resolving ethical dilemmas and making sound clinical decisions.

Understanding these regulations also benefits counselors directly. Knowledge of legal requirements reduces anxiety about potential violations and allows for more confident practice. It helps counselors establish clear boundaries with clients and collaborate effectively with other professionals. Perhaps most importantly, it enables counselors to focus on what matters most, providing effective therapeutic services to those in need.

This book addresses the specific laws and regulations applicable to professional clinical counselors, with particular attention to California's legal framework. However, many of the principles discussed apply broadly across jurisdictions, and the book notes important variations where relevant.

The chapters are organized to follow the natural progression of a counselor's career and practice responsibilities. We begin with the fundamental definition of professional clinical counseling and its scope of practice, then move through education and licensure requirements, standards for professional practice, ethical obligations, and specific legal duties such as mandated reporting and confidentiality.

Later chapters address specialized topics including record-keeping requirements, HIPAA compliance, psychiatric holds, telehealth practice, working with minors, and participation in legal proceedings. Each chapter includes practical examples, case studies, and templates to help readers apply the information to everyday situations.

Throughout the book, you'll find *Practice Point* sections highlighting key information and *Common Pitfall* warnings about frequently misunderstood regulations. The appendices include sample forms, checklists, and resources for further information.

It's worth noting what this book is not. It is not a substitute for legal advice in specific situations. When facing complex legal questions in your practice, consultation with an attorney familiar with mental health law remains essential. This book also does not replace the need for ongoing education about changing regulations. Laws evolve, and counselors must stay informed about new requirements affecting their practice.

What this book does provide is a solid foundation of legal knowledge that will help you practice with greater confidence and competence. Through a review of the laws and regulations that govern our profession, you can focus more fully on what brought you to this field, helping clients achieve positive change through the therapeutic relationship.

The practice of professional clinical counseling carries both privilege and responsibility. We are entrusted with clients' most personal struggles and vulnerabilities. The laws and regulations outlined in this book provide the framework within which we exercise that trust. By practicing within these guidelines, we protect our clients, our profession, and ourselves.

As you read through these chapters, I encourage you to approach the material not merely as rules to follow but as a structure that supports ethical practice. The regulations may sometimes seem burdensome, but they exist to uphold the core values of our profession: client welfare, respect for autonomy, professional competence, and social responsibility.

My hope is that this book will serve as a trusted companion throughout your counseling career, providing clarity when questions arise and confidence as you navigate the complex terrain of professional practice. The work you do matters deeply, and understanding the legal parameters of that work allows you to serve your clients with both compassion and competence.

CHAPTER ONE

EDUCATION AND LICENSURE REQUIREMENTS

EDUCATIONAL PATHWAYS AND DEGREE REQUIREMENTS

Business and Professions Code 4999.33 establishes the educational requirements for becoming a licensed professional clinical counselor in California. The Board of Behavioral Sciences (BBS) has approved specific clinical degrees that meet these requirements, which serve as the foundation for developing the knowledge and skills necessary for effective counseling practice.

To qualify for licensure as a professional clinical counselor, candidates must complete a master's degree in counseling or a closely related mental health field. This degree must consist of at least 60 semester units (or 90 quarter units) of graduate-level coursework from an accredited institution. The educational institution must hold regional accreditation, which confirms the school meets established standards for educational quality. Programs accredited by the Council for Accreditation of Counseling and Related Educational Programs (CACREP) are particularly valued, as they follow specific standards designed for counselor preparation.

The core curriculum mandated by Business and Professions Code 4999.33 includes several essential knowledge domains, each with minimum credit hour requirements:

Counseling theory and techniques requires a minimum of 3 semester units. This area introduces students to major therapeutic approaches such as cognitive-behavioral, person-centered, psychodynamic, and solution-focused methods. Students learn to evaluate these approaches and begin forming their own theoretical orientation.

Human growth and development requires at least 3 semester units covering theories of individual and family development across the lifespan. This coursework examines normal and abnormal personality development, human behavior patterns, developmental crises, and disability factors that affect clients.

Career development theory requires at least 3 semester units covering career development theories, occupational information sources, assessment tools, and techniques for facilitating career planning and decision-making.

Group counseling theory and practice requires a minimum of 3 semester units plus experiential components examining group dynamics, leadership styles, and theories of group counseling. Students learn about developmental stages of groups and methods for designing and facilitating various types of groups.

Assessment and testing requires at least 3 semester units covering standardized and non-standardized assessment techniques, test construction, and the appropriate use and interpretation of various assessment tools. Students learn about the limitations of assessment instruments and ethical considerations in their application.

Social and cultural diversity requires at least 3 semester units examining how factors such as culture, ethnicity, nationality, age, gender, sexual orientation, mental and physical characteristics, education, and socioeconomic status impact counseling relationships. Students develop awareness of their own cultural values while learning strategies for working with diverse populations.

Psychopathology requires at least 3 semester units covering the classification, diagnosis, and treatment of mental disorders according to current diagnostic systems like the DSM-5 TR. Students learn to recognize symptoms, understand causal factors, and develop appropriate treatment plans.

Research and program evaluation requires a minimum of 3 semester units introducing research methods, statistical analysis, and the application of research findings to counseling practice. This coursework helps counselors evaluate the effectiveness of their interventions.

Professional ethics requires a minimum of 3 semester units dedicated to ethical standards established by professional organizations like the American Counseling Association, legal requirements governing counseling practice, and decision-making models for resolving ethical dilemmas. Topics include confidentiality, informed consent, boundary issues, and cultural considerations.

Psychopharmacology requires at least 3 semester units covering the biological foundations of behavior and major classifications of commonly prescribed psychotropic medications. Students learn to identify medication indications, contraindications, and potential side effects, and to make appropriate referrals for medical evaluation.

Addictions counseling requires at least 3 semester units covering substance use disorders, co-occurring conditions, and various models of addiction treatment. Coursework examines prevention strategies, legal and medical aspects of addiction, and the role of support systems and community resources in recovery.

Crisis and trauma counseling requires at least 3 semester units addressing immediate and long-term responses to crises, trauma, and disasters. Students learn crisis theory, trauma assessment, and intervention techniques for supporting individuals with mental health needs during acute emergencies.

Advanced counseling and psychotherapeutic theories requires at least 3 semester units covering clinical applications of counseling theories, assessment strategies, and treatment planning. Students deepen their understanding of therapeutic relationships, psychopathology, and advanced intervention techniques.

Beyond these core areas, programs typically include specialized coursework in areas such as human sexuality, family systems, and spousal/partner abuse, amongst others for a minimum of 15 units.

Students must also complete a supervised practicum or internship that includes direct counseling experience. This requirement is fully detailed in the 'Practicum Requirements and Guidelines' section. Many programs also require students to complete a comprehensive examination or capstone project demonstrating their mastery of core counseling concepts and skills.

These educational requirements directly connect to the licensure process. After completing their degree, graduates must accumulate additional supervised experience hours as post-graduate associates before becoming eligible to take the licensure examination. The coursework completed during their master's program prepares them for this examination, which tests their understanding of counseling theories, ethical standards, assessment techniques, and other key knowledge areas.

OUT-OF-STATE EDUCATION EVALUATION

The California Board of Behavioral Sciences (BBS) maintains specific procedures for evaluating out-of-state education credentials when counselors from other states seek licensure in California (Business and Professions Code 4999.61). This evaluation process ensures that all practitioners meet California's standards regardless of where they completed their education. Understanding this process is essential for out-of-state counselors who wish to practice in California without repeating their entire educational journey.

When submitting out-of-state credentials for review, applicants must first complete the Application for Licensure, which includes sections specifically addressing out-of-state education. This application requires basic information about the applicant's degree program, including the institution name, location, degree title, and completion date. The application serves as the starting point for the credential evaluation process, but it's only the beginning of a thorough review.

Applicants must arrange for official transcripts to be sent directly from their educational institution to the BBS. These transcripts must be sealed and unopened to maintain their official status. The BBS will not accept transcripts submitted by the applicant, as this could compromise the integrity of the documents. For institutions that use electronic transcript services, the BBS accepts transcripts sent through secure, verifiable electronic methods.

The course-by-course evaluation represents the most detailed aspect of the credential review. The BBS examines each course on the applicant's transcript to determine whether it fulfills California's specific content requirements. Applicants are evaluated on 13 content areas outlined in Business and Professions Code 4999.33, as described in the 'Educational Pathways and Degree Requirements' section.

For each content area, the BBS looks for specific elements that must be covered in the coursework. For example, the multicultural counseling requirement must include instruction on counselors' cultural self-awareness, knowledge of cultural differences, and skills for working with diverse populations. The BBS may request course descriptions, syllabi, or other materials to determine whether courses adequately cover the required content.

The BBS uses a worksheet to track which requirements have been met and which remain outstanding. This worksheet becomes part of the applicant's file and guides any remediation that may be necessary. If gaps are identified, the BBS will specify exactly which content areas need additional coursework.

Out-of-state applicants face several additional requirements beyond the standard educational evaluation. They must document their supervised experience hours, which may have been completed under different guidelines than California requires. The BBS will evaluate these hours to determine how many can be credited toward California's requirements. Often, out-of-state applicants must complete additional supervised experience to meet California's standards. Applicants must also pass California's law and ethics examination, regardless of whether they've passed similar exams in other states.

Common challenges in the evaluation process include incomplete documentation, courses that partially but not fully meet California's requirements, and differences in how supervised experience was structured and documented. To address these challenges, applicants should:

1. Request detailed course descriptions and syllabi from their graduate programs well in advance of applying
2. Maintain complete records of all supervised experience, including supervisor qualifications and the nature of the clinical work performed
3. Begin the application process early, allowing time to address any deficiencies identified by the BBS
4. Consider consulting with a license preparation service familiar with California's requirements
5. Contact the BBS directly with specific questions about their individual situation

Applicants with coursework deficiencies may need to take additional graduate-level courses or complete supervised experience. See the 'International Credentials Assessment Process' section for a detailed explanation of common gaps and remediation strategies, many of which also apply to out-of-state applicants. For supervised experience shortfalls, they can register as Associate Professional Clinical Counselors and complete additional hours under supervision. In some cases, substantial experience as a licensed counselor in another state may partially offset educational deficiencies, though this is evaluated on a case-by-case basis.

INTERNATIONAL CREDENTIALS ASSESSMENT PROCESS

The California Board of Behavioral Sciences (BBS) maintains specific procedures for evaluating international counseling credentials that differ in several key aspects from the evaluation of out-of-state credentials. International applicants face unique challenges related to educational equivalency, documentation, and translation requirements (Business and Professions Code 4999.40). Counselors trained outside the U.S. can navigate licensure more confidently by becoming familiar with these procedures in advance.

International applicants must begin by submitting their credentials to a BBS-approved foreign credential evaluation service. The BBS accepts evaluations from members of the National Association of Credential Evaluation Services (NACES). This organization specialize in analyzing foreign educational credentials and determining their U.S. equivalency. Popular evaluation services include World Education Services (WES), Educational Credential Evaluators (ECE), and International Education Research Foundation (IERF).

When selecting an evaluation service, applicants should request a *"course-by-course"* evaluation rather than a basic credential evaluation. The course-by-course analysis provides detailed information about each course taken, including U.S. semester unit equivalents and course content descriptions. This level of detail is necessary for the BBS to determine whether the applicant's education meets California's specific content requirements as outlined in Business and Professions Code (BPC) Section 4999.33.

All documents submitted to the credential evaluation service must be official and sent directly from the educational institution. The evaluation service will not accept documents provided by the applicant, as this could compromise the integrity of the evaluation process. For institutions that no longer exist or are in countries experiencing political unrest, the evaluation service may have alternative verification procedures, but these are determined on a case-by-case basis.

Non-English documents require certified translations. The BBS accepts translations completed by:

1. A certified translator who is a member of the American Translators Association
2. The foreign credential evaluation service itself, if they offer translation services
3. A translation service that provides a certificate of accuracy
4. The educational institution issuing the original documents, if they offer official translation services

Self-translated documents are not accepted under any circumstances. The translation must include all information from the original document, including stamps, seals, and signatures. Both the original document and the certified translation must be submitted to the evaluation service.

The BBS recognizes several international accreditation bodies when evaluating foreign credentials. For programs in Canada, accreditation by the Canadian Counselling and Psychotherapy Association (CCPA) is recognized. For European programs, the European Association for Counselling (EAC) provides standards that may be considered. However, unlike with domestic CACREP accreditation, international accreditation does not automatically satisfy California's requirements. The BBS still conducts a detailed review of course content regardless of the program's accreditation status.

The credential equivalency determination process involves multiple steps. First, the evaluation service determines whether the applicant's degree is equivalent to a U.S. master's degree or higher. California requires a minimum of a master's degree in counseling or a related field with at least 60 semester units (or the equivalent) of graduate-level coursework.

Next, the BBS examines whether the program included the specific content areas required by California law. The BBS also verifies that the program included a practicum or supervised field experience component with at least 280 hours of face-to-face counseling experience. This requirement is specified in BPC Section 4999.33.

International applicants often need to complete additional coursework or training to meet California's requirements. Common areas where international programs may fall short include:

1. California-specific content: All applicants must complete coursework in California law and ethics (minimum 3 semester units) and child abuse assessment and reporting (minimum 7 hours).
2. Total unit count: Many international master's programs are shorter than U.S. programs and may not meet the 60-semester unit minimum.
3. Specific content areas: International programs may emphasize different aspects of counseling based on cultural or regional approaches to mental health.
4. Practicum hours: Some international programs have limited supervised practice components.

When deficiencies are identified, applicants must complete additional coursework at regionally accredited institutions in the United States. The BBS provides a detailed list of outstanding requirements, and applicants can take these courses at graduate schools offering counseling programs or through BBS-approved continuing education providers for certain topics.

International applicants face several common challenges during the evaluation process:

1. Documentation difficulties: Obtaining official transcripts from institutions in certain countries can be challenging, especially if political instability or natural disasters have affected record-keeping systems.
2. Educational system differences: Some countries structure higher education differently, making direct comparisons to U.S. semester units difficult.
3. Course content variability: Counseling approaches and theories taught internationally may differ substantially from those emphasized in U.S. programs.

4. Supervised experience documentation: Standards for documenting supervised practice vary widely across countries. 5. Timeline and cost: The international evaluation process typically takes longer and costs more than domestic credential reviews.

To navigate these challenges, international applicants should follow these step-by-step guidelines:

Step 1: Research California's requirements thoroughly before beginning the application process. Review the BBS website and BPC Sections 4999.30-4999.46 to understand the specific requirements.

Step 2: Contact a BBS-approved foreign credential evaluation service and request information about their process, timeline, and fees. Select a service that offers course-by-course evaluation.

Step 3: Gather all required documentation from your educational institution(s), including official transcripts, course descriptions, and practicum documentation. Request these documents well in advance, as obtaining them may take several months.

Step 4: Arrange for certified translations of all non-English documents through an approved translation service.

Step 5: Submit all documents to the credential evaluation service and pay the required fees. Be prepared for the evaluation to take 2-3 months or longer.

Step 6: Once you receive the evaluation report, review it carefully to understand which California requirements have been met and which remain outstanding.

Step 7: Submit your Application for Licensure or Registration to the BBS, including the foreign credential evaluation report and all supporting documentation.

Step 8: If the BBS identifies deficiencies, develop a plan to complete the required coursework at U.S. institutions. Consult with the BBS about specific courses that will satisfy the requirements.

Step 9: Complete any additional requirements, such as the California law and ethics examination, fingerprinting, and supervised experience hours.

Step 10: Maintain regular communication with the BBS throughout the process, as requirements may change or additional documentation may be requested.

The BBS provides specific guidance for international applicants in BPC Section 4999.40, which states that an applicant for licensure *"trained in an educational institution outside the United States shall demonstrate to the satisfaction of the board that he or she possesses a qualifying degree that is equivalent to a degree earned from a regionally accredited institution of higher education in the United States."*

When international applicants ensure they have a good understanding of these requirements and follow the established procedures, they can successfully navigate the credential evaluation process and work toward licensure in California. While the process is rigorous and often lengthy, it ensures that all counselors practicing in California meet the same high standards, regardless of where they received their training.

EXAMINATION PROCESS AND REQUIREMENTS

The California Board of Behavioral Sciences (BBS) requires candidates seeking licensure as Professional Clinical Counselors to successfully complete two examinations that assess both clinical knowledge and understanding of legal and ethical standards. These examinations serve as gatekeepers to ensure that only qualified professionals enter the field, protecting both the public and the integrity of the profession.

The examination process consists of two distinct tests: the California Law and Ethics Examination and the National Clinical Mental Health Counseling Examination (NCMHCE). Each examination evaluates different aspects of professional competency and must be passed sequentially as part of the licensure journey.

For the California Law and Ethics Examination, Associate Professional Clinical Counselors (APCCs) must apply within the first year of receiving their associate registration. According to Business and Professions Code (BPC) Section 4999.53, this examination specifically tests knowledge of California laws and regulations related to the practice of professional clinical counseling, as well as ethical standards established by professional organizations.

Eligibility for the Law and Ethics Examination begins once an individual receives their APCC registration number from the BBS. The application process requires submission of the *"Examination Eligibility Application"* form along with the current examination fee, which as of 2025 is $150. The BBS typically processes these applications within 4-6 weeks, after which candidates receive an eligibility notice allowing them to schedule their examination with the testing vendor.

The Law and Ethics Examination consists of 75 multiple-choice questions administered via computer at designated testing centers throughout California. Candidates have 90 minutes to complete the examination, which covers topics including:

- Confidentiality and privilege
- Mandated reporting requirements
- Scope of practice limitations
- Client rights and informed consent
- Record-keeping requirements
- Professional boundaries
- Advertising and professional statements
- Supervision requirements

If an APCC fails the Law and Ethics Examination, they may retake it after a 90-day waiting period. However, BPC Section 4999.55 requires that APCCs take the examination at least once per renewal cycle until passed. Failure to do so will result in the associate being unable to renew their registration until they have taken the examination at least once during that renewal period. They are also required to complete a three hour continuing education course on California laws and ethics.

Once an APCC has completed all other requirements for licensure, including the required 3,000 hours of supervised experience and any mandatory coursework, they become eligible to apply for the National Clinical Mental Health Counseling Examination (NCMHCE). This application requires submission of the *"Examination Eligibility Application"* form, current examination fee ($275 as of 20245), and verification that all other licensure requirements have been met.

The NCMHCE, developed by the National Board for Certified Counselors (NBCC), uses case studies, including eleven clinical scenarios that simulate the work of a mental health counselor engaging with a client across multiple sessions. Each case involves an intake narrative followed by 9–15 multiple-choice questions assessing the ability to identify, diagnose, and treat clinical concerns. Students demonstrate skills in analysis, treatment planning, and the application of counseling interventions over time.

The examination evaluates competency in:

- Professional Practice and Ethics
- Intake, Assessment, and Diagnosis
- Areas of Clinical Focus
- Treatment Planning
- Counseling Skills and Interventions
- Core Counseling Attributes

The NCMHCE consists of 130–150 items, with 100 items scored to determine a candidate's total score, based on the number of correct responses. Each scored multiple-choice question is worth one point. The passing score is determined through a standard setting process, where subject matter experts evaluate each item to define the performance of a Minimally Qualified Candidate (MQC). This score is then applied to other test forms through statistical equating, which adjusts for differences in difficulty across test versions. As a result, passing scores may vary slightly to ensure fairness across all exam forms.

For both examinations, the BBS contracts with a testing vendor that maintains multiple testing locations throughout California. Candidates can schedule their examinations online or by phone once they receive their eligibility notification. Testing centers offer appointments Monday through Saturday, with some locations providing evening hours to accommodate working professionals.

Preparation for these examinations requires a strategic approach. For the Law and Ethics Examination, candidates should thoroughly review:

1. The BBS Statutes and Regulations for LPCCs (available on the BBS website)
2. The California Business and Professions Code, particularly Sections 4999.10-4999.129
3. The American Counseling Association Code of Ethics
4. The California Association for Licensed Professional Clinical Counselors Ethical Standards

Many candidates supplement their studies with commercial preparation materials, including practice tests, study guides, and review courses. The BBS itself offers a Law and Ethics Review Guide that outlines the examination's content areas and provides sample questions.

For the NCMHCE, preparation should include:

1. Review of the NCMHCE content outline published by the NBCC
2. Study of the DSM-5 diagnostic criteria and treatment planning
3. Practice with case conceptualization and clinical decision-making
4. Familiarity with evidence-based practices for various mental health conditions

Several commercial preparation programs offer practice simulations that mirror the NCMHCE's case-based format. These programs help candidates become comfortable with the examination's unique structure and develop strategies for approaching the information-gathering and decision-making components.

The BBS provides reasonable accommodations for candidates with documented disabilities in accordance with the Americans with Disabilities Act. Candidates requiring accommodations must submit a Request for Accommodation form along with appropriate documentation when applying for examination eligibility. Accommodations may include extended testing time, readers, scribes, or modified testing environments.

After completing an examination, candidates receive preliminary results immediately at the testing center. However, these results are unofficial until verified by the BBS, which typically occurs within 2-4 weeks. Official results are mailed to candidates and also posted to their online BBS account.

For candidates who do not pass an examination, the BBS provides a performance feedback report identifying areas of strength and weakness. This feedback is valuable for focusing study efforts before retaking the examination. As mentioned earlier, candidates must wait 90 days before retaking either examination, and must pay the full examination fee for each attempt.

The BBS maintains strict security protocols for examination content. Candidates are prohibited from discussing specific examination questions with others or reproducing examination content in any form. Violation of these security measures can result in invalidation of examination results and potential disciplinary action against the candidate's registration or license.

Common pitfalls that candidates encounter during the examination process include:

1. Inadequate preparation time, particularly for the case-based format of the NCMHCE
2. Focusing solely on memorization rather than application of knowledge
3. Test anxiety that interferes with recall and decision-making

4. Mismanagement of examination time, particularly on the NCMHCE where cases vary in complexity
5. Failure to carefully read and follow instructions for each examination section

In addition to mastering the required content areas noted above, candidates should consider these practical strategies for maximizing exam success:

1. Begin preparation well in advance, ideally 3-6 months before the scheduled examination
2. Create a structured study schedule with specific goals for each session
3. Utilize multiple preparation resources, including practice examinations
4. Form or join study groups to discuss concepts and practice case formulation
5. Develop stress management techniques to control anxiety during the examination
6. Take care of physical needs by getting adequate rest, nutrition, and exercise before the examination
7. Arrive early at the testing center to complete check-in procedures without rushing

The examination process represents the final hurdle in the journey toward licensure as a Professional Clinical Counselor. While challenging, these examinations ensure that licensed professionals possess both the clinical knowledge and ethical understanding necessary to provide quality care to clients. By approaching the examination process with thorough preparation and a strategic mindset, candidates can successfully demonstrate their competence and join the ranks of licensed professional clinical counselors in California.

PRACTICUM REQUIREMENTS AND GUIDELINES

The practicum (internship/fieldwork/placement) experience serves as a foundational steppingstone in the educational journey of aspiring professional clinical counselors. California law establishes specific requirements to ensure students receive adequate supervised clinical experience before advancing to associate status. According to the California Business and Professions Code (BPC) Section 4999.33, all counseling programs must include supervised practicum or field study experience that meets rigorous standards.

The practicum component must include a minimum of 280 hours of face-to-face experience counseling individuals, families, or groups. This requirement is non-negotiable and represents the minimum threshold of direct client contact necessary to develop basic clinical skills. These 280 hours must consist entirely of direct counseling services, administrative tasks, observation hours, and other non-counseling activities cannot be counted toward this requirement.

Direct client contact hours encompass a range of counseling activities, including:

- Individual counseling sessions with adults, adolescents, or children
- Couples counseling sessions
- Family therapy sessions
- Group therapy facilitation
- Crisis intervention services
- Assessment and intake interviews that include therapeutic components

The BPC specifies that these hours must involve actual counseling interventions rather than merely observing others or discussing cases. Students must actively engage in the therapeutic process under appropriate supervision, applying the theoretical knowledge gained in their coursework to everyday clinical situations.

Practicum placements must occur in settings approved by the academic institution's counseling program. BPC Section 4999.36 outlines the parameters for acceptable practicum settings, which might include:

- University or college counseling centers

- Community mental health agencies
- Nonprofit counseling centers
- School-based counseling programs
- Hospital mental health departments
- Substance abuse treatment facilities
- Correctional facilities with counseling programs
- Other settings that provide direct mental health services to clients

These settings must have established protocols for clinical supervision and maintain formal agreements with the educational institution. The site must provide adequate facilities for confidential counseling sessions and access to clinical resources necessary for student learning.

Supervision during the practicum experience follows specific guidelines outlined in BPC Section 4999.36. Students must receive regular supervision from qualified professionals who can guide their clinical development and ensure client welfare. The supervision requirements include:

1. Weekly individual or triadic supervision (with one supervisor and two supervisees) provided by a qualified site supervisor
2. Regular group supervision provided by a program faculty member
3. A minimum of one hour of supervision for every five hours of direct client contact

Supervisor qualifications for practicum are clearly defined in BPC Section 4999.12(h). Supervisors must be:

- Licensed mental health professionals with at least two years of post-licensure experience
- Knowledgeable about the program's expectations, requirements, and evaluation procedures
- Trained in supervision methods and techniques

Qualified supervisors include Licensed Professional Clinical Counselors (LPCCs), Licensed Marriage and Family Therapists (LMFTs), Licensed Clinical Social Workers (LCSWs), Licensed Psychologists, and

Licensed Educational Psychologists. The supervisor must have held their license for at least two years and cannot have any disciplinary actions pending or imposed on their license.

Documentation requirements for practicum hours are extensive and must adhere to standards set by both the educational institution and the Board of Behavioral Sciences. Students must maintain detailed records of:

- Dates and duration of all client sessions
- Types of counseling services provided
- Client demographics (with appropriate confidentiality protection)
- Supervision hours received
- Evaluation forms completed by supervisors
- Learning goals and progress toward those goals

These records serve multiple purposes: they track progress toward the 280-hour requirement, provide material for supervision discussions, and may later be reviewed during the licensure application process. Most programs provide standardized forms for tracking these hours, which must be signed by both the student and supervisor on a weekly basis.

The integration of practicum experience with academic coursework represents a key component of counselor education. BPC Section 4999.33 requires that the practicum be integrated with the coursework experience. This integration typically occurs through:

1. Concurrent enrollment in practicum seminars that connect field experiences with theoretical concepts
2. Case presentation requirements that allow faculty and peers to provide feedback
3. Reflective assignments that encourage students to analyze their clinical work
4. Application of specific therapeutic techniques learned in coursework to clinical situations

This integration ensures that students don't simply accumulate hours but develop a thoughtful, theoretically grounded approach to counseling practice. The practicum seminar serves as a bridge between classroom learning and field experience, providing a structured environment for processing clinical challenges and successes.

To maximize the learning experience during practicum placement, students should implement several strategies:

First, approach site selection strategically. While the program will provide a list of approved sites, students should research each option carefully, considering the population served, theoretical orientation, supervision availability, and potential for learning specific skills. Selecting a site that aligns with career goals can provide valuable experience in a chosen specialty area.

Second, establish clear learning objectives at the beginning of the practicum. These objectives should be specific, measurable, and focused on developing core counseling competencies. Examples might include *"Demonstrate proficiency in conducting intake assessments"* or *"Apply cognitive-behavioral techniques with at least three clients."* Reviewing these objectives regularly with supervisors ensures focused professional development.

Third, actively seek diverse clinical experiences within the placement. While it may be comfortable to work with similar clients repeatedly, professional growth comes from exposure to varied presenting problems, demographics, and treatment approaches. Students should request opportunities to observe and work with different populations when possible.

Fourth, utilize supervision effectively by coming prepared with specific questions, concerns, and case material. Recording sessions (with client consent) provide valuable material for supervision discussions. Students should view supervision as a precious resource and maximize its benefit through thorough preparation.

Fifth, maintain comprehensive documentation beyond the minimum requirements. Detailed session notes, treatment plans, and reflections on interventions create a rich record of clinical development. These documents not only satisfy program requirements but also serve as learning tools for reviewing progress and identifying areas for growth.

Sixth, engage in regular self-reflection about personal reactions to clients and clinical work. Developing self-awareness about countertransference, biases, and emotional responses to challenging situations is essential for ethical practice. Journaling about these experiences can enhance self-understanding and professional identity development.

Seventh, connect with peers also completing practicum for additional support and perspective. Peer consultation provides opportunities to discuss challenges, share resources, and normalize the learning process. Many students find that peer relationships offer unique insights that complement formal supervision.

Finally, balance clinical responsibilities with self-care practices. Practicum experience can be emotionally demanding, particularly when working with clients in crisis or with trauma histories. Establishing sustainable self-care routines during practicum creates habits that will support career longevity.

The 280-hour practicum requirement represents just the beginning of supervised clinical experience. After completing the degree program, graduates must register as Associate Professional Clinical Counselors (APCCs) and accumulate an additional 3,000 hours of supervised experience before qualifying for licensure. The practicum lays the groundwork for this extended period of supervised practice, establishing fundamental skills and professional habits that will continue to develop throughout the pre-licensure period.

POST DGREE SUPERVISED PROFESSIONAL EXPERIENCE

Supervised professional experience serves as the foundation of counselor development, connecting classroom learning with experiential practice. California requires future Licensed Professional Clinical Counselors (LPCCs) to complete 3,000 hours of supervised professional experience before they can obtain licensure (BPC 4999.46). This training period helps counselors build the necessary skills to practice independently while receiving guidance from seasoned professionals.

The 3,000-hour requirement must be fulfilled with a mix of direct and indirect hours to ensure balanced clinical development. These hours must be accrued after registering as an Associate Professional Clinical Counselor (APCC) with the Board of Behavioral Sciences (BBS). The experience must include at least 1,750 hours of direct counseling experience with individuals, couples, families, or groups. This core requirement ensures that associates develop substantial face-to-face clinical skills across various therapeutic contexts. Up to 1,250 hours may come from non-counseling experience, including client-centered advocacy, consultation, assessment, research, direct supervisor contact, and workshops or training sessions.

Weekly supervision is required throughout the associate period. The BBS requires one hour of individual supervision or two hours of group supervision (with no more than eight supervisees) for every week in which experience is claimed. For weeks in which an associate provides more than 10 hours of direct counseling, additional supervision is required at a ratio of one hour of individual supervision (or two hours of group supervision).

Individual supervision involves one supervisor meeting with one or two supervisees if triadic, providing focused attention on specific cases and the associate's professional development. This format allows for in-depth discussion of challenging cases and personalized feedback. Group supervision, involving one supervisor and between three and eight supervisees, offers the benefit of peer learning and exposure to a wider range of clinical perspectives. Associates must receive a minimum of 52 weeks of supervision that includes at least one hour of individual supervision or two hours of group supervision per week.

The BBS maintains strict requirements regarding supervisor qualifications. Approved supervisors must be licensed mental health professionals who have held their license for at least two years. Eligible supervisors include Licensed Professional Clinical Counselors, Licensed Marriage and Family Therapists, Licensed Clinical Social Workers, Licensed Psychologists, and Licensed Physicians certified in psychiatry by the American Board of Psychiatry and Neurology. Additionally, supervisors must complete a supervision course before beginning supervision and a course every two years thereafter.

Supervisors must maintain a current and valid California license without any disciplinary actions that would affect their ability to supervise. They must also sign a *"Supervision Agreement"* with each supervisee before supervision begins, outlining the responsibilities of both parties, the supervisor's qualifications, and the scope and methods of supervision. This agreement serves as a contract that clarifies expectations and provides a framework for the supervisory relationship.

Documentation and tracking requirements for supervised experience are extensive and must be maintained meticulously. Before beginning to accrue hours, associates must register with the BBS and receive a registration number. They must also complete and submit a *"Supervision Agreement"* form within 60 days of commencing supervision. This form documents the supervisory relationship and outlines the scope of supervised experience.

Weekly logs must be maintained to track hours in each category of experience. These logs should include dates, hours worked in each category and supervision received. Supervisors must sign these logs weekly to verify their accuracy. Many associates use BBS-provided forms or electronic tracking systems designed specifically for this purpose.

According to the California Code of Regulations Title 16, Section 1821, supervisors must complete a written evaluation of the associate's performance yearly. These evaluations should address the associate's strengths, areas for improvement, and progress toward licensure requirements. Both the supervisor and associate should sign these evaluations, and they should be retained for submission with the licensure application.

When supervision ends, whether due to completion of hours, a change in employment, or a change in supervisors, a *"Experience Verification"* form must be completed. This form verifies the total hours accrued under that supervisor and must be signed by both parties. Associates should obtain this documentation promptly when a supervisory relationship ends, as locating former supervisors years later can be challenging.

The BBS limits associates to a maximum of 40 hours of experience per week. This cap helps prevent burnout and ensures that associates have adequate time to reflect on their clinical work and integrate their learning. Hours beyond this weekly maximum cannot be counted toward the 3,000-hour requirement, even if they were legitimately worked and supervised.

Triadic supervision, where one supervisor meets with two supervisees, counts as individual supervision. This format offers a middle ground between the intensity of one-on-one supervision and the diversity of group supervision. It allows for more personalized attention than group supervision while still providing the benefit of peer learning.

As mentioned previously, the BBS recognizes various settings for gaining supervised experience. These include nonprofit and charitable organizations, schools, colleges, universities, governmental entities, licensed health facilities, and private practices. Associates working in private practices must be employees, not independent contractors, and must receive regular supervision from a qualified supervisor.

Telehealth services can count toward supervised experience hours, provided they comply with all relevant laws and ethical guidelines. The supervisor must be competent in delivering services via telehealth and must provide appropriate supervision for this modality. Associates should document which hours were accrued through telehealth services.

Common pitfalls during the supervision process can delay licensure or result in hours being disallowed. One frequent mistake is failing to properly register with the BBS before beginning to accrue hours. Any experience gained before registration is officially processed cannot be counted toward licensure requirements (unless they met the 90-day rule, BPC 4999.46(b)(1)(a).

Another common error involves inadequate documentation. Associates sometimes fail to obtain signatures on weekly logs or neglect to obtain the right amount of supervision to clinical hour ratio. Maintaining organized records from the beginning of the associate period can prevent scrambling to categorize hours retrospectively when applying for licensure. When applying for licensure, missing documentation can result in hours being disallowed, potentially delaying the licensure process by months or even years.

Some associates mistakenly believe that all clinical work qualifies toward licensure hours. However, work performed as an independent contractor and hours accrued without proper supervision do not count. Associates should clarify with the BBS if they are uncertain whether specific work arrangements qualify.

Supervision interruptions can also cause problems. If an associate's supervisor becomes temporarily unavailable due to illness, vacation, or other circumstances, alternative supervision must be arranged if the associate wishes to continue accruing hours. Any work performed without supervision cannot be counted toward licensure requirements.

The supervised experience period represents an essential developmental phase for counselors, providing structured support as they apply theoretical knowledge in practice-based settings. By carefully following the BBS requirements, associates can ensure that their hours count toward licensure while maximizing their professional growth during this formative period.

HOUR TRACKING AND DOCUMENTATION

Accurate documentation of supervised professional experience hours is the backbone of the licensure process for Associate Professional

Clinical Counselors (APCCs). The California Board of Behavioral Sciences (BBS) requires meticulous record-keeping to verify that candidates have fulfilled all requirements before granting licensure. This systematic tracking not only satisfies regulatory requirements but also helps associates monitor their progress toward professional goals.

The BBS has established specific documentation requirements outlined in the Business and Professions Code (BPC) Section 4999.46. These requirements ensure that all supervised experience is properly verified and meets the standards for licensure. Associates must maintain detailed records of all clinical work, supervision received, and professional activities throughout their pre-licensure period.

Weekly logs form the foundation of the documentation system. These logs must record all hours worked in specific categories as defined by the BBS. Categories include direct counseling and indirect experiences like client-centered advocacy, consultation, assessment, research, direct supervisor contact, and professional enrichment activities. Each entry should include the date, number of hours in each category, and supervision received.

The BBS provides official Weekly Summary of Experience Hours forms (logs) that clearly distinguish between different categories of experience to ensure compliance with specific hour requirements. Logs should categorize direct and indirect hours according to the supervision structure outlined in the 'Post Degree Supervised Professional Experience' section.

Supervision details must be documented with particular care. Logs should record whether supervision was individual, triadic, or group format, the duration of each supervision session, and the supervisor's name and license number. This information is essential for verifying that the associate received the required one hour of individual supervision (or two hours of group supervision) for every week in which experience is claimed, as mandated by BPC Section 4999.46.2.

Again, supervisors must sign weekly logs to verify their accuracy. The BBS recommends obtaining these signatures promptly, ideally at the end of each supervision session or work week. Waiting to collect signatures can lead to complications if a supervisor becomes unavailable or details become difficult to recall. Some associates maintain duplicate copies of signed logs as a safeguard against loss or damage.

Beyond weekly logs, the BBS requires several formal documents throughout the supervision process. The Supervision Agreement must be completed within 60 days of commencing supervision with each supervisor. This form documents the supervisory relationship, outlines the scope and methods of supervision, and verifies the supervisor's qualifications. Both the supervisor and associate must retain copies of this agreement throughout the supervision period.

Written evaluations must be completed by supervisors every year as specified in 16 CCR § 1821. These evaluations should assess the associate's clinical skills, professional development, and progress toward licensure requirements. While the BBS does not provide a standard form for these evaluations, they should be signed by both the supervisor and associate and retained for submission with the licensure application.

When a supervisory relationship ends, whether due to completion of hours, change in employment, or other circumstances, an Experience Verification form must be completed. This form summarizes the total hours accrued under that supervisor in each category and must be signed by both parties. The BBS strongly recommends obtaining this documentation immediately when supervision ends, as locating former supervisors years later can be challenging.

For associates working in multiple settings or with multiple supervisors simultaneously, separate documentation must be maintained for each supervisory relationship. Each supervisor can only verify the hours for which they provided supervision, and hours cannot be double counted across settings. Clear organization of these parallel records is essential to avoid confusion during the licensure application process.

The BBS allows both paper and electronic documentation systems, provided they capture all required information and maintain appropriate security and confidentiality. Paper systems typically involve physical binders with printed forms, while electronic systems range from spreadsheets to specialized tracking applications. Regardless of the format, associates should maintain backup copies of all documentation in a secure location.

Electronic tracking systems have gained popularity for their convenience and organizational benefits. Platforms like TrackYourHours.com offer specialized tools designed specifically for mental health professionals accruing hours toward licensure in California. These systems automatically categorize hours according to BBS requirements, calculate running totals, flag potential compliance issues, and generate reports for licensure applications.

TrackYourHours.com and similar platforms typically include features such as digital supervisor signatures, cloud storage of documentation, and alerts when approaching hour thresholds in various categories. While these systems streamline the tracking process, associates remain responsible for ensuring the accuracy and completeness of all entries. The BBS accepts reports generated by these platforms provided they contain all required information.

Whether using paper or electronic systems, associates should prepare for potential BBS audits of their experience hours. The BBS randomly selects a percentage of licensure applications for detailed verification, requiring submission of all supporting documentation. To prepare for this possibility, associates should maintain organized files containing:

1. Original signed weekly logs for all experience hours
2. Supervision Agreement forms for each supervisor
3. Supervisor evaluations
4. Experience Verification forms
5. Documentation of supervisor qualifications

6. Any additional correspondence with the BBS regarding experience hours

These records should be retained years after licensure is granted, as for supervisors a minimum of seven years after termination of supervision as specified in BPC Section 4999.46.5. Some professionals recommend maintaining these records indefinitely as evidence of professional training and development.

The BBS also requires documentation of specific training for certain clinical situations. For example, associates working with children or conducting child abuse assessments must document the completion of required training in these areas. Similarly, associates providing services via telehealth must document compliance with telehealth regulations and appropriate supervision for this modality.

Best practices for maintaining accurate and complete records include:

1. Establishing a consistent schedule for updating logs, ideally daily or at minimum weekly
2. Creating a checklist of required documentation to ensure nothing is overlooked
3. Implementing a filing system that organizes records chronologically and by supervisor
4. Regularly reviewing hour totals in each category to ensure balanced progress
5. Discussing documentation requirements with supervisors at the outset of the relationship
6. Maintaining open communication with supervisors about any documentation concerns
7. Periodically auditing one's own records to identify and address any deficiencies
8. Securing all client-related documentation in compliance with HIPAA and state privacy laws

Associates should also familiarize themselves with the specific BBS forms required for their license type. The forms for LPCCs differ from those for other license types such as LMFTs or LCSWs. Using incorrect forms can result in delays or rejection of experience hours.

The documentation process, while administratively demanding, serves an important purpose beyond regulatory compliance. It creates a comprehensive record of professional development that associates can reference throughout their careers. Detailed logs often reveal patterns in clinical interests, strengths, and areas for growth that can inform future professional development and specialization decisions.

LICENSE APPLICATION PROCESS

The journey to becoming a licensed professional clinical counselor begins with a thorough understanding of the application process. In California, the Board of Behavioral Sciences (BBS) oversees this process, which involves multiple steps designed to ensure that only qualified individuals receive licensure. The application process typically begins after completing your master's degree program and before starting your supervised professional experience.

Your first step is to apply for registration as an Associate Professional Clinical Counselor (APCC). This registration is necessary before you can begin accruing supervised experience hours toward licensure. The application package for APCC registration includes several key components that must be submitted together to avoid delays in processing.

The primary application form requires personal information, educational history, and professional background details. You'll need to provide your legal name, contact information, social security number, and birth date. The form also asks about previous registrations or licenses in counseling or related fields, both in California and other states. Be prepared to disclose any denied, suspended, or revoked professional licenses, as well as any criminal convictions.

Educational documentation forms a substantial portion of your application package. You must submit official transcripts sent directly from your graduate institution to the BBS. These transcripts must show completion of a qualifying master's degree in counseling or a closely related field. Additionally, you'll need to submit a Program Certification form completed by your graduate program's director or authorized representative. This form verifies that your program meets California's educational requirements for counseling licensure.

For those with degrees from out-of-state institutions, additional documentation is required. You'll need to submit course descriptions, syllabi, and possibly a written explanation of how your coursework meets California's requirements. International applicants must first have their credentials evaluated by an approved evaluation service before submitting their application.

The background check requirements are stringent and non-negotiable. All applicants must complete a Live Scan fingerprinting process through an approved vendor. The Live Scan form, which is included in the application package, must be completed by both you and the fingerprinting agency. The fingerprints are used to conduct background checks through both the California Department of Justice and the Federal Bureau of Investigation. These checks identify any criminal history that might affect your eligibility for licensure.

If you have a criminal history, you may need to provide court documents and a personal statement explaining the circumstances. Minor infractions typically don't prevent licensure, but the BBS evaluates each case individually, considering factors such as the nature of the offense, when it occurred, and evidence of rehabilitation.

The fee structure for the application process includes several components. As of this writing, the APCC registration application fee is $150, though this amount is subject to change. The Live Scan fingerprinting service charges its own fee, which typically ranges from $60 to $100 depending on the provider. These fees are non-refundable, even if your application is denied, so it's essential to ensure your application is complete and accurate before submission.

Payment methods accepted by the BBS include personal checks, money orders, and cashier's checks made payable to the *"Behavioral Sciences Fund."* Credit card payments are not accepted for initial applications. When submitting payment, include your name and *"APCC Application"* on the memo line of your check to ensure proper processing.

The timeline for application processing varies based on the BBS's current workload, but typically ranges from 4 to 8 weeks for complete applications. Incomplete applications or those requiring additional review may take significantly longer. The BBS processes applications in the order they are received, and checking your application status can be done through the BBS website using your application number.

Once your APCC registration is approved, you'll receive a registration number that remains valid for six years. This registration allows you to begin accruing supervised experience hours toward licensure. It's important to note that you cannot begin counting hours until your APCC registration is officially approved.

Common application errors can significantly delay the processing of your application. These include:

- Incomplete forms with missing information or signatures
- Failure to include all required documentation
- Discrepancies between names on different documents (due to marriage or legal name changes)
- Insufficient fees or incorrect payment methods
- Illegible handwriting on application forms
- Missing or incomplete Live Scan information
- Failure to disclose required information about past convictions or disciplinary actions

To avoid these errors, carefully review all application instructions before beginning the process. Use the checklist provided by the BBS to ensure you've included all required components. Consider having a colleague or mentor review your application before submission to catch any oversights.

After completing your supervised professional experience requirements (3,000 hours over at least two years), you'll be eligible to apply for the LPCC examination eligibility. This application process shares many similarities with the initial APCC registration but includes additional forms documenting your supervised experience.

The examination application requires submission of Experience Verification forms signed by each of your supervisors, Weekly Summary forms documenting your accrued hours, and Supervisor Responsibility Statements from each supervisor. These forms must account for all hours being claimed toward licensure.

The examination application fee is separate from your initial registration fee and must be submitted with your application. Upon approval of your examination application, you'll be eligible to take the California Law and Ethics Examination and, upon passing that, the National Clinical Mental Health Counseling Examination (NCMHCE).

After passing both examinations, you'll submit a final application for licensure as an LPCC, along with the associated fee. This application is typically straightforward if you've successfully completed all previous steps in the process.

Throughout the entire licensure journey, maintaining clear communication with the BBS is essential. If you change your address, name, or employment, you must notify the BBS within 30 days. All communications should include your APCC registration number for proper identification.

If you encounter problems during the application process, the BBS offers several resources for assistance. Their website provides detailed FAQs, application instructions, and contact information. For specific questions about your application, email communication is preferred and typically receives a response within 3-5 business days.

To ensure a smooth application process, create a dedicated folder or digital file to organize all your licensure documents. Keep copies of everything you submit to the BBS, including a record of when materials were sent. Track all communication with the BBS, noting dates, topics discussed, and the names of representatives you speak with.

Here's a comprehensive checklist for your APCC application submission:

- Completed and signed application form with all questions answered
- Official transcripts sent directly from your graduate institution
- Program Certification form completed by your graduate program
- Completed Live Scan form with fingerprinting agency information
- Application fee in the form of check or money order
- Documentation of legal name changes (if applicable)
- Conviction/discipline disclosure forms and supporting documentation (if applicable)
- Course descriptions and syllabi (for out-of-state applicants)
- Credential evaluation report (for international applicants)
- Copy of your driver's license or other government-issued ID
- Self-addressed, stamped envelope for receipt confirmation (optional but recommended)

If you are (or will be) an APCC applicant, you should carefully follow these guidelines and maintain thorough documentation throughout the process so that you can navigate the licensure application system efficiently. Remember that the application process is designed not just as a bureaucratic hurdle but as a means of ensuring that all licensed counselors meet the high standards necessary to protect public safety and provide quality mental health care.

CHAPTER TWO

SCOPE OF PROFESSIONAL COUNSELING

DEFINING PROFESSIONAL CLINICAL COUNSELING

Professional clinical counseling in California is defined by the California Business and Professions Code (BPC) Section 4999.20, which provides the legal framework for understanding what constitutes legitimate counseling practice. According to this statute, professional clinical counseling means *"the application of counseling interventions and psychotherapeutic techniques to identify and remediate cognitive, mental, and emotional issues, including personal growth, adjustment to disability, crisis intervention, and psychosocial and environmental problems."* This definition serves as the basis for determining who may practice as a licensed professional clinical counselor (LPCC) in the state and what activities fall within their scope of practice.

The legal definition contains several key components that warrant closer examination. First, the reference to *"counseling interventions and psychotherapeutic techniques"* establishes that professional counseling involves structured approaches based on established therapeutic methods, not simply friendly advice or casual conversation. These interventions must be grounded in recognized counseling theories and evidence-based practices that the counselor has been trained to implement.

The phrase *"identify and remediate"* points to the assessment and treatment functions of counseling. LPCCs must possess the skills to properly evaluate a client's situation, recognize patterns of thought and behavior, and implement appropriate interventions to address identified issues. This diagnostic component distinguishes professional counseling from supportive relationships that may offer comfort but lack clinical assessment.

The statute goes on to specify the types of issues that fall within a counselor's purview: *"cognitive, mental, and emotional issues."* This language acknowledges the interconnected nature of human experience, recognizing that problems may manifest in thoughts (cognitive), overall mental health, and emotional responses. For example, a client experiencing workplace anxiety might exhibit negative thought patterns about their abilities (cognitive), emotional distress when thinking about work (emotional), and potentially broader mental health impacts like depression or sleep disturbances.

The inclusion of *"personal growth"* in the definition acknowledges that counseling isn't solely focused on pathology or problems. Many clients seek counseling to enhance their self-understanding, improve relationships, or develop better coping skills even when not experiencing a diagnosable condition. An LPCC might work with a client who wants to develop better communication skills or process a life transition such as becoming a parent, situations that represent growth opportunities rather than disorders.

"Adjustment to disability" specifically recognizes the role counselors play in helping clients adapt to physical or mental conditions that affect daily functioning. This might involve helping a client who has recently experienced a physical injury adjust to new limitations or working with someone managing a chronic condition to develop coping strategies and reframe their identity in light of their changed circumstances.

"Crisis intervention" acknowledges the acute, time-sensitive work counselors often perform. This could include supporting clients through suicidal ideation, acute grief reactions, trauma responses, or other urgent situations requiring immediate attention and stabilization. For instance, an LPCC might provide crisis counseling to a client who has just experienced

a traumatic event, focusing on safety planning, emotional regulation, and connecting with support resources.

The final component, *"psychosocial and environmental problems,"* broadens the scope to include issues stemming from a client's social context and environment. This might involve helping clients navigate relationship difficulties, workplace challenges, housing insecurity, or cultural adjustment issues. This element recognizes that mental health doesn't exist in isolation from social and environmental factors.

To illustrate how this definition translates into practice, consider the following scenarios:

A 35-year-old self-identified woman seeks counseling after her divorce. The LPCC helps her process grief and loss (emotional issues), challenges negative thoughts about her self-worth (cognitive issues), develops strategies for co-parenting (psychosocial problems), and supports her in establishing a new identity and future goals (personal growth).

A college student experiences panic attacks before exams. The counselor teaches anxiety management techniques (remediation of emotional issues), helps identify and restructure catastrophic thinking patterns (cognitive issues), and works with the student to develop better study habits and communicate with professors about accommodations (environmental problems).

A veteran returns from deployment with symptoms of PTSD. The LPCC provides trauma-focused therapy (mental health issues), helps the client manage flashbacks and hypervigilance (emotional and cognitive issues), supports reintegration into civilian life (adjustment), and connects them with veteran support groups (psychosocial and environmental support).

The law also addresses the administration and interpretation of tests. According to BPC 4999.20(c), LPCCs may administer and interpret certain tests *"designed to measure aptitudes, abilities, achievements, interests, personality characteristics, disabilities, and mental, emotional, and behavioral disorders."* However, this excludes projective personality, neuropsychological testing, or individually administered intelligence tests, areas that typically require specialized training in psychology.

What distinguishes professional clinical counseling from other supportive relationships is the combination of formal training, ethical obligations, and the application of established therapeutic techniques. While friends, family members, clergy, or mentors may offer valuable support and guidance, professional counseling involves:

1. Formal education and training: LPCCs in California must complete a master's or doctoral degree in counseling or a related field, accumulate 3,000 hours of supervised experience, and pass licensing examinations.

2. Ethical and legal obligations: Professional counselors are bound by ethical codes (such as the American Counseling Association Code of Ethics) and legal requirements regarding confidentiality, mandated reporting, and standard of care.

3. Evidence-based interventions: LPCCs utilize therapeutic approaches grounded in research and established theory rather than personal opinion or anecdotal experience.

4. Clinical assessment skills: Professional counselors are trained to assess mental health conditions, evaluate risk factors, and develop structured treatment plans.

5. Professional boundaries: Unlike informal supportive relationships, counseling maintains clear professional boundaries regarding the nature, purpose, and limitations of the relationship.

For example, a friend might listen to someone's relationship problems and offer advice based on personal experience, while an LPCC would assess patterns of communication and attachment, identify underlying issues, and implement specific therapeutic techniques to address these problems. The friend offers support; the counselor provides treatment.

Similarly, a life coach might help a client set and achieve personal or professional goals but lacks the training to address underlying mental health conditions that might be impeding progress. An LPCC can work on goal setting while also addressing anxiety, depression, or trauma that might be affecting the client's functioning.

The California Association of Marriage and Family Therapists (CAMFT) and the California Association for Licensed Professional Clinical Counselors (CALPCC) provide additional guidance on interpreting these legal definitions, offering resources to help practitioners understand the nuances of their scope of practice. The Board of Behavioral Sciences (BBS), which regulates LPCCs in California, also publishes clarifications and updates on scope of practice issues through its website and newsletters.

Understanding this legal definition is essential not only for compliance but also for ethical practice. By recognizing the boundaries of professional counseling, practitioners can ensure they provide services within their competence while making appropriate referrals when client needs extend beyond their scope of practice or expertise.

PSYCHOLOGICAL TESTING PARAMETERS

So, let's talk a bit more about administering those tests to clients! Professional clinical counselors must navigate specific legal boundaries when it comes to psychological testing. The California Business and Professions Code (BPC) Section 4999.20 outlines the scope of practice for Licensed Professional Clinical Counselors (LPCCs), including important limitations on psychological testing. Understanding these parameters helps counselors practice legally and ethically while ensuring clients receive appropriate assessment services.

The BPC explicitly states that LPCCs may administer and interpret certain types of tests but with clear restrictions. As explained earlier in the 'Defining Professional Clinical Counseling' section, BPC §4999.20

outlines the general scope of LPCC practice. This section focuses specifically on how that scope applies to psychological testing. This provision allows counselors to use assessments that help understand client functioning in practical contexts.

Specifically, LPCCs may administer, score, and interpret tests of personality, behavior, interpersonal relationships, attitudes, interests, and values. These assessments help counselors gather information about client characteristics that inform treatment planning. For example, a counselor might use the Beck Depression Inventory-II to assess the severity of a client's depressive symptoms, the Minnesota Multiphasic Personality Inventory (MMPI-2) to evaluate personality characteristics and psychopathology, or relationship inventories like the Dyadic Adjustment Scale to assess couple functioning.

Career assessment represents another area where LPCCs have testing privileges. The BPC permits counselors to administer and interpret instruments that measure vocational interests, aptitudes, and skills. These include assessments like the Strong Interest Inventory, the Self-Directed Search, and the Myers-Briggs Type Indicator when used for career exploration purposes. Such tools help clients identify potential career paths aligned with their personal characteristics and preferences.

However, the law establishes firm boundaries around certain types of psychological testing. Section 4999.20(c) explicitly prohibits LPCCs from "the use of projective techniques in the assessment of personality, individually administered intelligence tests, neuropsychological testing, or utilization of a battery of three or more tests to determine the presence of psychosis, dementia, amnesia, cognitive impairment, or criminal behavior." These assessments require specialized training in neuropsychology typically obtained through doctoral-level education in psychology. Does this mean an LPCC could never use the PAI? Based on this definition, as long as a battery three or more… is not used to assess those specific conditions. LPCCs should verify with the BBS prior to the use of any assessments they are not sure is within their scope of practice.

Educational and cognitive testing presents another area with clear limitations. LPCCs may not administer or interpret standardized intelligence tests, cognitive ability tests, or achievement tests used for educational placement or disability determination. These include instruments like the Wechsler Intelligence Scale for Children (WISC), the Woodcock-Johnson Tests of Achievement, or the Stanford-Binet Intelligence Scales. Such assessments fall within the scope of practice for school psychologists, educational psychologists, and clinical psychologists with appropriate training.

The law also addresses qualifications necessary for administering different types of assessments. For tests that LPCCs are permitted to use, the BPC requires that counselors have education and training to administer, score and interpret these instruments. This typically means formal coursework in assessment during graduate education, supervised experience with specific instruments, and ongoing professional development to maintain competence.

Many test publishers impose additional qualification requirements beyond legal standards. These publishers often use classification systems that restrict access to certain assessments based on education level, professional credentials, and specialized training. For example, Pearson Assessment's qualification levels range from A (tests available to professionals with relevant graduate degrees) to C (tests requiring doctoral-level training and specialized expertise). LPCCs must adhere to both legal requirements and publisher qualifications when selecting assessment tools.

Documentation requirements for testing represent another important aspect of assessment practice. When conducting assessments within their scope, LPCCs must maintain thorough records that include:

1. The reason for assessment and specific referral questions
2. Informed consent documentation showing the client understood the purpose, process, and limitations of testing
3. Raw test data and scoring worksheets
4. Interpretation notes and summary

5. How the results were communicated to the client
6. Recommendations based on assessment findings
7. Any referrals made based on test results

These documentation practices protect both clients and counselors by creating a clear record of the assessment process and ensuring appropriate use of test results.

Making proper decisions about psychological testing requires careful consideration of several factors. First, counselors must honestly evaluate whether a particular assessment falls within their legal scope of practice. When uncertain, consulting the specific language of BPC Section 4999.20 provides necessary guidance. Second, counselors should assess their own competence with the instrument, considering their training, experience, and comfort level with administration and interpretation.

Third, LPCCs must determine whether the assessment meets the client's needs or if a referral would better serve them. For example, if a client presents with symptoms suggesting possible attention-deficit/hyperactivity disorder (ADHD), the counselor might recognize that comprehensive neuropsychological testing would provide the most accurate diagnosis. Rather than attempting to assess ADHD with behavior rating scales alone, the ethical counselor would refer the client to a psychologist qualified to conduct a full neuropsychological evaluation.

The referral process requires thoughtful communication with clients. When explaining the need for referral, counselors should emphasize how specialized testing will benefit the client rather than focusing on the counselor's limitations. For instance, instead of saying *"I'm not allowed to do that kind of testing,"* a more client-centered approach would be: *"To get the most accurate understanding of your attention difficulties, I recommend working with Dr. Johnson, who specializes in comprehensive ADHD assessments. Her evaluation will give us detailed information about your cognitive processing that will help guide our work together."*

Collaboration with other professionals often enhances assessment outcomes. When referring clients for testing outside their scope, LPCCs can maintain therapeutic continuity by:

1. Obtaining appropriate release of information forms
2. Communicating relevant background information to the testing professional
3. Reviewing assessment results to incorporate findings into ongoing counseling
4. Helping clients understand and apply test results to their therapeutic goals

This collaborative approach respects professional boundaries while ensuring clients receive integrated care.

Regardless of the breadth of scope available to the licensee or registrant, it is expected that they will refer clients to other licensed healthcare professionals when client issues are outside their scope of education, training, and experience. You are not likely to know how to treat every problem found in the DSM 5 TR. This refers not to just scope of practice (again the legal aspects of this that we were talking about) but the scope of competence. The question you must always ask is, *"Am I competent enough to help this client? Can I provide the appropriate level of services that is adequate for their mental, emotional, and psychological need?"*

When we talk about the scope of competence, we are talking about what you know and what you can do as informed by your education, training, and experience. There is no expectation that you will be able to treat every client issue that you come across, that's probably just not possible for any psychotherapist. With cultural considerations, family dynamics, interpersonal dynamics, and psychological wellness concerns, there may be issues and situations that you are unfamiliar with. If you have no experience or no relevant training, it would be inappropriate for you to continue to provide services. Here the scope of practice might allow you to work with the client, but your scope of competence is lacking, and therefore, it would be inappropriate.

It is quite possible that some therapists have a scope of competence that exceeds others because of their education, their own experience, and their professional training, while another therapist may not be as competent in some areas although they both may have very similar educational backgrounds. The great thing about scope of competence is that you can expand it so you can become more competent in a clinical area. So, let's say you want to be more competent in working with clients that have severe and persistent mental illness specific to schizophrenia, you can go and obtain additional training. You can take classes, attend workshops, read up on that particular diagnosis, and receive supervision as you learn to become competent in working with this diagnosis. Note: You cannot expand your scope of practice unless identified explicitly in the law or you obtain an additional license that has that expanded scope. An example would be obtaining licensure as a psychologist.

Note that BPC 2908 does state that LPCC *can* do work of a psychological nature, with some conditions, as long as " they do not hold themselves out to the public by any title or description of services incorporating the words "psychological," "psychologist," "psychology," "psychometrist," "psychometrics," or "psychometry," amongst other stipulations.

TREATMENT PLANNING AND ASSESSMENT

Treatment planning begins with a thorough understanding of the client's needs, challenges, and goals. Professional clinical counselors must develop structured, individualized treatment plans that serve as roadmaps for the therapeutic journey while meeting legal and ethical requirements. The process combines clinical judgment with documentation standards that protect both clients and practitioners.

Initial assessment forms the foundation of effective treatment planning. When a client first enters counseling, LPCCs conduct a complete evaluation that typically spans one to three sessions. This assessment phase gathers essential information about presenting problems, symptom history, previous treatment experiences, current functioning, and relevant background factors. The information collected during this phase directly informs diagnosis and treatment recommendations.

EXAMPLES

Counselor Rebecca demonstrated effective initial assessment with her new client, Carlos, who sought help for relationship difficulties. During their first session, Rebecca explained the assessment process: *"Over our first few meetings, I'll be asking questions about different areas of your life to understand what brings you here and how I can best help. This helps us create a plan that addresses your specific needs."* She then conducted a semi-structured interview covering Carlos's presenting concerns, relationship history, family background, mental health history, substance use patterns, and current coping strategies. Rebecca documented this information in a standardized intake form, noting both Carlos's subjective reports and her objective observations of his affect, thought patterns, and interpersonal style.

The biopsychosocial framework provides a useful structure for complete assessment. This approach examines biological factors (medical conditions, medication use, sleep patterns, substance use), psychological elements (emotional states, thought patterns, coping mechanisms), and social dimensions (relationships, cultural background, employment, living situation). Gathering data across emotional, cognitive, and contextual domains helps counselors form a complete picture of each client's experience.

For example, counselor Michael used a biopsychosocial approach with his client Leila, who presented with anxiety symptoms. His assessment documented biological factors (recent thyroid diagnosis, caffeine consumption, disrupted sleep), psychological elements (perfectionistic thinking, catastrophizing, avoidance behaviors), and social contexts (high-pressure work environment, recent move away from support system, cultural expectations from family). This complete picture allowed Michael to develop a treatment plan addressing multiple dimensions of Leila's experience rather than focusing solely on symptom reduction.

Standardized assessment tools complement clinical interviews by providing objective measures of symptom severity and functional impairment. These instruments help establish baselines for tracking progress and may identify issues not readily apparent in conversation. Common screening tools include the Patient Health Questionnaire-9 (PHQ-9) for depression, Generalized Anxiety Disorder-7 (GAD-7) for anxiety, PTSD Checklist (PCL-5) for trauma symptoms, and the Alcohol Use Disorders Identification Test (AUDIT) for substance use concerns.

Counselor Jason incorporated standardized assessment with his client Wei, who described feeling *"stressed and overwhelmed."* Jason administered both the PHQ-9 and GAD-7, discovering that Wei's scores indicated moderate depression (PHQ-9 score of 12) but severe anxiety (GAD-7 score of 18). This assessment helped clarify that while Wei experienced both conditions, anxiety symptoms were more prominent and likely warranted primary attention in treatment planning. Jason documented these scores in Wei's chart, noting: *"Assessment indicates anxiety symptoms are more severe than depressive symptoms, with particular elevation in worry, restlessness, and difficulty relaxing. Treatment will prioritize anxiety management strategies while monitoring depressive symptoms."*

Risk assessment constitutes an essential component of initial evaluation. Counselors must screen for suicidal ideation, homicidal thoughts, and abuse or neglect situations that may require immediate intervention. This screening should occur during initial assessment and continue throughout treatment as risk factors can emerge at any point in the therapeutic process.

Counselor Alisha demonstrated appropriate risk assessment with her client Derek, who mentioned feeling *"like giving up"* during their intake session. Alisha asked direct questions about suicidal thoughts, plans, means, and intent. When Derek acknowledged passive suicidal ideation but denied active plans, Alisha conducted a thorough safety assessment, documenting protective factors (strong connection to children, religious beliefs against suicide, willingness to seek help) and risk factors (recent job loss, history of depression, social isolation). She developed a safety plan with Derek, including coping strategies, emergency contacts, and agreement to remove firearms from his home temporarily. Alisha documented this assessment and plan in detail, noting: *"Client endorsed passive SI without plan or intent. Safety plan developed and provided to client in writing. Client agreed to contact crisis services if thoughts intensify and demonstrated understanding of plan by restating key components."*

Diagnostic considerations within the LPCC scope require careful attention to both clinical presentation and legal parameters. According to California Business and Professions Code Section 4999.20, LPCCs can diagnose mental health conditions using the Diagnostic and Statistical Manual of Mental Disorders (DSM-5) because of the "and the use, application, and integration of the coursework and training required by Sections 4999.32 and 4999.33", in which they learn diagnostic principles. Counselors must ensure that their diagnostic decisions reflect both the limits of their legal scope and their actual clinical training and experience.

Counselor Victor appropriately approached diagnosis with his client Amara, who described persistent sadness, sleep disturbance, and difficulty concentrating following her divorce six months earlier. Victor conducted a thorough assessment, ruling out medical conditions by confirming Amara had recently seen her physician. He documented his diagnostic reasoning: *"Client presents with depressed mood, anhedonia, sleep disturbance, concentration difficulties, and fatigue persisting for 6+ months following divorce. Symptoms cause substantial distress and impairment in social and occupational functioning. Medical causes have been ruled out through recent physical. Differential diagnosis considered adjustment disorder with depressed mood, but symptom duration and severity support diagnosis of F33.1 Major Depressive Disorder, moderate, single episode. Will monitor for bipolar features as treatment progresses."*

When clients present with symptoms suggesting conditions outside the counselor's scope or expertise, an appropriate referral becomes essential. As outlined in Business and Professions Code Section 4999.20(d), LPCCs must recognize the limitations of their competence and make appropriate referrals when necessary. Conditions requiring specialized assessment might include complex neurological disorders, severe psychiatric conditions requiring intensive treatment, or presentations suggesting medical etiology.

Counselor Priya recognized her diagnostic limitations when client Jackson described unusual sensory experiences and disorganized thinking patterns. Rather than attempting to diagnose what appeared to be early psychosis, Priya documented: *"Client presents with symptoms requiring specialized assessment beyond my scope of practice, including possible thought disturbances and perceptual abnormalities. Discussed with client the importance of comprehensive evaluation. Provided referral to Dr. Ramirez at the XZY Intervention Clinic with client's agreement. Will maintain contact with client to provide support during referral process and coordinate care following assessment."*

Once assessment is complete, the formal treatment planning process begins. Effective treatment plans include several key components: identified problems/diagnoses, measurable goals, specific interventions, timeframes, and evaluation methods. These elements create accountability and provide clear direction for both counselor and client.

Problem statements describe the specific issues to be addressed in treatment, directly connected to assessment findings and diagnostic conclusions. These statements should be concrete, specific, and focused on the client's experience rather than theoretical constructs.

For example, counselor Darius worked with client Sophia, who met criteria for Generalized Anxiety Disorder. Rather than simply listing the diagnosis, Darius documented specific problem statements: *"1) Persistent excessive worry across multiple life domains that client cannot control; 2) Physical tension manifesting as headaches and muscle pain; 3) Sleep disturbance characterized by difficulty falling asleep due to racing thoughts; 4) Avoidance of decision-making due to fear of making mistakes."*

Goals translate problem statements into positive, achievable outcomes. Effective treatment goals follow the SMART framework: Specific, Measurable, Achievable, Relevant, and Time-bound. This approach creates clarity about what success looks like and how progress will be evaluated.

Counselor Lucia developed SMART goals with her client Mateo, who struggled with social anxiety. Rather than setting a vague goal like *"reduce anxiety,"* Lucia documented: *"1) Client will reduce subjective anxiety in social situations from current SUDS rating of 8/10 to 4/10 by implementing cognitive restructuring and breathing techniques in at least three social encounters per week, within 3 months; 2) Client will increase social engagement by participating in at least one group activity weekly for 30+ minutes without leaving early, within 4 months; 3) Client will reduce avoidance behaviors by completing 75% of items on his fear hierarchy with anxiety levels below 5/10, within 6 months."*

Objectives break goals into smaller, sequential steps that build toward the larger outcome. These short-term targets create momentum and provide opportunities to celebrate progress along the way. Objectives should be concrete actions the client will take rather than changes the counselor hopes to see.

For Mateo's first goal of reducing subjective anxiety, Lucia developed these objectives: *"1) Client will learn and practice diaphragmatic breathing daily for 2 weeks, demonstrating proper technique in session; 2) Client will identify and record 3 anxiety-provoking thoughts daily for 2 weeks; 3) Client will develop and practice 2 alternative responses to each identified thought; 4) Client will implement breathing and cognitive techniques during one brief social interaction weekly, then two, then three."*

Interventions specify the therapeutic approaches, techniques, and activities the counselor will use to help the client achieve their goals. These should align with evidence-based practices appropriate for the client's diagnosis and circumstances while remaining within the counselor's competence.

CRISIS INTERVENTION BOUNDARIES

Professional clinical counselors regularly encounter clients in crisis, requiring clear understanding of intervention boundaries and protocols. Crisis intervention represents a distinct skill set within the counseling profession, with specific legal parameters governing appropriate response. While LPCCs are trained to address many crisis situations, they must recognize when a situation exceeds their scope of practice and requires additional resources (BPC 4999.20(d)).

Crises appropriate for counselor intervention include suicidal ideation without immediate intent, acute anxiety or panic attacks, grief reactions, trauma responses, relationship conflicts, and situational stressors. These situations, while urgent, typically allow for assessment and intervention within the therapeutic relationship.

Suicidal risk assessment falls within the LPCC scope but requires specific protocols. Counselors must directly assess ideation, plan, means, intent, and protective factors. When client Marcus mentioned thoughts of suicide during a routine session, counselor David immediately shifted to a structured assessment: *"I appreciate you sharing those thoughts with me. I need to ask some specific questions about these feelings to understand how to best help you. Have you thought about how you might harm yourself? Do you have access to those means? Have you decided when you might act on these thoughts?"* David documented Marcus's responses verbatim, noting that Marcus acknowledged passive thoughts of *"not wanting to be here"* but denied specific plans, means, or intent.

For clients experiencing suicidal ideation without immediate risk, counselors develop safety plans that include coping strategies, social supports, means restriction, emergency contacts, and professional resources. These plans should be documented and provided to clients in writing. Counselor Naomi created a detailed safety plan with client Tara, who experienced intermittent suicidal thoughts. The plan identified specific warning signs (isolation, stopping medication, increased alcohol use), coping strategies (grounding techniques, physical exercise, calling supportive friends), emergency contacts (sister, roommate), and crisis resources (local crisis line, nearest emergency department). Naomi documented: *"Safety plan developed collaboratively and provided to client in writing. Client demonstrated understanding by restating key components and identifying which strategies she feels most likely to use."*

However, immediate suicidal risk exceeds standard counseling intervention. When clients present with current intent, detailed plan, available means, and few protective factors, counselors must initiate emergency protocols. Counselor Ben recognized this boundary when client Aisha revealed she had pills at home and planned to take them that evening. Ben maintained engagement with Aisha while activating office emergency procedures, which included having a colleague contact emergency service while Ben continued supporting Aisha. Ben documented: *"Client presented with active suicidal intent, specific plan to overdose on medication tonight, access to means, and diminished protective factors following recent relationship loss. Emergency protocol initiated per practice policy. Maintained therapeutic connection while arranging emergency evaluation. Client transported to XYZ Hospital ED by ambulance at 2:45pm. Provided relevant clinical information to emergency personnel with client's verbal consent."*

Homicidal risk assessment follows similar parameters. Counselors must evaluate threats toward others, determining specificity, means, access to potential victims, and history of violence. When client Ray expressed anger toward his former business partner during a session, counselor Gabriela assessed: *"You mentioned wanting to 'make him pay.'*

Can you tell me more about what you mean by that? Have you thought about harming him physically? Do you have any specific plans? Do you know where he lives or works?" Gabriela documented Ray's responses, noting that while he expressed intense anger, he denied violent intentions and demonstrated appropriate reality testing about consequences.

The duty to warn and protect potential victims (which we will talk about thoroughly in this book) represents a critical legal obligation that overrides confidentiality when specific threats exist. Most states have established clear protocols for this duty following the Tarasoff case. Counselor Kevin faced this situation when client Trevor disclosed specific plans to harm his ex-wife, stating he knew her schedule and had purchased a weapon. Kevin implemented the state-mandated duty to warn protocol: he notified Trevor that confidentiality would be broken due to the serious threat, contacted local law enforcement to report the threat, and called Trevor's ex-wife to warn her of the potential danger. Kevin documented each step taken, including times of calls, names of officials contacted, and information provided.

Natural disasters and community crises may require counselors to provide psychological first aid while connecting clients to broader emergency services. During a regional wildfire, counselor Maria implemented her practice's disaster response plan, contacting current clients to assess their safety and immediate needs. For displaced clients, she provided brief supportive interventions focused on immediate coping while connecting them with Red Cross services for practical assistance. Maria documented these contacts, noting: *"Brief supportive contact provided to client following evacuation from Paradise Hills area. Basic needs assessment completed. Client currently safe at sister's home but experiencing acute stress symptoms. Provided grounding techniques and connected client with disaster relief services at community center. Will follow up in 48 hours to reassess needs."*

Substance-related emergencies present complex intervention boundaries. While counselors can address substance use disorders therapeutically, acute intoxication or withdrawal requiring medical intervention exceeds counseling scope. Counselor Thomas recognized this boundary when client Diane arrived visibly intoxicated, slurring speech and unable to maintain balance. Rather than proceeding with the session, Thomas implemented the practice's intoxication protocol: *"Session discontinued due to client's apparent intoxication. Assessed for immediate safety concerns. Client denied suicidal thoughts but was unable to safely transport herself. Arranged safe transportation with client's spouse who was contacted with client's permission. Provided resources for medical detoxification and rescheduled appointment for assessment when sober."*

Similarly, withdrawal symptoms requiring medical monitoring exceed counseling intervention. When client James reported severe shaking, sweating, and elevated heart rate after stopping alcohol consumption, counselor Whitney recognized potential dangerous withdrawal and facilitated immediate medical evaluation rather than continuing with counseling. Whitney documented: *"Client presenting with apparent alcohol withdrawal symptoms including tremors, diaphoresis, tachycardia, and confusion. Explained need for medical evaluation. Called client's emergency contact (brother) with permission to arrange transport to urgent care. Provided referral information for medically-supervised detoxification program. Will follow up after medical clearance."*

Documentation during crisis situations must be particularly thorough, including assessment details, interventions provided, resources offered, referrals made, and follow-up plans. This documentation serves both clinical and legal purposes, demonstrating appropriate standard of care. Effective crisis documentation includes:

1. Objective observations of client presentation
2. Direct quotes of concerning statements
3. Assessment questions asked and client responses
4. Risk level determination with supporting rationale
5. Interventions implemented
6. Resources provided

7. Consultations sought
8. Referrals made
9. Follow-up plan
10. Time frames for each action taken

Consultation during crisis situations provides essential support for appropriate decision-making. Counselors should establish relationships with supervisors or colleagues who can provide immediate consultation when needed. Counselor Derek documented his consultation process during a client crisis: *"Consulted with clinical supervisor Dr. Rivera regarding client's ambiguous statements about self-harm. Discussed assessment findings and intervention options while maintaining client confidentiality. Based on consultation, implemented additional screening questions and determined low imminent risk. Will continue to monitor in weekly sessions."*

Collaboration with emergency services requires understanding of local resources and protocols. Counselors should maintain updated contact information for local crisis teams, emergency departments, and mobile assessment units. When counselor Stephanie needed to facilitate emergency psychiatric evaluation for client Jamal, she documented: *"Contacted county mobile crisis team at 3:15pm with client's permission. Provided relevant clinical information including current presentation, history of bipolar disorder, medication compliance issues, and previous hospitalization history. Mobile team arrived at office at 4:05pm and conducted evaluation. Team determined inpatient evaluation warranted. Provided Jamal with information about what to expect during evaluation process. Mobile team transported client to Riverside Behavioral Health at 4:45pm. Called client's mother (emergency contact) with Jamal's permission to inform of hospitalization."*

BOUNDARIES WITH OTHER PROFESSIONS

Professional clinical counselors operate within a mental health ecosystem that includes several related but distinct professions. Understanding these boundaries helps counselors practice ethically, collaborate effectively, and make appropriate referrals when client needs extend beyond their scope of practice. While all mental health professionals share the common goal of supporting psychological wellbeing, each discipline brings unique training, perspectives, and legal authorizations to their work.

When comparing clinical counseling with psychology, several key distinctions emerge. Psychologists typically complete doctoral-level education (Ph.D., Psy.D., or Ed.D.) with extensive training in psychological assessment, research methods, and specialized interventions. In contrast, LPCCs generally hold master's degrees with focused training in counseling techniques and therapeutic relationships. This educational difference translates into practical distinctions in service delivery.

Psychologists possess unique testing privileges that allow them to administer, score, and interpret standardized psychological assessments. For example, when working with a client who exhibits symptoms that might indicate a learning disorder, an LPCC would recognize the need for formal cognitive and achievement testing. Rather than attempting to diagnose the learning disorder themselves, the ethical LPCC would refer the client to a psychologist for comprehensive assessment while potentially continuing to provide supportive counseling for the client's emotional concerns.

A practical example of appropriate collaboration occurred when counselor Michael began working with 14-year-old Aiden, who struggled with school performance and social anxiety. During their sessions, Michael noticed patterns suggesting possible attention difficulties and executive functioning challenges. Recognizing the limits of his scope, Michael discussed with Aiden's parents the benefits of a formal psychological evaluation. With their agreement, he referred them to a child psychologist specializing in neurodevelopmental assessments while continuing to help Aiden develop coping strategies for anxiety. The psychologist later diagnosed ADHD, and the two professionals coordinated their approaches, the psychologist providing specific recommendations for academic accommodations based on test results, while Michael incorporated these insights into their ongoing therapeutic work.

The boundary between psychiatry and clinical counseling centers primarily on the medical model and prescription privileges. Psychiatrists are medical doctors (M.D. or D.O.) who complete medical school followed by specialized residency training in psychiatric medicine and Psychiatric Mental Health Nurse Practitioners (PMHNP) have earned a masters or Doctor of Nursing degree and are trained in psychiatric nursing. This specialized background allows them to prescribe medications, conduct physical examinations, order and interpret laboratory tests, and address the biological aspects of mental health conditions.

LPCCs approach mental health through a counseling lens, focusing on talk therapy, behavioral interventions, and emotional processing without the authority to prescribe medications. This distinction creates natural opportunities for collaboration. For instance, when a counselor works with a client experiencing severe depression that doesn't improve with counseling alone, the counselor might suggest a psychiatric consultation (prescribing provider) to evaluate whether medication could be beneficial as part of the treatment plan.

Consider the case of counselor Sarah, who had been treating Elena for anxiety using cognitive-behavioral techniques. Despite making some progress, Elena continued to experience debilitating panic attacks that interfered with her daily functioning. Sarah discussed the potential benefits of medication as an adjunctive treatment and, with Elena's permission, referred her to a prescribing provider. The provider prescribed an anti-anxiety medication while Sarah continued providing weekly therapy. They communicated regularly (with Elena's written consent) to monitor her response to the combined treatment approach. This collaboration respected professional boundaries while providing Elena with comprehensive care that neither professional could offer alone.

Interprofessional collaboration often presents ethical challenges regarding information sharing and role clarity. When multiple mental health professionals work with the same client, clear communication boundaries must be established. This requires obtaining specific written consent from clients before sharing information, limiting shared information to what is necessary for coordination of care, and clearly defining each professional's role in the treatment process.

For example, when an LPCC and PMHNP collaborate on a client's care, they should establish at the outset: who will address which aspects of treatment, how frequently they will communicate, what information will be shared, and how disagreements about treatment direction will be resolved. The client should be fully informed about and involved in these decisions.

The ethical LPCC also recognizes when a client's needs would be better served by a different type of mental health professional. Signs that might indicate the need for referral include: when a client requires services outside the counselor's scope of practice (such as psychological testing or medication), when the client's needs match another profession's specialized training (such as intensive case management or family systems work), or when the complexity of the case suggests a team approach would be beneficial.

In all cases, referrals should be made thoughtfully, with clear explanation to clients about the rationale, and with attention to maintaining therapeutic rapport throughout the transition process. The goal is always to ensure clients receive the most appropriate and effective care, even when that means acknowledging the limitations of one's own professional scope.

EMERGING PRACTICE AREAS

The counseling profession continues to evolve in response to societal changes, technological advances, and new research findings. As the field expands, professional clinical counselors face both opportunities and challenges when incorporating emerging practices into their work. Understanding how these new approaches fit within established legal and ethical frameworks is essential for maintaining professional integrity while meeting clients' changing needs.

Technology-assisted counseling represents one of the most rapidly developing areas within the profession. While telehealth services gained widespread acceptance during the COVID-19 pandemic, the boundaries of digital therapeutic engagement extend far beyond video sessions. Mobile applications designed to supplement traditional therapy now offer between-session support through guided meditations, mood tracking, thought records, and skill-building exercises. When incorporating these tools, counselors must verify that recommended applications comply with privacy regulations and clearly communicate to clients that these technologies supplement rather than replace professional services.

Text-based counseling services, whether through secure messaging platforms or specialized therapeutic texting services, present unique documentation challenges. Unlike traditional sessions with clear beginning and end times, text exchanges may occur sporadically throughout the day or week. Counselors utilizing these modalities must establish clear boundaries regarding response times and emergency protocols while maintaining comprehensive records of all therapeutic exchanges. A sample policy might state: *"Messages will be responded to within 24 business hours. This service is not monitored 24/7 and should not be used for emergencies. If you experience a mental health emergency, please contact the crisis line at [number] or go to your nearest emergency room."*

Virtual reality (VR) applications for exposure therapy represent another technological frontier. These tools allow counselors to create controlled environments for clients to practice coping with anxiety-provoking situations, from public speaking to height phobias. Before implementing VR interventions, counselors must ensure they have received appropriate training in both the technology itself and the therapeutic protocols it supports. Documentation should include specific VR scenarios utilized, duration of exposure, client response, and any adverse effects experienced.

Artificial intelligence tools designed to analyze communication patterns or suggest therapeutic interventions raise complex questions about clinical judgment and responsibility. While these technologies may offer valuable insights, the counselor remains accountable for all treatment decisions. When utilizing AI-augmented tools, counselors should document their independent assessment of any AI-generated suggestions and maintain their clinical authority in determining appropriate interventions.

Specialized population services have expanded as counselors develop expertise in working with specific groups with unique needs. Trauma-informed care for veterans, refugees, and survivors of human trafficking requires specialized knowledge of both psychological impacts and relevant support systems. Counselors working with these populations must document their specialized training and clearly delineate when clients' needs exceed their expertise, necessitating collaboration or referral.

LGBTQ+ affirmative counseling has evolved from basic cultural competence to specialized approaches addressing the unique mental health challenges faced by sexual and gender minorities. Counselors providing gender-affirming care must understand both the psychological aspects of gender identity and the medical pathways available to clients. When writing letters supporting gender-affirming medical interventions, counselors should follow established professional guidelines such as those from the World Professional Association for Transgender Health (WPATH) and clearly document their assessment process.

Services for neurodivergent individuals, including those with autism spectrum conditions, ADHD, and learning differences, have expanded beyond traditional deficit-focused models to strength-based approaches. Counselors working with these populations should document their understanding of neurodiversity-affirming practices and any accommodations made to standard therapeutic techniques. For example: *"Session modified to include visual schedule and 5-minute movement breaks every 20 minutes to accommodate client's processing style and attention needs."*

Perinatal mental health services addressing pregnancy, childbirth, and early parenting challenges require knowledge of both psychological processes and physiological factors. Counselors in this specialty must document careful screening for conditions like postpartum depression and psychosis while maintaining clear referral pathways to medical providers when needed. Documentation might include: *"Administered Edinburgh Postnatal Depression Scale (score 15, indicating moderate depression symptoms). Discussed results with client and coordinated care with OB/GYN Dr. Smith with client's written consent."*

Integrative treatment approaches combining traditional counseling methods with complementary practices continue to gain acceptance. Mind-body interventions such as clinical hypnosis, biofeedback, and guided imagery require specialized training and certification. Counselors utilizing these techniques must document their qualifications, the specific protocols followed, and client response. For example: *"Conducted 20-minute progressive muscle relaxation training following Bernstein & Borkovec protocol. Client reported decrease in subjective anxiety from 8/10 to 4/10 and demonstrated reduced muscle tension as measured by shoulder posture."*

Somatic approaches focusing on the body's role in processing emotions and experiences have expanded from specialized trauma treatments to broader applications. Counselors incorporating techniques like somatic experiencing or sensorimotor psychotherapy should document their training in these modalities and maintain clear boundaries between counseling interventions and physical therapies requiring different licensure. Documentation might specify: *"Used somatic awareness techniques to help client identify physical sensations associated with anxiety. Guided client in tracking body sensations while discussing work stressors. Client identified chest tightness preceding worry thoughts."*

Nutritional counseling as it relates to mental health represents an area of growing interest but potential scope confusion. While counselors may educate clients about research on nutrition-mental health connections, they must avoid prescribing specific diets or supplements, which falls within the scope of registered dietitians and medical providers. Appropriate documentation might include: *"Discussed research on omega-3 fatty acids and mood. Provided educational handout on foods containing these nutrients. Recommended consultation with primary care physician regarding potential supplements."*

New intervention techniques continue to emerge from research and clinical innovation. Acceptance and Commitment Therapy (ACT), Compassion-Focused Therapy (CFT), and other *"third wave"* cognitive-behavioral approaches have expanded the counselor's toolkit. When implementing these approaches, counselors should document their training, the specific techniques utilized, and their rationale for selecting these interventions for particular clients.

Eye Movement Desensitization and Reprocessing (EMDR) and other trauma-specific protocols require certification beyond basic counseling credentials. Counselors must document completion of appropriate training programs and ongoing consultation or supervision when learning these specialized techniques. Session notes should clearly indicate which phase of the protocol was implemented and client response: *"Completed Phase 3 (Assessment) of EMDR protocol for target memory of car accident. Identified negative cognition 'I am unsafe' with validity of 2/7 and positive cognition 'I can handle difficult situations' with validity of 4/7. Subjective Units of Distress (SUD) rated at 8/10."*

Psychedelic-assisted therapy represents an emerging area with complex legal considerations. While some jurisdictions have approved certain psychedelic substances for therapeutic use, counselors must understand both state and federal regulations before engaging in this work. In locations where these treatments are legal, counselors typically work as part of multidisciplinary teams including medical providers who administer the substances. Documentation must clearly delineate the counselor's role in preparation and integration sessions versus medical aspects of treatment.

When evaluating whether an emerging practice fits within their scope, counselors should apply a systematic assessment process:

1. Training and competence evaluation: Have I received adequate training in this approach? Can I demonstrate competence through education, supervised experience, or certification?
2. Regulatory alignment: Does this practice comply with my state's definition of counseling and scope of practice laws? Does it require additional licensure or certification?
3. Evidence assessment: Is there research supporting this approach for my client population? What is the quality of this evidence?
4. Risk-benefit analysis: What are the potential risks of this approach? Do the likely benefits outweigh these risks for this specific client?
5. Ethical consideration: Does this approach align with counseling ethics codes? Are there potential conflicts with principles like nonmaleficence or professional boundaries?
6. Consultation: Have I consulted with colleagues, supervisors, or my professional association about this practice?
7. Documentation plan: Can I clearly document my decision-making process, the interventions used, and client response?

A counselor considering incorporating animal-assisted therapy might document this assessment process: *"Completed 40-hour certification in animal-assisted interventions through [organization].*

Reviewed state regulations confirming therapy animals permitted in professional offices with proper certification. Examined research showing benefits for clients with trauma history similar to client's presentation. Identified minimal risks given client's positive history with animals and absence of allergies. Consulted with colleague who has 5 years' experience in animal-assisted therapy. Will document specific interventions, client response, and any adverse events in session notes."

As the counseling profession continues to expand, maintaining clear boundaries while embracing innovation requires ongoing education and careful evaluation. Counselors are highly encouraged to meet legal and ethical guidelines by thoroughly documenting their decision-making process and ensuring new approaches align with legal and ethical requirements in order to responsibly incorporate emerging practices that enhance client care.

CHAPTER THREE

PROFESSIONAL PRACTICE STANDARDS

CREATING COMPLIANT INFORMED CONSENT DOCUMENTS

Although the term 'informed consent' is not explicitly defined in California statutes or regulations, it is a foundational practice standard. Informed consent is both a legal and ethical concept, reflecting the counselor's obligation to ensure clients understand the nature of treatment and their rights. Its inclusion under practice standards reflects its role in establishing the therapeutic relationship and meeting the standard of care. This process goes beyond simply having a client sign a form, it represents a meaningful exchange of information that empowers clients to make educated decisions about their care.

It should be noted that *Cobbs v. Grant* (1972) established several fundamental elements of informed consent critical to professional counseling. The case clarified that clients must be informed of potential benefits and risks of treatment, alternatives to the proposed treatment, and their right to accept or decline services. Counselors must also accurately describe their qualifications and avoid misrepresentation of scope, ensuring clients are not led to believe the counselor has the same training or authority as a psychologist or psychiatrist. This is important so that the client can make the best decision possible for themselves. As required under California Business and Professions Code §2290.5, counselors must obtain and document verbal or written informed consent prior to delivering telehealth services.

A legally compliant informed consent document must include several essential components. First, it must clearly identify the counselor, including name, license type, license number, and contact information. This establishes the professional's credentials and authority to provide services. Second, it must outline the nature and purpose of counseling, including potential benefits and limitations. Third, it must address confidentiality and its limits, particularly regarding mandated reporting situations. Fourth, it must detail financial arrangements, including fees, insurance billing, and cancellation policies. Finally, it must explain client rights, including the right to terminate therapy at any time. While most counselors obtain informed consent in writing, California law does not require this in all cases. Verbal informed consent is acceptable, especially when writing poses a barrier due to language, cultural norms, or ability. Regardless of how consent is obtained, it must be documented in the client record.

When crafting the treatment description section, begin with a clear explanation of your therapeutic approach. For example: *"I primarily utilize cognitive-behavioral therapy (CBT), which focuses on identifying and changing unhelpful thought patterns and behaviors. This approach is active and may include homework assignments between sessions." Avoid technical jargon that clients might not understand. Include information about session length (typically 45-50 minutes), frequency (usually weekly to start), and expected duration of treatment when possible. Be honest about limitations, stating something like: "While many clients benefit from counseling, outcomes vary, and there are no guarantees of specific results."*

The confidentiality section requires particular attention due to its legal implications. Start with a strong statement affirming confidentiality: *"Information shared in our sessions is confidential and will not be disclosed without your written permission."* Then clearly outline exceptions mandated by law: *"However, there are specific situations where I am legally required to break confidentiality: (1) if you present an imminent danger to yourself or others; (2) if there is suspected abuse or neglect of a child, elderly person, or dependent adult; (3) if I receive a court order requiring disclosure; or (4) if you use insurance benefits, as I must provide certain information to your insurer."*

For telehealth services, add specific language about electronic communication: *"While I take extensive measures to protect your privacy during telehealth sessions, including using HIPAA-compliant platforms, no electronic communication can be guaranteed 100% secure. By consenting to telehealth services, you acknowledge and accept these limitations."*

The fee structure section should be transparent and comprehensive. Include your standard fee, any sliding scale options, insurance billing procedures, and payment methods accepted. Be explicit about cancellation policies: *"A full session fee will be charged for appointments canceled with less than 24 hours' notice, except in cases of emergency. Insurance typically does not cover missed sessions."* Also address potential fee increases: *"Fees may be adjusted periodically. You will receive at least 30 days' notice before any fee change takes effect."*

Emergency procedures must be clearly outlined to manage client expectations and ensure safety. Include language such as: *"I am not available 24/7 for emergencies. If you experience a mental health emergency, please call the National Suicide Prevention Lifeline at 988, go to your nearest emergency room, or call 911."* Provide your policy for between-session contact: *"For non-urgent matters, you may leave me a message at [phone number]. I typically return calls within 24 business hours. Brief calls (under 10 minutes) are not charged; longer calls may be billed at my prorated hourly rate."*

The client rights and responsibilities section should empower clients while setting appropriate boundaries. Include statements like: *"You have the right to ask questions about any aspect of therapy, to discuss your treatment plan, and to request changes to your treatment approach. You have the right to end therapy at any time, and I can provide referrals if needed."* Regarding responsibilities, include: *"For therapy to be effective, your active participation is essential. This includes attending scheduled sessions, completing agreed-upon between-session activities, and providing honest feedback about your progress and our work together."*

When drafting informed consent documents, avoid these common pitfalls:

1. Using overly technical language that clients may not understand
2. Making absolute guarantees about confidentiality without clearly stating exceptions
3. Being vague about fees, billing practices, or cancellation policies
4. Failing to address electronic communication and social media policies
5. Omitting information about record-keeping practices
6. Not explaining the process for termination of services
7. Using a generic template without customizing it to your specific practice

Counselors must assess whether the client has the legal and cognitive capacity to provide informed consent. Clients with dementia, significant intellectual disability, or those under conservatorship may require that consent be obtained from a legally authorized representative. When working with minors under the age of 12, counselors should obtain consent from a guardian and seek the minor's assent by explaining services in age-appropriate language and confirming their willingness to participate.

Sample language for a social media policy might include: *"To maintain professional boundaries and protect your confidentiality, I do not accept friend or contact requests from current or former clients on social networking sites. I will not search for you online without your permission except in emergency situations where I have reason to believe you may be in danger."*

For record-keeping practices, you might state: *"I maintain clinical records that include your contact information, diagnosis, treatment plan, session notes, and billing information. These records are stored securely in accordance with professional standards and state law. You have the right to request access to your records, though in rare cases I may deny access if I believe viewing them would be harmful to you."*

Regarding termination, include language such as: *"Either of us may decide to end therapy at any time. Ideally, termination occurs when treatment goals have been substantially achieved. If you decide to terminate therapy, I recommend discussing this decision in session to ensure appropriate closure and to address any ongoing concerns."*

The informed consent document should also address technology use in practice: *"I use encrypted email for scheduling and administrative matters. However, email is not completely secure, so please do not include sensitive clinical information in emails. Text messaging is used only for scheduling purposes and should not include clinical content."*

For group therapy settings, add specific language about the limits of confidentiality: *"While I am bound by confidentiality rules, I cannot guarantee that other group members will maintain your privacy. All group members are asked to respect confidentiality, but this cannot be legally enforced."*

When working with couples or families, address potential conflicts of interest: *"When working with couples or families, I maintain a 'no secrets' policy. Information shared with me individually may be shared in joint sessions if I determine it is in the best interest of the therapeutic process."*

Before implementing your informed consent document, use this compliance checklist:

1. Does the document clearly identify you, your credentials, and your contact information?
2. Does it explain your therapeutic approach and what clients can expect from treatment?
3. Does it address confidentiality and all legally mandated exceptions?
4. Are fees, payment policies, and insurance procedures clearly outlined?

5. Does it explain emergency procedures and between-session contact policies?
6. Are client rights and responsibilities clearly stated?
7. Does it address record-keeping practices and client access to records?
8. Does it explain policies regarding electronic communication and social media?
9. Does it outline the process for termination of services?
10. Is the language clear, free of jargon, and accessible to clients?
11. Does it include a signature line for the client, the counselor, and the date?
12. Has it been reviewed by a legal professional familiar with mental health law in California?

Remember that informed consent is an ongoing process, not a one-time event. Regularly review and update your informed consent document to reflect changes in your practice, professional standards, or legal requirements. Discuss the document with clients at the beginning of treatment, encourage questions, and revisit relevant sections as needed throughout the therapeutic relationship. This document serves not only as a legal safeguard but as a therapeutic tool that clarifies expectations and empowers clients to engage fully in the counseling process.

ETHICAL FEE SETTING AND BILLING

Setting appropriate fees for counseling services requires balancing professional value with client accessibility while adhering to ethical standards. The process begins with a thorough market analysis of your geographic location, as fee norms vary significantly across regions. In metropolitan areas like San Francisco or Los Angeles, standard therapy rates typically range from $150-250 per session, while rural California communities might average $80-120. This regional variation reflects differences in cost of living, population density, and local economic conditions.

Beyond location, your education and experience level substantially impact appropriate fee structures. Recent graduates with associate registrations generally charge 20-30% less than fully licensed professionals with several years of experience. Specialized training or certifications in high-demand treatment approaches like EMDR, DBT, or specialized trauma work often justify premium rates, as these skills represent additional investment in professional development and offer specialized value to clients.

If you operate under a fictitious business name (DBA), you must disclose the name of the business and clearly identify the licensed counselor(s) who own or manage the practice. This ensures clients understand who is legally responsible for their care. Practice expenses form another key consideration in ethical fee setting. Calculate your monthly overhead costs, including office rent, utilities, electronic health record systems, professional liability insurance, continuing education, license renewal fees, professional memberships, and administrative support. For example, a counselor in a mid-sized California city might face monthly expenses like:

* Office rent: $800-1,200
* Professional liability insurance: $30-60
* Electronic health record system: $50-100
* Professional association dues: $25-40
* Continuing education: $50-100
* Administrative costs: $100-200

Dividing these total monthly expenses by your expected number of client hours provides your break-even rate, the minimum you must charge to cover basic practice costs before accounting for your professional compensation.

Insurance panel participation introduces additional fee considerations. Most insurance companies establish fee schedules that dictate reimbursement rates regardless of your standard fees. Before joining panels, request their fee schedules and calculate whether participation aligns with your financial needs. Many California counselors maintain a mixed practice model, accepting some insurance clients while reserving slots for private-pay clients at their full rate.

When establishing your fee structure, document your decision-making process, noting market research, overhead calculations, and professional value considerations. This documentation serves both ethical and practical purposes, providing justification for your rates and a reference point for future fee adjustments.

Proper billing documentation begins with clear, written fee agreements incorporated into your informed consent documents. These agreements should specify:

1. Your standard session fee
2. Session length (typically 45-50 minutes)
3. Payment timing (due at time of service, monthly billing, etc.)
4. Accepted payment methods
5. Cancellation policy and associated fees
6. Insurance billing procedures, if applicable
7. Fee adjustment policies and frequency
8. Additional charges for services like letter writing, record preparation, or court appearances

For example, a cancellation policy might state: *"A full fee will be charged for appointments canceled with less than 24 hours' notice except in cases of emergency or illness. Insurance companies do not reimburse for missed sessions, so you will be responsible for this charge."*

For court-related services, specify hourly rates and minimum charges: *"Court appearances, depositions, or legal consultations are billed at $200 per hour with a four-hour minimum, plus travel time. Document preparation for legal purposes is billed at $150 per hour."*

Sliding scale implementation requires thoughtful structure to maintain both accessibility and sustainability. Rather than arbitrary fee reductions, develop a systematic approach based on documented financial need. A common method uses a percentage of the federal poverty guidelines adjusted for household size. For example:

* Household income below 200% of federal poverty level: 40% discount
* Household income 201-300% of federal poverty level: 30% discount
* Household income 301-400% of federal poverty level: 20% discount
* Household income 401-500% of federal poverty level: 10% discount

Document your sliding scale policy in writing, including eligibility criteria, verification requirements, and reassessment frequency. Clients receiving reduced fees should complete a financial disclosure form and provide documentation such as tax returns or pay stubs. Include language indicating that sliding scale spots are limited and subject to availability.

For example: *"I offer a limited number of sliding scale spots based on financial need and current practice capacity. Eligibility is determined by household income relative to the federal poverty guidelines. Documentation of financial status is required annually to maintain reduced fee arrangements."*

Payment arrangement protocols address situations where clients need flexibility beyond sliding scale options. These arrangements might include installment plans, delayed billing, or temporary fee reductions during financial hardship. Document all payment arrangements in writing, specifying:

1. The agreed-upon payment amount
2. Payment schedule and due dates
3. Duration of the arrangement
4. Consequences for missed payments
5. Process for renegotiation if needed

For example: *"We have agreed that your $120 session fee will be paid in two $60 installments on the 1st and 15th of each month. This arrangement will be reviewed after three months. If a payment is missed, we will discuss the situation in our next session and may need to adjust our arrangement."*

Billing statements must meet both ethical and legal requirements. Each statement should include:

1. Your name, license type, and license number
2. Practice address and contact information
3. Client name and identifier
4. Service dates
5. Service codes (CPT codes if insurance is involved)
6. Fee charged
7. Payments received
8. Current balance
9. Payment due date

For insurance billing, additional elements are required:

1. Your NPI number
2. Tax identification number
3. Diagnosis code (ICD-10)
4. Place of service code
5. Client insurance information including policy and group numbers

Maintain meticulous records of all financial transactions, including copies of statements, payment receipts, and insurance claims. These records should be stored securely in compliance with HIPAA requirements and retained according to state record-keeping guidelines.

Several common ethical scenarios arise in counseling billing practices. One frequent challenge involves clients who accumulate unpaid balances. When this occurs, address the issue directly in session rather than avoiding the uncomfortable topic. For example: *"I've noticed your account has an outstanding balance of $360 for our last three sessions. I'd like to discuss how we might address this and whether there are financial concerns affecting your ability to pay."*

If a client cannot pay their balance, explore options such as temporarily reducing the fee, creating a payment plan, or, in extreme cases, referring to a provider with lower fees or free services. Document all discussions and agreements regarding unpaid balances.

Another common scenario involves insurance denials. When claims are denied, promptly notify clients of their financial responsibility while offering to appeal the denial if appropriate. For example: *"Your insurance has denied coverage for our session on May 15, stating it wasn't medically necessary. You're responsible for the $130 fee, but I'm happy to file an appeal if you'd like. In the meantime, would you prefer to pay this balance now or should we set up a payment plan?"*

Gift offers from clients present another ethical billing challenge. The California Board of Behavioral Sciences and the American Counseling Association ethics codes caution against accepting substantial gifts that could create dual relationships or boundary confusion. Small tokens of appreciation may be acceptable, but should be documented in the client's record. When declining gifts, do so tactfully: *"I appreciate your thoughtfulness, but accepting gifts beyond a small token could complicate our professional relationship. Your continued work in therapy is the best gift you can give."*

Bartering arrangements, where services are exchanged instead of payment, require careful consideration. While not explicitly prohibited, bartering introduces potential complications including dual relationships, valuation disputes, and tax reporting issues. If considering a barter arrangement, document:

1. Why the arrangement is clinically appropriate
2. How the services are valued
3. The specific exchange terms
4. Potential risks discussed with the client
5. Contingency plans if the arrangement becomes problematic

For example: *"Client has requested to exchange graphic design services for therapy sessions. We have agreed that 2 hours of design work equals one therapy session. This arrangement will be reviewed monthly and terminated if it interferes with therapeutic progress."*

Fee increases require thoughtful implementation. Provide clients with at least 30 days' written notice before implementing any fee change. Explain the reasons for the increase and be prepared to discuss its impact on continuing treatment. For example: *"Effective September 1, my session* *fee will increase from $130 to $140. This is my first fee adjustment in three years and reflects increases in practice expenses and cost of living. Please let me know if you have any concerns about this change."*

The No Surprises Act, which took effect January 1, 2022, adds another layer to ethical billing practices. This federal law requires that Professional Clinical Counselors provide Good Faith Estimates (GFEs) of expected charges to uninsured and self-pay clients. According to California Business and Professions Code §4999.90, counselors must provide clear information about fees and billing practices as part of informed consent. The GFE requirement aligns with this existing obligation while adding specific documentation requirements.

When preparing GFEs, include:

- A detailed explanation of your diagnosis and treatment plan
- Expected number and frequency of sessions
- Estimated total cost based on the anticipated treatment duration
- Statement that actual costs may vary based on treatment progress

California Business and Professions Code §4999.75 also requires that counselors maintain accurate records of all professional services rendered, including financial transactions. For specific record retention requirements, see the 'Documentation and Legal Compliance' section. Regular review of these practices, consultation with colleagues when ethical questions arise, and prioritizing client welfare in financial decisions form the foundation of ethical billing in professional counseling.

ADVERTISING AND MARKETING LEGAL BOUNDARIES

Marketing counseling services requires careful attention to both professional standards and legal requirements. California law establishes specific parameters for how Professional Clinical Counselors can advertise their services while protecting consumers from misleading claims. Section 1811 of the California Code of Regulations (16 CCR) forms the foundation of these regulations, requiring all advertisements to clearly identify the license type and status of the practitioner.

When creating any marketing materials, counselors must include their complete license designation. For example, *"Jaylin Smith, LPCC #12345"* or *"Jordyn Doe, Registered Associate Professional Clinical Counselor (APCC) #98765 (Supervised by Casey Sims, LPCC #12345)."* Counselors practicing as associates or trainees are required to inform clients of their registration status and provide their supervisor's full name, license number, and contact information in both informed consent and marketing materials. This transparency allows potential clients to verify credentials and understand the practitioner's level of experience and authority. BPC 4999.90 further specifies that advertisements must not contain false, misleading, or deceptive statements, including any implications that the counselor can provide services beyond their scope of practice.

Social media has become an essential marketing channel for many counselors, but it presents unique challenges for maintaining professional standards. When establishing a social media presence, counselors should create separate professional and personal accounts to maintain appropriate boundaries. Professional accounts should clearly display license information in the profile biography section and avoid casual language that might diminish professional credibility.

Content shared on social media platforms must adhere to the same standards as other advertising materials. BPC Section 651 prohibits making claims that professional services can cure specific conditions or guaranteeing results. Instead, focus on sharing educational content about mental health topics, practice updates, and general information about counseling approaches would likely be the best approach in advertising.

Website development offers counselors extensive opportunities to showcase their services while maintaining compliance with legal requirements. Your website's homepage should prominently display your name, license type, and license number. The *"About"* page should include detailed information about your education, training, and approach to counseling, being careful not to exaggerate qualifications or make claims about specialized expertise without appropriate training.

BPC Section 651 requires that descriptions of services accurately represent what you can legally provide as an LPCC or APCC. The service description page should outline your areas of focus while avoiding terms like *"expert," "specialist,"* or *"certified"* unless you hold formal certifications in those areas. For APCCs, websites must clearly indicate that services are provided under supervision and include the supervisor's name and license information.

Fee information must be transparent and consistent with what clients will actually pay. The California Board of Behavioral Sciences (BBS) regulations prohibit *"bait and switch"* tactics where advertised rates differ from actual charges. If offering a sliding scale or insurance-based services, clearly explain how fees are determined to avoid confusion.

Professional networking represents another important marketing avenue for counselors. When distributing business cards or brochures at networking events, ensure these materials include your complete license information as required by BPC Section 651. Professional directories, both online and print, must accurately represent your qualifications and services. Many counselors join platforms like Psychology Today or TherapyDen, which provide structured profiles that help ensure compliance with advertising regulations.

Print materials remain valuable marketing tools despite the digital shift. Brochures, flyers, and business cards must include the same license information required in other formats. BPC Section 651 applies to all advertising regardless of medium. When designing print materials, avoid stock photos that might misrepresent your practice demographics or create unrealistic expectations about counseling outcomes.

Educational outreach through workshops, presentations, and community events offers counselors opportunities to demonstrate expertise while serving the public good. When advertising these events, BPC Section 651 still applies, requiring clear identification of your license status. Marketing materials for workshops should accurately describe the content and avoid promising specific outcomes for attendees.

When presenting at community events, counselors can distribute materials that comply with advertising regulations while providing valuable information. These events allow for direct interaction with potential clients, but counselors must maintain professional boundaries even in these more casual settings. Avoid offering on-the-spot clinical advice, which could create an inappropriate counseling relationship outside proper channels.

Terms implying medical expertise beyond a counselor's scope are also prohibited. PCCs cannot use terms like *"psychoanalyst," "neuropsychologist,"* or *"psychiatrist"* unless they hold those specific credentials. Similarly, counselors cannot advertise services that fall outside their scope of practice, such as medication management or certain types of psychological testing as outlined in BPC Section 4999.20.

The following examples illustrate compliant versus problematic marketing statements:

Compliant: *"I provide cognitive-behavioral therapy for adults experiencing anxiety and depression."*

Problematic: *"I specialize in rapid anxiety cure techniques that provide immediate relief."*

Compliant: *"As an LPCC, I offer counseling services to help clients develop coping strategies for life challenges."*

Problematic: *"My unique therapeutic approach guarantees you'll overcome your problems in just five sessions."*

Compliant: *"I work with clients experiencing relationship difficulties, using evidence-informed approaches."*

Problematic: *"My revolutionary couples therapy technique has a 95% success rate in saving marriages."*

The BBS has the authority to review advertising materials during investigations, and having an archive of past marketing content can help demonstrate compliance. This documentation should include screenshots of social media posts, copies of print materials, and records of website changes over time. The key principles, transparency about credentials, accuracy in service descriptions, and avoiding guarantees or exaggerated claims, apply across all marketing channels. When in doubt about a specific marketing approach, consulting with colleagues, supervisors, or legal advisors can help ensure that promotional efforts enhance rather than compromise professional standing.

DOCUMENTATION AND LEGAL COMPLIANCE

Documentation serves as the backbone of ethical and legally sound counseling practice. Every client interaction, assessment, treatment decision, and outcome must be recorded with precision and care. Proper documentation not only protects counselors from liability but also ensures quality client care and facilitates communication among treatment providers.

Session notes represent the most frequent form of documentation in counseling practice. The SOAP format (Subjective, Objective, Assessment, Plan) provides a structured approach that meets both clinical and legal requirements. The Subjective component captures the client's self-reported experiences, concerns, and goals, ideally using direct quotes when possible. For example: *"Client stated, 'I've been having trouble sleeping since my promotion last month. I lie awake worrying about making mistakes at work.'"* The Objective section documents observable behaviors and clinical observations without interpretation. This might include: *"Client arrived 10 minutes late, appeared fatigued with slumped posture and frequent yawning. Made minimal eye contact during first half of session, increased engagement when discussing coping strategies."* The Assessment portion contains the counselor's professional analysis and clinical impressions: *"Client presents with symptoms consistent with adjustment disorder with anxiety related to recent job promotion. Sleep disturbance appears to be exacerbating anxiety symptoms, creating a cycle of worry and fatigue."* Finally, the Plan section outlines next steps: *"Will introduce sleep hygiene practices and thought recording for anxious rumination. Scheduled next appointment for 5/15 at 2pm. Will assess effectiveness of sleep interventions and determine need for additional anxiety management techniques."*

Some practices prefer the DAP format (Data, Assessment, Plan), which consolidates subjective and objective information into the Data section. A sample DAP note might read: *"Data: Client reported increased conflict with teenage son over homework completion and curfew. Described feeling 'at the end of my rope' and 'unable to get through to him.' Client became tearful when discussing recent argument that ended with son slamming door and refusing to speak for two days. Assessment: Client struggling with developmentally appropriate adolescent separation behaviors but lacking effective communication strategies to maintain connection while enforcing boundaries. Plan: Introduced concept of validation before problem-solving. Role-played conversation scenarios. Client will practice reflective listening this week and track interactions in parent-child communication log."*

Regardless of format, session notes must include certain essential elements: date, start and end times, location (including whether telehealth), participants, interventions used, client response to interventions, risk assessment when indicated, and plan for continued treatment. Notes should be completed as soon as possible after sessions, ideally within 24 hours, to ensure accuracy.

Treatment plan documentation forms the roadmap for counseling services. A properly documented treatment plan includes presenting problems, diagnosis (if within scope), measurable goals, specific interventions, and anticipated timeframes. Each identified problem should connect to specific goals and interventions. For example:

Problem: Client experiences panic attacks in social situations, leading to avoidance of work meetings and social gatherings.

Goal: Client will reduce panic symptoms in social situations from daily occurrence to no more than once weekly within 3 months.

Objectives:

1. Client will identify and challenge catastrophic thoughts using thought records daily for 6 weeks.
2. Client will practice diaphragmatic breathing for 5 minutes twice daily for 4 weeks.
3. Client will gradually increase exposure to anxiety-provoking social situations using hierarchy developed in session.

Interventions:

1. Provide psychoeducation on cognitive-behavioral model of panic.
2. Teach and practice cognitive restructuring techniques.
3. Introduce and rehearse breathing and grounding exercises.
4. Develop and implement graduated exposure hierarchy.

Timeframe: 12 weekly sessions with reassessment at session 6.

Treatment plans should be developed collaboratively with clients and updated regularly as treatment progresses. Documentation should reflect client input and agreement with the plan, often including the client's signature. When goals are achieved or require modification, the treatment plan should be formally updated with documentation of the rationale for changes.

Progress monitoring records track advancement toward treatment goals. These records may include standardized measures, client self-reports, and counselor observations. For example, a counselor working with a client experiencing depression might document: *"PHQ-9 score decreased from 18 (baseline) to 12 (week 4), indicating moderate improvement in depressive symptoms. Client reports increased energy and has resumed daily walks. Sleep remains disrupted but has improved from 3-4 hours to 5-6 hours nightly. Client continues to experience anhedonia and social withdrawal."* Progress notes should specifically reference treatment plan goals and objectives, noting movement toward or away from targets.

Risk assessment documentation requires particular attention to detail. When clients present with suicidal or homicidal ideation, self-harm behaviors, or other safety concerns, documentation must thoroughly capture the assessment process, risk determination, and safety planning. A sample risk assessment note might include: *"Client endorsed passive suicidal ideation ('Sometimes I think it would be easier if I wasn't here') but denied active ideation, plan, intent, or preparatory behaviors. Denied history of suicide attempts. Identified children and religious beliefs as protective factors. Contracted verbally for safety. Provided crisis resources including National Suicide Prevention Lifeline. Developed written safety plan that client will keep in phone case. Plan includes warning signs, coping strategies, social supports, and emergency contacts. Client demonstrated understanding by restating key components of safety plan."*

Termination documentation closes the clinical record appropriately when counseling concludes. Termination notes should include the reason for ending treatment, summary of progress, remaining concerns, recommendations, and any referrals provided. For example: *"Treatment concluded today by mutual agreement after 16 sessions. Client has achieved primary goals of reducing panic attacks (none in past month) and returning to work meetings without avoidance.*

Client reports continued mild anxiety in novel social situations but feels confident using cognitive restructuring and breathing techniques independently. Reviewed relapse prevention strategies and situations that might warrant return to treatment. Provided referral to community support group for ongoing maintenance. Client aware they can return for booster sessions if needed."

Legal compliance requirements for documentation vary by jurisdiction but typically include:

1. Timeliness: Notes completed within established timeframes (usually 24-48 hours)
2. Security: Records stored securely with appropriate access controls

3. Legibility: Clear, readable documentation (whether handwritten or electronic)
4. Authorship: Signature, credentials, and date on all entries
5. Corrections: Proper procedures for amending records (single line through errors, initialed and dated)
6. Retention: Adherence to state-mandated record retention periods

Electronic health records (EHRs) present both opportunities and challenges for documentation. While EHRs can improve organization, accessibility, and legibility, they may also introduce risks related to template overuse and copy-paste functions. When using EHRs, counselors should:

1. Customize templates to reflect individual client presentations
2. Avoid excessive auto-population of content
3. Review all documentation for accuracy before finalizing
4. Ensure appropriate security measures including encryption and secure login procedures
5. Maintain awareness of audit trails that track all access to records

Documentation becomes particularly important in high-risk situations. When working with mandated clients, those involved in legal proceedings, or cases with potential for litigation, counselors should implement enhanced documentation practices:

1. Increase detail regarding client statements and behaviors
2. Document all communications with other professionals or systems
3. Note client attendance, punctuality, and adherence to treatment recommendations
4. Record all attempts to address non-compliance
5. Maintain copies of all signed agreements and informed consent discussions

Sample documentation for a mandated client might include: *"Client arrived 15 minutes late for court-ordered anger management session. When addressed, client stated, 'Traffic was bad, not my fault.' Reviewed attendance requirements per court order (no more than 2 absences permitted). Client signed attendance sheet. Completed Module 3 on identifying anger triggers. Client initially minimized responsibility stating, 'People just know how to push my buttons,' but later identified work stress as contributing factor. Practiced thought-stopping technique with moderate engagement. Client completed homework assignment from previous session (anger log) but left two days blank without explanation. Reviewed homework requirements and potential consequences of non-compliance. Client will continue anger log and practice thought-stopping daily before next session. Report on attendance and participation will be sent to referring probation officer on 5/30 as required."*

Ultimately, effective documentation balances thoroughness with efficiency. Records should contain sufficient detail to demonstrate appropriate care without unnecessary information that could create liability or violate client privacy. Structured documentation and routine review support legally sound recordkeeping while promoting consistent, high-quality care.

PROFESSIONAL COMMUNICATIONS PROTOCOL

Professional communication forms the backbone of ethical counseling practice, establishing clear boundaries and expectations while protecting both clients and counselors. Licensed Professional Clinical Counselors (LPCCs) in California must navigate various communication channels with careful attention to legal requirements, confidentiality concerns, and professional standards. The California Business and Professions Code requires that LPCCs maintain professional standards in all communications related to their practice.

When communicating with clients via email or text messages, counselors must implement specific safeguards to maintain confidentiality and professional boundaries. Before initiating electronic communications, counselors should obtain written consent that acknowledges the risks and limitations of these methods. This consent should be documented in the client's record as required by California Business and Professions Code Section 4999.75, which mandates adequate records of all professional services.

A sample electronic communication consent form should include:

1. Acknowledgment of potential privacy risks
2. Expected response times
3. Appropriate content for electronic communications
4. Emergency protocols (clarifying that email/text are not appropriate for emergencies)
5. Fee policies for time spent on electronic communications
6. Record-keeping practices for electronic messages

For example, the consent might state: *"I understand that email and text communications are not completely secure and that while my therapist takes reasonable precautions to protect my privacy, confidentiality cannot be guaranteed. I agree to use these methods only for non-urgent matters such as scheduling."*

When using email with clients, counselors should employ encrypted email services that comply with HIPAA requirements. Regular email services like Gmail or Yahoo do not provide adequate security for protected health information. Messages should include confidentiality disclaimers such as: *"This message contains confidential information and is intended only for the individual named. If you are not the named recipient, you should not disseminate, distribute, or copy this email. Please notify the sender immediately if you have received this email by mistake."*

Text messaging presents particular challenges due to limited security features. Best practices include:

1. Using HIPAA-compliant texting platforms rather than standard SMS
2. Limiting text content to scheduling and brief administrative matters
3. Avoiding clinical discussions via text
4. Setting clear boundaries regarding response times
5. Documenting substantive text exchanges in the client's record

Professional correspondence with colleagues, insurance companies, and other entities requires equal attention to confidentiality and professionalism. When corresponding about client matters, counselors should:

1. Use letterhead that clearly displays license type and number as required by Business and Professions Code Section 651
2. Include only necessary client information
3. Obtain appropriate releases before sharing information
4. Maintain copies of all correspondence in the client's record
5. Use secure methods for transmitting protected health information

Letters of referral deserve special consideration, as they involve sharing client information with other providers. These letters should:

1. Be concise and focused on relevant clinical information
2. Include only information authorized by the client's release
3. Clearly state the purpose of the referral
4. Provide contact information for follow-up questions
5. Document the referral in the client's record

For example, a properly structured referral letter might begin: *"I am writing regarding my client, [Name], who has provided written authorization for this communication (authorization attached). I am referring [Name] for psychiatric evaluation due to symptoms of depression that have not responded adequately to psychotherapy alone."*

Inter-professional communications require balancing collaboration with confidentiality. When consulting with other professionals about client care, counselors must:

1. Obtain specific written consent from clients before sharing information

2. Limit disclosed information to what is necessary for consultation purposes
3. Document consultations in the client's record
4. Maintain professional tone and language
5. Respect professional boundaries and scope of practice

The California Business and Professions Code Section 4999.90 identifies unprofessional conduct as including the unauthorized disclosure of confidential information, underscoring the importance of proper authorization for inter-professional communications.

When participating in treatment teams or coordinated care settings, counselors should establish clear protocols for information sharing that comply with both HIPAA and California's Confidentiality of Medical Information Act (Civil Code Section 56 et seq.). These protocols might include:

1. Regular team meetings with documented attendance
2. Standardized formats for sharing essential information
3. Clear documentation of team decisions and rationales
4. Processes for resolving disagreements about treatment approaches
5. Mechanisms for maintaining client confidentiality in team settings

Crisis response protocols require particularly careful communication planning. California law establishes specific duties related to dangerous clients, including the Tarasoff duty to protect potential victims (codified in Civil Code Section 43.92). When facing client crises, communication protocols should include:

1. Clear procedures for immediate response to suicidal or homicidal ideation
2. Scripts for communicating with emergency services
3. Documentation requirements for crisis situations
4. Notification procedures for supervisors or consultants
5. Follow-up communication plans with clients after crises

For suicide risk, communications should follow an established protocol such as:

1. Direct assessment of suicidal ideation, plan, means, and intent
2. Clear documentation of risk assessment and safety planning
3. Communication with emergency contacts when warranted
4. Coordination with crisis services or emergency departments
5. Documented follow-up communications

When fulfilling the duty to warn and protect, counselors must carefully document:

1. The assessment that led to the determination of danger
2. Reasonable efforts to communicate the threat to the potential victim
3. Notifications to law enforcement
4. The rationale for clinical decisions made during the crisis
5. Follow-up actions taken to address the underlying issues

The California Board of Behavioral Sciences emphasizes that proper documentation of crisis communications is essential for both client care and risk management. Business and Professions Code Section 4999.90 identifies failure to maintain adequate records as grounds for disciplinary action.

Documentation of all professional communications forms an essential part of the client record. California regulations require that records be *"consistent with sound clinical judgment, the standards of the profession, and the nature of the services being rendered"* (California Code of Regulations, Title 16, Section 1815.1).

When documenting communications, counselors should:

1. Record the date, time, and method of significant communications
2. Summarize the content and outcome of important exchanges
3. Note any clinical decisions made based on communications
4. Document follow-up plans or actions
5. Include copies of written communications in the client record

Phone conversations with clients or other professionals should be documented with the same care as in-person sessions. A phone contact note might include:

1. Date and time of the call
2. Duration of the conversation
3. Participants in the call
4. Summary of topics discussed
5. Any decisions or plans made
6. Follow-up actions required

For example: *"5/15/2025, 3:15-3:30 PM: Phone call with client regarding increased anxiety symptoms following job loss. Client denied suicidal ideation but reported difficulty sleeping and persistent worry. Reviewed coping strategies and scheduled urgent session for tomorrow at 10:00 AM. Client agreed to use deep breathing exercises and call crisis line if symptoms worsen."*

Risk management for electronic communications requires specific attention in today's digital environment. The California Board of Behavioral Sciences has identified several areas of concern regarding electronic communications, including confidentiality breaches, boundary violations, and documentation deficiencies.

To manage these risks, counselors should:

1. Develop and implement a written electronic communication policy
2. Use only HIPAA-compliant platforms and devices for client communications
3. Maintain separate professional and personal accounts for all digital communications
4. Implement strong password protection and encryption for all devices
5. Establish regular backup procedures for electronic records
6. Conduct periodic security audits of communication systems
7. Obtain cyber liability insurance coverage

Social media presents particular challenges for professional boundaries. The California Board of Behavioral Sciences advises that counselors:

1. Avoid accepting client friend or connection requests
2. Maintain strict privacy settings on personal accounts

3. Establish clear policies regarding social media interactions
4. Avoid searching for client information on social media
5. Consider the impact of professional social media content on clients

When breaches in electronic communication occur, counselors must follow notification requirements under both HIPAA and California's Information Practices Act (Civil Code Section 1798.29). These laws require notification of affected individuals when certain types of personal information have been compromised. Licensed Professional Clinical Counselors can fulfill their legal and ethical obligations while providing effective care to clients. Regular review and updating of communication policies ensures ongoing compliance with evolving regulations and technological changes.

PRACTICE POLICIES AND PROCEDURES

A well-structured policy and procedure manual serves as the foundation for a professional clinical counseling practice, providing clarity for both clients and staff while ensuring legal compliance. Appointment scheduling policies establish expectations for both clients and counselors. These policies might include information about session length (typically 45-50 minutes), frequency of appointments, and methods for scheduling. For example, a policy could state: *"Initial appointments are 60 minutes in length, with follow-up sessions lasting 50 minutes. Appointments may be scheduled by phone, through our secure client portal, or in person at the conclusion of your session."*

Cancellation policies protect the practice while respecting client circumstances. A standard policy might require 24-48 hours' notice for cancellations to avoid a fee, with exceptions for emergencies. For instance: *"We request 24 hours' notice for cancellations. Late cancellations or missed appointments may result in a charge of $75, which is not billable to insurance. This fee may be waived for emergencies or illness at the discretion of your counselor."* The Business and Professions Code Section

4999.90(n) prohibits charging for services not rendered, so cancellation policies must be clearly communicated and agreed to in advance.

Rescheduling procedures should outline how clients can reschedule appointments and any limitations on this process. A policy might state: *"Rescheduling within the same week is subject to availability. We will make every effort to accommodate your schedule, but cannot guarantee immediate openings."* This helps manage client expectations while maintaining practice efficiency.

Wait list management becomes necessary when a practice reaches capacity. A transparent policy might explain: *"When our schedule is full, we maintain a wait list and contact clients in the order received when openings become available. We may ask about your scheduling flexibility to help match you with appropriate openings."* This approach balances fairness with practical considerations.

Emergency procedures are essential for client safety and risk management. A comprehensive emergency policy includes:

- Definition of what constitutes an emergency (suicidal ideation, homicidal thoughts, psychosis)
- Instructions for contacting emergency services (911)
- Crisis line information (National Suicide Prevention Lifeline: 988)
- After-hours contact procedures for the practice
- Follow-up protocols after emergencies

For example: *"If you experience a mental health emergency outside of session, please call 911 or go to your nearest emergency room. You may also call the National Suicide Prevention Lifeline at 988. For urgent but non-emergency situations, you may call our office and select the urgent message option. A counselor will return your call within 4 hours during business days."*

The policy should also address counselor availability between sessions: *"While your counselor is not available for crisis intervention between scheduled appointments, urgent messages will be returned within*

24 business hours. For immediate assistance, please use the emergency resources provided."

Client rights and responsibilities form a central component of practice policies, reflecting both legal requirements and ethical standards. Under California Civil Code Section 56.10 (the Confidentiality of Medical Information Act) and HIPAA, clients have specific rights regarding their treatment and records.

A client rights section might include:

- Right to confidentiality with clear explanation of limits (mandated reporting, danger to self/others)
  Right to access records as provided by Health and Safety Code Section 123110
- Right to informed consent before treatment
- Right to refuse treatment or request referral
- Right to be treated with dignity and respect
- Right to participate in treatment planning
- Right to file complaints with the Board of Behavioral Sciences

Client responsibilities balance these rights and might include:

- Providing accurate information about symptoms and history
- Actively participating in treatment
- Following agreed-upon treatment plans
- Attending scheduled appointments
- Paying agreed-upon fees
- Notifying the counselor of changes in condition
- Respecting practice policies

Privacy practices must align with both HIPAA and California's stringent privacy laws. The California Confidentiality of Medical Information Act (Civil Code Section 56 et seq.) provides additional protections beyond HIPAA in many cases.

A Notice of Privacy Practices should include:

- How client information may be used and disclosed
- Client rights regarding their information
- Practice responsibilities to protect information
- How to file a complaint regarding privacy violations
- Contact information for privacy questions

The policy should address electronic communications: *"Email and text communications are not completely secure. We use encrypted email for sensitive communications and limit text messages to scheduling matters. Please do not include detailed clinical information in electronic messages."*

Social media policies have become increasingly important. A clear policy might state: *"To maintain professional boundaries and protect your confidentiality, our counselors do not accept friend or connection requests from current or former clients on personal social media accounts. We maintain a professional page for practice information only."*

Payment policies must be transparent and compliant with both California law and the federal No Surprises Act. Business and Professions Code Section 4999.90(n) identifies failure to provide a fee disclosure statement as unprofessional conduct.

A comprehensive payment policy includes:

- Current fee schedule for all services
- Insurance billing procedures and client responsibilities
- Copayment and deductible collection practices
- Payment methods accepted
- Late payment policies and any interest charges
- Financial hardship considerations and sliding scale availability

For example: *"Payment is expected at the time of service unless other arrangements have been made. We accept cash, checks, and major credit cards. Insurance copayments are collected at each visit. If your insurance denies coverage, you will be responsible for the full fee. We offer a sliding scale for clients experiencing financial hardship, based on household income and family size."*

Specialized policies may be needed for specific services or populations. Telehealth services require additional policies addressing technology requirements, emergency procedures for remote clients, and state-specific regulations. Group therapy needs policies on confidentiality among participants and attendance requirements. Policies for minors must address consent requirements, involvement of parents/guardians, and confidentiality limitations.

CHAPTER FOUR

MANDATED REPORTING FOR MINORS

UNDERSTANDING REASONABLE SUSPICION STANDARDS

Determining reasonable suspicion of child abuse or neglect requires careful observation and professional judgment. California law establishes specific parameters for mandated reporters, including Professional Clinical Counselors. According to California Penal Code Section 11166(a)(1), mandated reporters must report when they have *"reasonable suspicion"* that a child has experienced abuse or neglect. This standard doesn't require certainty or proof, but rather a reasonable belief based on observable facts.

Physical indicators often provide the most concrete evidence for reasonable suspicion. These might include unexplained bruises, burns, or fractures, particularly when they appear in unusual locations such as the torso, back, or buttocks. For example, loop-shaped marks could indicate being struck with a cord, while hand-shaped bruises might suggest grabbing or slapping. Burns with clear demarcation lines or in the shape of objects (like cigarettes or irons) rarely occur accidentally. According to the California Department of Social Services guidelines, multiple injuries in various stages of healing particularly warrant attention, as they suggest repeated harm rather than isolated incidents.

Behavioral signs, while less definitive, can strengthen reasonable suspicion when combined with other indicators. Children experiencing abuse might display extreme behaviors, excessive compliance or aggression, inappropriate sexual knowledge for their age, fear of certain adults, or reluctance to go home. The California Board of Behavioral Sciences (BBS) training materials note that sudden changes in behavior, such as a previously outgoing child becoming withdrawn, merit further assessment. Business and Professions Code Section 4999.33(d)(9) requires LPCCs to be trained in recognizing these behavioral patterns as potential indicators of abuse.

Patterns are particularly telling when establishing reasonable suspicion. A single bruise might have many innocent explanations, but repeated injuries, especially with inconsistent explanations, raise legitimate concerns. California Penal Code Section 11166 acknowledges this by emphasizing that mandated reporters should consider the totality of circumstances. For instance, if a child repeatedly comes to counseling with new injuries and the explanations provided seem implausible or change over time, this pattern strengthens reasonable suspicion.

Distinguishing between accidental injuries and potential abuse requires careful assessment. Children naturally experience bumps and bruises through play and normal activities. Accidental injuries typically occur on bony prominences like knees, elbows, shins, and foreheads. In contrast, injuries to soft tissue areas like cheeks, thighs, or the abdomen more commonly suggest non-accidental trauma.

The explanation provided for an injury warrants careful consideration. Explanations inconsistent with the injury type, severity, or the child's developmental capabilities raise concerns. For example, a counselor might question reasonable suspicion when a parent claims a non-mobile infant *"fell while running."* Similarly, delayed medical attention for serious injuries without reasonable explanation could indicate neglect under California Penal Code Section 11165.2.

Cultural considerations add complexity to reasonable suspicion assessments. California's diverse population means counselors encounter families with varying child-rearing practices, discipline approaches, and medical beliefs. Business and Professions Code Section 4999.32(c)(1)(F) requires cultural competence in clinical assessment. While cultural sensitivity matters, California law makes clear that cultural practices never justify actions causing serious physical harm or emotional damage. For example, certain traditional healing practices like *"cao gio"* (coin rubbing) might leave marks resembling bruising but represent cultural health interventions rather than abuse. Counselors must distinguish between cultural practices and actual abuse through careful assessment and, when needed, consultation.

Consider these examples illustrating the reasonable suspicion threshold:

Situation likely meeting the threshold: A 7-year-old client has multiple bruises in various healing stages on her upper arms and back. When asked, she becomes anxious and says, *"I'm not supposed to talk about that."* The parent offers different explanations on different occasions, none matching the injury patterns. This scenario combines physical indicators, behavioral responses, and inconsistent explanations, creating reasonable suspicion requiring a report.

Situation likely not meeting the threshold: A 10-year-old has a bruise on his shin. He enthusiastically explains he got it playing soccer, which aligns with the location and appearance of the injury. The child shows no fear or anxiety when discussing the injury or his home life. This represents a typical childhood injury with a consistent, developmentally appropriate explanation.

Situation requiring further assessment: A 4-year-old appears unwashed and wears the same clothes to several sessions. She occasionally mentions being hungry. While these signs could indicate neglect, they might also reflect temporary family hardship or poverty. When whether this would require reporting, a counselor might sensitively gather more information about the family's circumstances while monitoring for additional indicators.

California Penal Code Section 11166 emphasizes that mandated reporters need not be certain of abuse, reasonable suspicion suffices. The law protects mandated reporters acting in good faith from civil or criminal liability, even if the investigation determines no abuse occurred. Conversely, failing to report when reasonable suspicion exists can result in misdemeanor charges per PC 11166(c) and professional discipline by the Board of Behavioral Sciences.

For clinical counselors navigating these complex determinations, a structured decision-making framework can help evaluate potential cases:

- Document observable facts: Record specific physical, behavioral, and environmental observations without interpretation. Note the child's exact statements using quotation marks.

- Assess explanations: Evaluate whether explanations for injuries or concerning behaviors align with the physical evidence and the child's developmental capabilities.

- Consider patterns: Look for repeated concerns over time rather than isolated incidents.

- Apply developmental lens: Consider whether the situation is consistent with the child's developmental stage and abilities.

- Evaluate severity and immediacy: Assess whether the situation presents immediate danger requiring emergency response.

- Consult when uncertain: California and HIPAA law permits consultation with colleagues while maintaining confidentiality. Consultation can clarify thinking without delaying necessary reports. It may be important to consult directly with the receiving agency.

- Document decision-making: Record the factors considered, consultations sought, and rationale for reporting or not reporting.

The California Penal Code defines reportable categories including physical abuse, sexual abuse, emotional abuse, and neglect. Physical abuse includes non-accidental infliction of physical injury, while sexual abuse encompasses sexual assault, exploitation, and trafficking. Emotional abuse involves non-physical mistreatment causing serious emotional damage evidenced by severe anxiety, depression, or aggressive behavior. Neglect includes failure to provide adequate food, clothing, shelter, supervision, or medical care.

It is important to note that, unlike other sections of the mandated reporting law that use the word *"shall,"* California Penal Code Section 11166.05 uses the word *"may."* This section allows, but does not require, a report when a mandated reporter has knowledge of or reasonably suspects that a child is suffering serious emotional damage or is at substantial risk of such harm. The law specifies that this must be evidenced by observable states of being or behavior, including but not limited to severe anxiety, depression, withdrawal, or aggressive behavior toward self or others. In other words, a report may be made when there is actual knowledge or reasonable suspicion that these emotional or behavioral indicators are present.

When reasonable suspicion exists, California Penal Code Section 11166 requires an immediate (or as soon as is practicably possible) phone report to child protective services or law enforcement, followed by a written report within 36 hours. The report should include the counselor's name and contact information, the child's information, and specific concerns prompting the report (PC 11167(a).

Throughout this process, counselors must balance their mandated reporting obligations with maintaining the therapeutic relationship. The California Board of Behavioral Sciences recommends transparency with clients about mandated reporting obligations during the informed consent process. When making a report becomes necessary, counselors can explain the process in age-appropriate terms, emphasizing their concern for safety rather than blame or judgment.

IMMEDIATE RESPONSE PROTOCOL

When a counselor suspects child abuse or neglect, immediate and appropriate action is essential. California law establishes specific protocols that Professional Clinical Counselors need to follow. This structured approach helps protect the child while fulfilling legal obligations under California Penal Code Section 11166.

Initial Steps:

Document the exact circumstances that led to suspicion

When abuse indicators emerge during a session, thorough documentation forms the foundation of an effective response. Begin by recording exactly what you observed using objective language. Note physical indicators with specific descriptions rather than interpretations: *"Three circular burns approximately 1cm in diameter on right forearm"* rather than *"cigarette burns."* Document the child's exact words using quotation marks: *"My stepdad gets really mad and hits me with his belt"* rather than *"Child reported physical abuse."*

Include contextual information about when and how the disclosure or observation occurred. Was it spontaneous or in response to a question? What was the child's emotional state during disclosure? Note the date, time, and setting of the disclosure or observation.

California Business and Professions Code requires LPCCs to maintain records that accurately reflect client interactions, and failure to do so is unprofessional conduct under 4999.90(v). Your documentation might become part of legal proceedings, so avoid speculation or diagnosis in your notes.

A sample documentation entry might read:

"4/15/2025, 3:15 PM: During today's session, Jamie (8) had visible bruising on both upper arms, approximately 2-3 inches in diameter, purple/blue in color. When asked about the bruises, Jamie stated, 'My mom's boyfriend grabbed me really hard because I spilled my juice.' Jamie

became tearful while sharing this information. When asked if this had happened before, Jamie nodded and said, 'He gets mad a lot.' Jamie expressed fear about returning home today."

Gather essential information without conducting an investigation

While mandated reporters need sufficient information to make a report, California Penal Code Section 11166(a) clarifies that counselors should not conduct their own investigations. The distinction between appropriate information gathering and investigation lies in purpose and approach.

Appropriate information gathering involves:
- Listening to spontaneous disclosures
- Asking non-leading, clarifying questions when necessary
- Documenting observable indicators
- Collecting information needed for the mandated report

Inappropriate investigation includes:
- Repeated questioning about the incident
- Asking leading questions that suggest answers
- Interviewing potential witnesses or alleged perpetrators
- Examining the child's body beyond readily observable areas
- Attempting to collect physical evidence

When a child discloses potential abuse, you might gather essential information with open-ended questions like:
- *"Can you tell me more about what happened?"*
- *"When did this happen?"*
- *"Has something like this happened before?"*
- *"Who was there when this happened?"*

Avoid questions that could influence the child's account, such as:
- *"Did your father hit you?"*
- *"Were you scared when your mother did that?"*
- *"That must have hurt a lot, right?"*

Here it should be emphasized that gathering basic information for reporting purposes differs from conducting a forensic interview. The latter requires specialized training and typically occurs through child protective services or law enforcement.

Assess immediate safety risks

California Penal Code Section 11165.9 recognizes that some situations require emergency response. Assessing immediate safety helps determine whether standard reporting procedures suffice or if emergency intervention is necessary.

Consider these factors when evaluating immediate risk:

- Is the child expressing fear about returning home?
- Are there threats of imminent harm to the child?
- Does the child have access to basic necessities (food, shelter, supervision)?
- Is the alleged perpetrator currently in the home with access to the child?
- Does the situation involve severe physical injury requiring medical attention?
- Is there a history of escalating violence?

If immediate danger exists, California Penal Code Section 11165.9 permits contacting law enforcement directly rather than child protective services. Document your risk assessment and rationale for emergency response.

A sample risk assessment note might read:

"Based on Jamie's disclosure of ongoing physical abuse, expressed fear of returning home today, and statement that 'he said he'd really hurt me if I told anyone,' I've determined there is an immediate safety risk requiring emergency response rather than standard reporting procedures."

Contact appropriate authorities

California Penal Code Section 11166(a) requires mandated reporters to make two reports: an immediate phone report followed by a written report within 36 hours. The following are typically the items that would be included, for not limited to:

For the phone report:

1. Contact either child protective services or law enforcement in the county where the child lives
2. Provide your name, position, and contact information
3. Share the child's name, address, present location, and relevant family information
4. Describe the specific concerns and observations that led to your report
5. Note any immediate safety concerns
6. Request the name of the intake worker and a report number
7. Ask about next steps and whether you should take any additional actions

For the written report:

1. Complete Form SS 8572 (Suspected Child Abuse Report)
2. Include all information from your phone report plus any additional details
3. Submit within 36 hours of the phone report
4. Keep a copy for your records, as required by California Code of Regulations Title 16, Section 1845

Same Report – Multiple Providers

Note that BPC 11166(h) states " When two or more persons, who are required to report, jointly have knowledge of a known or reasonably suspected instance of child abuse or neglect, and when there is agreement among them, the telephone report may be made by a member of the team selected by mutual agreement and a single report may be made and signed by the selected member of the reporting team. Any member who has knowledge that the member designated to report has failed to do so shall thereafter make the report."

Responding to a Child's Disclosure

How a counselor responds to a child's disclosure can significantly impact both the child's wellbeing and the effectiveness of subsequent interventions.

When a child begins to disclose:

- Remain calm and listen attentively
- Find a private space where the conversation won't be interrupted
- Allow the child to speak at their own pace
- Use the child's vocabulary for body parts
- Avoid displaying shock or disgust, which might shame the child

Example dialogue:

Child: *"I don't want to go home today."* Counselor: *"Can you tell me more about that?"* Child: *"My uncle comes over on Thursdays. He makes me do things I don't like."* Counselor: *"Thank you for telling me. Can you help me understand what kinds of things he makes you do?"* Child: *"He makes me touch his private parts and says it's our secret game."* Counselor: *"I'm glad you told me about this. It sounds like something that might be making you feel uncomfortable or unsafe. It's my job to help keep you safe, so I'll need to talk to some people who can help make sure this doesn't happen anymore. Would it be okay if I asked you a couple more questions so I can better understand what's been happening?"*

After a disclosure:

- Acknowledge the child's courage: *"Thank you for telling me. That took a lot of bravery."*

- Reassure without making promises: *"I'm going to do what I can to help keep you safe"* rather than *"I promise your uncle will never bother you again."*
- Explain next steps in age-appropriate terms: *"I need to talk to some people whose job it is to help keep kids safe. They might want to talk with you too."*
- Address fears about what happens next: *"You're not in trouble. The adults are responsible for making sure kids are safe."*

Example dialogue for explaining reporting:

Counselor: *"I want to explain what will happen next. There are special people whose job it is to help keep kids safe. I need to call them and tell them what you shared with me today."* Child: *"Will I get in trouble? My uncle said I'd get in trouble if I told."* Counselor: *"You are not in trouble at all. You did exactly the right thing by telling me. Adults are supposed to keep children safe, and what you described isn't okay. Sometimes kids worry they might have done something wrong, but this is not your fault."*

CONSENSUAL SEXUAL ACTIVITY GUIDELINES

California law establishes specific guidelines for mandated reporters regarding consensual sexual activity among minors. Professional Clinical Counselors must navigate these requirements carefully, balancing their legal obligations with therapeutic relationships. Under California Penal Code Section 11165.1(a), not all consensual sexual activity between minors requires a mandated report, but certain circumstances do trigger reporting obligations.

Age Parameters and Reporting Requirements

California Penal Code Section 11165.1 defines reportable sexual conduct involving minors based on several key factors. The law recognizes that some sexual activity between minors of similar ages might not constitute abuse requiring intervention. However, specific age differences and circumstances trigger mandatory reporting. Because these situations require good clinical judgement and legal knowledge, counselors are encouraged to review the various laws including, but note limited to PC 261.5, 285, 288, and 289. Several other laws, statues and court cases include this information: Cal. Rptr. 762, 769 (3rd Dist. Ct. App. 1989); 226 Cal. Rptr. 361, 381 (1st Dist. Ct. App. 1986); 73 Cal. Rptr. 2d 331, 333 (1st Dist. Ct. App. 1998).

1. **Consider Age Difference Thresholds:**

    - When one partner is under 14 years old and the other partner is 14 years or older.

    - When one partner is 14 or 15 years old and the other partner is at least 21 years old.

    - When one partner is 16 or 17 years old and the other partner is at least 21 years old.

2. **Consensual Activity Between Similar-Aged Minors:**

    - Sexual activity between minors of similar ages (both under 14, or where the age difference is minimal) might not require reporting if truly consensual and non-coercive.

    - However counselors must assess for power imbalances, coercion, or exploitation even when ages are similar.

Clinical Judgment Considerations

When evaluating consensual sexual activity between minors, PCCs must exercise clinical judgment in several areas:

1. **Assessing True Consent:** Counselors should evaluate whether the sexual activity was truly consensual by considering:
    - Cognitive and emotional development of both parties
    - Presence of intellectual or developmental disabilities

- Power dynamics in the relationship
- History of coercion or manipulation
- Influence of substances

2. **Determining Exploitation:** Even when ages don't automatically trigger reporting, counselors must assess for exploitation:
    - Presence of gifts, money, or favors in exchange for sexual activity
    - Promises of special treatment or threats of negative consequences
    - Use of authority positions (e.g., team captain, club president)
    - Manipulation of trust or emotional vulnerability

3. **Evaluating Harm:** Counselors consider potential harm:
    - Physical injuries or health consequences
    - Emotional distress or trauma symptoms
    - Impact on the minor's relationships with family and peers
    - Effects on academic performance or daily functioning

A counselor might document this assessment as follows:

"Client A (15) disclosed consensual sexual activity with Partner B (16). Assessment indicates: relationship of 6 months duration; no power differential observed; both parties initiated activity; no evidence of coercion or exploitation; both demonstrate age-appropriate understanding of the relationship; no physical or emotional harm reported. Based on these factors and current California law, this does not appear to meet reporting criteria. Will continue to monitor for changes in dynamics or emerging concerns."

Case Studies and Reporting Obligations

1. **Case Study 1: Age Difference Requiring Report:**

   Maya (13) discloses during therapy that she has been sexually active with her girlfriend, Samal (15). She describes the relationship as loving and consensual, stating that she initiated their first sexual encounter.

   Analysis: Despite Maya's perception of the relationship as consensual, the counselor determined that laws and statutes require a report when one partner is under 14 and the other is 14 or older. The counselor determines that they must report this situation to Child Protective Services or law enforcement, regardless of the apparent consensual nature.

   Documentation Note: *"Client (13) disclosed sexual activity with 15-year-old partner. Despite client's description of relationship as consensual and non-coercive, California law requires reporting when one partner is under 14 and the other is 14 or older. Made verbal report to County CPS on 01/16/2025 at 3:45 PM (Report #CPS2025-8742) and submitted written report within 36 hours. Explained reporting obligation to client with sensitivity to therapeutic alliance."*

2. **Case Study 2: Similar Ages, No Report Required**

   Tyler and Jordan, both 15, have been dating for six months and recently became sexually active. Tyler discloses this during counseling, describing a mutually respectful relationship with no pressure or coercion.

   Analysis: As both minors are the same age, the counselor determines there is no automatic reporting requirement. The counselor's assessment finds no evidence of coercion, exploitation, or harm. In this case, the counselor determines reporting is not required, but the counselor should provide education on healthy relationships and sexual health.

   Documentation Note: *"Client (15) disclosed consensual sexual activity with partner (also 15). Assessment indicates mutual consent, no power differential, no coercion or exploitation, and no evidence of physical or emotional harm. Based on a review of applicable California law and clinical assessment, this does not meet reporting criteria. Provided education on healthy relationships, consent, and sexual health resources."*

3. **Case Study 3: Power Differential Requiring Report**

   Alex (16) discloses sexual activity with Casey (17), who is the captain of Alex's sports team and has threatened to cut Alex's playing time if the relationship ends. Alex expresses feeling trapped and unable to say no to sexual demands.

   Analysis: Although the age difference doesn't trigger automatic reporting, the power differential and coercion elements make this reportable. The relationship involves exploitation and emotional harm, meeting the definition of sexual abuse requiring a report.

   Documentation Note: *"Client (16) disclosed sexual relationship with team captain (17) involving coercion through threats regarding playing time. Assessment indicates presence of power differential, exploitation, and emotional distress. Despite similar ages, the coercive elements meet reporting criteria. Made verbal report to County CPS on 01/18/2025 at 2:15 PM (Report #CPS2025-8901)."*

Inappropriate Use of Guidelines to Maintain Secrecy

It is essential to understand that these guidelines should never be used to justify keeping disclosures of sexual assault, molestation, or other criminal behavior secret, even when requested by a minor client. Counselors should be aware that therapeutic relationship does not supersede the counselor's legal obligation as a mandated reporter under PC 11166(a).

When a minor asks a counselor to keep sexual abuse or assault confidential, several ethical and legal principles apply:

1. **Legal Primacy:** The legal duty to report suspected abuse overrides any professional confidentiality between counselor and

client. This means that regardless of therapeutic concerns, the reporting obligation takes precedence.

2. **Client Safety:** The primary purpose of mandated reporting is to protect vulnerable individuals from harm. Keeping abuse secret potentially leaves the minor and others at risk for continued victimization.

3. **Therapeutic Integrity:** While reporting might temporarily disrupt the therapeutic relationship, honesty about reporting obligations from the outset of therapy establishes clear boundaries and expectations. California should engage in transparency about the limits of confidentiality.

4. **Supportive Reporting:** Counselors can maintain therapeutic alliance by:

    - Explaining reporting requirements compassionately
    - Involving the minor in the reporting process when appropriate
    - Continuing to provide support throughout the investigation
    - Addressing fears about consequences of reporting

PENALTIES, LEGAL PROTECTIONS AND IMMUNITY

California law establishes clear penalties for mandated reporters who fail to report suspected child abuse or neglect. Under California Penal Code §11166(c), a mandated reporter who fails to report known or reasonably suspected child abuse or neglect is guilty of a misdemeanor punishable by up to six months in county jail, a fine of up to $1,000, or both imprisonment and fine. This legal obligation applies to Licensed Professional Clinical Counselors (LPCCs), Associate Professional Clinical Counselors (APCCs), and Trainees as specified in California

Penal Code §11165.7(a)(21), (38), and (39), which explicitly identifies them as mandated reporters.

The penalties increase substantially for cases where the failure to report results in serious harm. If a child suffers great bodily injury or death because a mandated reporter failed to report suspected abuse, the penalty increases to up to one year in county jail, a fine of up to $5,000, or both, as outlined in Penal Code §11166.01(b). These enhanced penalties reflect the serious consequences that can result from a counselor's inaction.

Beyond criminal penalties, PCCs could face professional discipline from the Board of Behavioral Sciences (BBS) for failing to fulfill mandated reporting obligations. Under Business and Professions Code §4999.90, unprofessional conduct includes violating any of the provisions of the chapter or any regulation adopted by the board. Since mandated reporting is incorporated into professional standards through reference to the Penal Code, failure to report could result in license suspension, revocation, or other disciplinary action.

Civil liability presents another potential consequence. While mandated reporters generally receive immunity for good faith reports (discussed below), no such protection exists for failing to report. A counselor who fails to report suspected abuse could be sued by the victim if the failure to report resulted in continued harm. In Landeros v. Flood (1976), the California Supreme Court established that professionals could be held liable for failing to diagnose and report child abuse.

To balance these significant penalties, California law provides several important legal protections for mandated reporters who fulfill their obligations. These protections aim to encourage reporting by reducing concerns about potential negative consequences for the reporter. The basis of these protections is immunity from civil and criminal liability. California Penal Code §11172(a) states that mandated reporters *"shall not be civilly or criminally liable for any report required or authorized by this article."* This immunity applies to all mandated reporters, including LPCCs, APCCs, and Trainees who make reports as required by law.

The scope of this immunity is broad but not unlimited. It covers reports made *"even if the mandated reporter acquired the knowledge or reasonable suspicion of child abuse or neglect outside of their professional capacity or outside the scope of their employment."* This means that counselors who learn about potential abuse in social settings or other contexts outside their professional role still receive immunity when reporting.

However, immunity only applies to good faith reporting. The law specifically states that immunity does not extend to a counselor who makes a report they "knew that the report was false or was made with reckless disregard of the truth or falsity of the report." This good faith requirement serves as a check against malicious or deliberately false reports.

In Krikorian v. Barry (1987), a California court upheld immunity for a therapist who reported suspected sexual abuse based on a child's statements and behaviors during play therapy. Though the investigation did not substantiate the abuse, the court found the therapist had reasonable suspicion and acted in good faith, thus qualifying for immunity.

Confidentiality protections represent another important safeguard for mandated reporters. California Penal Code §11167(d) states that *"the identity of all persons who report under this article shall be confidential and disclosed only"* to specified agencies and individuals involved in the investigation or judicial proceedings. This confidentiality protection helps shield reporters from potential retaliation.

The law further protects mandated reporters from employment consequences. California Labor Code §1102.5 prohibits employers from retaliating against employees who disclose information to government agencies when they have reasonable cause to believe the information reveals a violation of law. This provision could protect counselors who face adverse employment actions after making mandated reports.

Despite these protections, counselors face certain legal obligations and limitations when making mandated reports. Understanding these parameters helps counselors navigate the reporting process effectively while minimizing legal risks. First, counselors must understand that mandated reporting obligations override client confidentiality. Business and Professions Code §4999.20 defines the practice of professional clinical counseling as including the application of counseling interventions to assist individuals with *"achieving more effective personal, social, educational, and vocational development and adjustment."* While this practice typically involves confidentiality, California Evidence Code §1027 and PC 11166 create an exception to the psychotherapist-patient privilege in cases involving child abuse.

This means that when a counselor has reasonable suspicion of child abuse or neglect, the legal obligation to report supersedes any ethical or professional duty of confidentiality. In People v. Stritzinger (1983), the California Supreme Court affirmed that the child abuse reporting law creates a valid exception to the psychotherapist-patient privilege.

Second, counselors must report within the timeframes specified by law. California Penal Code §11166(a) requires an immediate telephone report (or as soon as is practicably possible), followed by a written report within 36 hours. Failure to adhere to these timeframes could potentially compromise immunity protections and expose the counselor to penalties for non-compliance.

Third, counselors should understand the limits of their role in the reporting process. The law requires reporting of reasonable suspicions, not conducting investigations. In fact, attempting to investigate beyond gathering information necessary for the report could potentially interfere with official investigations and exceed the counselor's professional boundaries.

Fourth, counselors must maintain appropriate documentation of their observations, assessments, and reporting actions. While not explicitly required by the mandated reporting law, proper documentation serves as evidence of compliance with legal obligations and supports claims of good faith reporting if challenged.

In summary, California law establishes a framework of penalties and protections that govern mandated reporting for clinical counselors. The penalties for failing to report are substantial, including criminal charges, professional discipline, and potential civil liability. However, counselors who fulfill their reporting obligations in good faith receive broad immunity from legal consequences related to their reports.

To navigate this system effectively, counselors could:

- Report promptly when reasonable suspicion exists, without attempting to investigate or confirm abuse
- Document observations, assessments, and reporting actions thoroughly
- Understand that mandated reporting obligations override confidentiality concerns
- Maintain awareness of the scope and limitations of immunity protections
- Stay current on changes to relevant laws and regulations

CHAPTER FIVE

ADULT MANDATED REPORTING

UNDERSTANDING ADULT ABUSE CATEGORIES

California law establishes specific protections for vulnerable adults, requiring Professional Clinical Counselors to report suspected abuse. Under California Welfare and Institutions Code (WIC) Section 15610.27, an *"elder"* is defined as any person 65 years of age or older. A *"dependent adult,"* as defined in WIC Section 15610.23, includes any person between 18 and 64 years who has physical or mental limitations that restrict their ability to carry out normal activities or protect their rights, including those with physical or developmental disabilities or whose physical or mental abilities have diminished due to age.

Physical Abuse

Physical abuse of elders and dependent adults encompasses any form of bodily injury, pain, or impairment resulting from non-accidental means. According to WIC Section 15610.63, this includes but not limited to:
- Direct physical assault (hitting, slapping, pushing)
- Inappropriate use of drugs or physical restraints

- Force-feeding
- Physical punishment of any kind

Indicators that counselors might observe include:

- Unexplained bruises, welts, or fractures in various stages of healing
- Bilateral bruising on upper arms (suggesting shaking)
- Clustered bruises on trunk (indicating repeated harmful contact)
- Burns with distinctive patterns (cigarette burns, rope burns, immersion burns)
- Unexplained lacerations to face, lips, mouth, torso, or back
- Broken eyeglasses or frames

A subtle example often overlooked involves an elderly client who appears with multiple bruises explained away as *"just being clumsy."* The caregiver might consistently answer questions directed at the client, minimizing injuries or providing implausible explanations for wounds. In such cases, counselors could note discrepancies between injuries and explanations, particularly when the pattern repeats over time.

Emotional/Psychological Abuse

Emotional abuse, defined in WIC Section 15610.53, involves subjecting an elder or dependent adult to fear, agitation, confusion, severe depression, or other forms of serious emotional distress through threats, intimidation, or other abusive conduct.

Warning signs include:

- Unusual behavior typically attributed to dementia (rocking, sucking, biting)
- Extreme withdrawal or agitation
- Fearfulness or paranoia
- Contradictory statements not resulting from mental confusion
- Reluctance to talk openly
- Implausible stories

A less obvious example might involve a dependent adult who appears increasingly withdrawn during sessions. Upon careful questioning, the counselor learns that the client's caregiver routinely threatens to place them in an institution if they *"cause trouble"* or *"complain too much."* This form of emotional manipulation creates fear and compliance without leaving physical evidence.

Financial Abuse

Financial abuse, as outlined in WIC Section 15610.30, occurs when a person or entity takes, secretes, appropriates, obtains, or retains real or personal property of an elder or dependent adult for wrongful use, with intent to defraud, or through undue influence.

Indicators include:

- Sudden changes in bank account or banking practices
- Unexplained withdrawal of large sums of money
- Adding names to the elder's signature card
- Unauthorized ATM withdrawals
- Abrupt changes in a will or other financial documents
- Unexplained disappearance of funds or valuable possessions
- Discovery of an elder's signature being forged
- Sudden appearance of previously uninvolved relatives claiming rights to possessions

An example might involve a counselor noticing that an elderly client mentions being unable to afford medications despite having adequate retirement income. Further exploration reveals that a family member has convinced the client to add them to bank accounts for *"convenience"* but has been systematically withdrawing funds for personal use while telling the elder that their pension has been reduced.

Sexual Abuse

Sexual abuse, defined in WIC Section 15610.63, includes sexual assault or battery, rape, sodomy, oral copulation, sexual penetration, or lewd or lascivious acts upon an elder or dependent adult.

Signs that might indicate sexual abuse include but not limited to:

- Bruises around breasts or genital area
- Unexplained vaginal or anal bleeding
- Torn, stained, or bloody underclothing
- Sexually transmitted diseases
- Difficulty walking or sitting without obvious cause
- An elder's report of being sexually assaulted

A less recognized scenario might involve a dependent adult with cognitive impairments who shows increasing distress before bathing or toileting assistance from a particular caregiver. The client may lack the verbal ability to report abuse but demonstrates physical resistance or emotional distress that warrants further assessment.

Neglect

California law distinguishes between neglect by caregivers and self-neglect, both requiring mandated reporting. Caregiver neglect, defined in WIC Section 15610.57, refers to the failure of responsible persons to provide care for an elder or dependent adult, including failure to:

- Assist with personal hygiene
- Provide food, clothing, or shelter
- Provide medical care
- Prevent malnutrition or dehydration
- Protect from health and safety hazards

REASONABLE SUSPICION STANDARDS

Reasonable suspicion in adult abuse cases represents a legal standard that balances protecting vulnerable adults while respecting their autonomy. In California, this standard is defined under Welfare and Institutions Code § 15630 states that counselors make reports when they have "observed or has knowledge of an incident that reasonably appears to be physical abuse, as defined in Section 15610.63, abandonment, abduction, isolation, financial abuse, or neglect, or is told by an elder or dependent adult that they have experienced behavior..." Professional Clinical Counselors must understand this definition to fulfill their mandated reporting obligations effectively.

- **Scenario 1: Physical Abuse Indicators**

During a therapy session, your 75-year-old client with mild cognitive impairment shows unusual bruising on her wrists and arms. When you inquire about the marks, she becomes anxious and says, *"My son gets frustrated when I can't remember things. Sometimes he grabs me too hard, but he doesn't mean it."* She adds that she's afraid to upset him because she depends on him for housing and transportation.

In this scenario, reasonable suspicion clearly exists. You have observed physical indicators (bruising), received a direct disclosure about rough handling, and identified a power imbalance that increases vulnerability. Under Welfare and Institutions Code § 15630(b)(1), you must report this suspicion of physical abuse.

- **Scenario 2: Financial Abuse Indicators**

A 68-year-old client mentions that his nephew recently moved in with him after losing his job. Over several sessions, you notice the client appears increasingly anxious about finances. Today, he mentions that his nephew *"helps"* with his banking now, but he seems confused about recent transactions and says, *"I thought I had more money in my account."* When you explore further, he becomes evasive and changes the subject.

This scenario presents indicators of potential financial abuse. While no direct disclosure has occurred, the pattern of increasing anxiety, confusion about finances, and evasiveness when discussing money matters, combined with a new living arrangement, creates reasonable suspicion that financial exploitation may be occurring. California Welfare and Institutions Code § 15610.30 defines financial abuse of an elder or dependent adult, and the threshold for reporting has likely been met.

- **Scenario 3: Ambiguous Situation**

Your client is a 58-year-old woman with chronic health issues who lives with her sister. She occasionally mentions that her sister *"gets on her case"* about taking medications and following doctors' orders. Today she comments, *"My sister locked the pantry again because she says I'm not following my diet."* The client seems annoyed but not distressed by this behavior.

This scenario falls into a gray area. The sister's behavior could be interpreted as controlling or as an attempt to support medical compliance. To determine if reasonable suspicion exists, you would need to gather more information about the nature of their relationship, whether the client has decision-making capacity, and whether the restrictions are causing harm or distress. This situation illustrates the importance of professional judgment in applying the reasonable suspicion standard.

If you determine that reasonable suspicion exists, California Welfare and Institutions Code § 15630(b) requires you to report to the appropriate adult protective services agency or law enforcement immediately or as soon as practicably possible by telephone, followed by a written report within two working days.

Common pitfalls in applying the reasonable suspicion standard include:

1. **Waiting for certainty**: Some counselors hesitate to report until they have definitive proof of abuse. This misunderstands the standard, which requires only reasonable suspicion, not certainty.

2. **Conducting personal investigations**: Attempting to gather evidence beyond what emerges naturally in the therapeutic context can compromise both the therapeutic relationship and the official investigation. Your role is to report reasonable suspicion, not to investigate.

3. **Overreliance on client self-report**: While client statements are important, reasonable suspicion may exist even when a client denies abuse, particularly when observable indicators contradict those denials or when cognitive impairment affects reliability.

4. **Misinterpreting cultural practices**: Cultural differences in family dynamics, caregiving approaches, and communication styles can sometimes be misinterpreted as signs of abuse. However, cultural considerations should inform your assessment without preventing reporting when genuine abuse indicators are present.

5. **Failing to document the basis for suspicion**: Thorough documentation of the specific observations and information that led to your suspicion is essential for both the protection of the client and your own professional liability.

6. **Confusing the threshold for different types of abuse**: Some counselors incorrectly believe that physical abuse requires a lower threshold for reporting than emotional or financial abuse. In reality, reasonable suspicion applies equally to all forms of abuse defined in Welfare and Institutions Code § 15610.

7. **Allowing countertransference to cloud judgment**: Personal reactions to clients or their family members can sometimes interfere with objective assessment. Consultation with colleagues can help maintain objectivity.

Reporting Timeframes

California law establishes specific timeframes for reporting:

Emergency Reporting Timeframes

Under Welfare and Institutions Code § 15630(b)(1), for emergency situations:

- Initial Report: An oral report must be made immediately or as soon as practicably possible by telephone.
- Written Follow-up: A written report must be submitted within two (2) working days of the telephone report.

GATHERING REQUIRED REPORT INFORMATION

When preparing to report suspected adult abuse in California, Professional Clinical Counselor need to gather specific information to ensure reports are thorough and actionable. California Welfare and Institutions Code Section 15630 outlines the legal obligation for mandated reporters to provide certain details when reporting elder or dependent adult abuse.

Reporting Agency Requirements

Different counties in California might have specific forms or reporting procedures. According to California Welfare and Institutions Code Section 15630, reports could be made to either APS or law enforcement, depending on the situation.

Adult Protective Services Reporting:

- Most counties accept telephone reports followed by written documentation
- Some counties have online reporting systems

- Reports typically include the information outlined in the template above
- APS might request additional information during their investigation

Law Enforcement Reporting:

- Required in emergency situations or when a crime has potentially occurred
- Might require more detailed information about the suspected criminal activity
- Could involve immediate response and intervention

Facility Reporting:

- If abuse occurs in a licensed facility, additional reporting to licensing agencies might be required
- California Department of Public Health or Department of Social Services might have specific reporting requirements

Balancing Reporting Requirements and Therapeutic Relationship

Counselors should also consider the importance of the therapeutic relationship. When gathering information for a mandated report:

- Be transparent about your obligations as a mandated reporter
- Explain the reporting process and what information will be shared
- Acknowledge the impact reporting might have on your therapeutic relationship
- Continue to provide support throughout the reporting process
- Document your efforts to maintain the therapeutic alliance while fulfilling legal obligations

INTERACTING WITH ADULT PROTECTIVE SERVICES

Adult Protective Services (APS) serves as California's primary agency responsible for investigating reports of abuse, neglect, and exploitation of vulnerable adults. Professional Clinical Counselors frequently interact with APS as mandated reporters and sometimes as ongoing collaborators in client care. Understanding how to navigate these interactions professionally ensures both compliance with legal obligations and optimal client outcomes.

Understanding APS Authority and Scope

Adult Protective Services operates under the authority granted by the California Welfare and Institutions Code (WIC) Sections 15600-15765, commonly known as the Elder Abuse and Dependent Adult Civil Protection Act. This legislation establishes APS's jurisdiction over cases involving:

- Adults aged 65 and older
- Dependent adults (18-64) with physical or mental limitations that restrict their ability to protect themselves

APS has the authority to:

- Receive and investigate reports of abuse or neglect
- Conduct in-person assessments
- Develop safety plans
- Connect vulnerable adults with community resources
- Petition for protective orders when necessary
- Collaborate with law enforcement in criminal cases

However, APS faces important limitations that counselors should recognize:

- APS cannot force services on competent adults who refuse assistance
- They typically cannot remove adults from their homes without court intervention
- Investigation timelines vary by county and case priority

- Resources and response capabilities differ significantly across counties

Collaborative Approach to APS Interactions

The most effective interactions with APS reflect a collaborative approach that honors legal reporting duties while preserving the integrity of the therapeutic relationship. A therapeutic focus can inform how counselors approach APS interactions:

- View reporting as potentially therapeutic rather than punitive
- Consider how APS resources might complement therapeutic goals
- Recognize that safety stabilization often enables deeper therapeutic work
- Approach APS as allied professionals with complementary expertise
- Maintain appropriate boundaries while facilitating necessary information sharing

Addressing Common Client Concerns

Clients often have specific worries when learning about a mandated report. Preparing responses to these concerns helps maintain the therapeutic relationship:

Concern: *"Will the person hurting me find out I told you?"*

Response: *"Your safety is my priority. The report focuses on the concerning situation, not on who reported it. While APS doesn't typically reveal who provided information, I can't guarantee complete confidentiality in all circumstances. Let's talk about specific safety concerns you have and develop a plan to address them."*

Concern: *"I don't want to leave my home/family member."*

Response: *"Making a report doesn't automatically mean you'll need to relocate. APS typically focuses on finding ways to increase safety while respecting your choices. You have the right to accept or decline services they offer, as long as you're able to make those decisions. Let's discuss what options might work best for your situation."*

Concern: *"I shouldn't have told you, now everything will get worse."*

Response: *"I understand this feels frightening. Sharing your experience took courage, and it's natural to worry about what happens next. Many people find that connecting with resources actually helps improve difficult situations. We can work together on strategies to manage any challenges that arise from the report."*

These responses acknowledge client autonomy while providing realistic information about the reporting process, consistent with the California Code of Ethics for LPCCs.

PENALTIES, LEGAL PROTECTIONS FOR REPORTERS

Professional Clinical Counselors in California face serious legal consequences for failing to report suspected elder or dependent adult abuse. California Welfare and Institutions Code §15630(h) establishes that failure to report physical abuse, abandonment, isolation, financial abuse, or neglect of an elder or dependent adult is a misdemeanor, punishable by up to six months in county jail, a fine of up to $1,000, or both imprisonment and fine. For cases involving serious bodily injury or death, the penalties increase significantly, with potential jail time extending to one year.

The California Board of Behavioral Sciences, which regulates PCCs under Business and Professions Code §4999, may also impose professional discipline for failure to fulfill mandated reporting obligations. This disciplinary action might range from citations and fines to probation, suspension, or even revocation of a professional license. The Board considers failure to report abuse a violation of professional standards that could indicate unfitness to practice.

Beyond criminal penalties and professional discipline, counselors who fail to report abuse might face civil liability. If a client suffers additional harm that could have been prevented through proper reporting, the counselor might be named in a civil lawsuit seeking damages for negligence. California courts have established that mandated reporters have a duty of care toward vulnerable adults, and failure to report suspected abuse could constitute a breach of that duty.

While these penalties underscore the seriousness of reporting obligations, California law also provides substantial protections for mandated reporters who fulfill their duties in good faith. These protections help ensure that counselors can report suspected abuse without fear of legal repercussions or professional harm.

The main focus of these protections is immunity from liability. Under California Welfare and Institutions Code §15634(a), mandated reporters who report suspected elder or dependent adult abuse are immune from civil or criminal liability for making the report. This immunity applies even if the investigation ultimately determines that abuse did not occur, provided the report was made in good faith.

The *"good faith"* standard means that the reporter genuinely believed, based on the information available to them at the time, that abuse might be occurring. This standard does not require certainty or proof beyond a reasonable doubt. Instead, it acknowledges that mandated reporters must often make difficult judgments based on limited information. As long as the report isn't knowingly false or made with reckless disregard for the truth, the immunity protection applies.

For example, if an LPCC reports suspected financial abuse based on a client's statements about unusual withdrawals from their bank account, and the investigation later reveals that the transactions were legitimate, the counselor would still be protected from liability because they had reasonable grounds for suspicion at the time of reporting.

California law also protects the confidentiality of mandated reporters. Welfare and Institutions Code §15633 specifies that the identity of persons who report suspected elder or dependent adult abuse shall be confidential and disclosed only among agencies investigating the report, or as required by court order. This confidentiality provision helps shield reporters from potential harassment or retaliation.

There are, however, certain exceptions to this confidentiality. The reporter's identity might be disclosed:

- To the licensing agency when Adult Protective Services or law enforcement refers the case for investigation of unlicensed care facilities
- When the reporter waives confidentiality
- By court order when deemed necessary for the administration of justice

Even with these exceptions, the law generally aims to protect reporter identity whenever possible. This protection extends to court proceedings, where efforts are made to maintain confidentiality unless disclosure is essential to the case.

When a counselor makes a report, they might worry about the impact on their therapeutic relationship with the client. The law recognizes this concern and provides guidance on maintaining professional boundaries while cooperating with investigations.

California Evidence Code §1010-1027 establishes psychotherapist-patient privilege, which generally protects confidential communications between counselors and clients. However, Evidence Code §1024 creates an exception to this privilege when the therapist has reasonable cause to believe that the patient is dangerous to themselves or others. This exception aligns with the mandated reporting requirements for abuse situations that present danger to vulnerable adults.

When cooperating with investigations, counselors could maintain professional boundaries by:

- Limiting disclosure to information relevant to the reported abuse

- Consulting with legal counsel or supervisors about specific requests for information
- Documenting all communications with investigators
- Being transparent with clients about obligations while expressing continued support

The California Attorney General's Office has clarified that mandated reporters are expected to cooperate with investigating agencies by providing necessary information related to the reported abuse. However, this cooperation does not require disclosure of information beyond the scope of the investigation or unrelated to the suspected abuse.

For counselors concerned about potential conflicts between their reporting duties and therapeutic relationships, the American Counseling Association's Code of Ethics (which many California counselors follow alongside state law) provides guidance on balancing legal requirements with client welfare. While the code acknowledges the primacy of legal obligations, it also emphasizes the importance of maintaining trust and transparency with clients whenever possible.

In practice, this might mean explaining to clients at the outset of therapy the limits of confidentiality, including mandated reporting requirements. When a situation arises that necessitates a report, counselors could, when safe and appropriate, inform the client about the report and the reasons for it. This transparency, while not always possible in high-risk situations, can help preserve the therapeutic relationship.

The California Department of Social Services, which oversees Adult Protective Services programs, provides resources for mandated reporters that include guidance on navigating the reporting process while maintaining professional relationships. These resources emphasize that reporting is ultimately an act of client advocacy, not betrayal, as it aims to connect vulnerable adults with needed services and protection.

For counselors who face challenges related to reporting, such as threats of retaliation or concerns about maintaining client relationships, several resources are available:

- The Board of Behavioral Sciences offers consultation on ethical and legal questions
- Professional associations like the California Association for Licensed Professional Clinical Counselors provide guidance and support
- Legal counsel specializing in mental health law can advise on complex situations
- Clinical supervision offers a space to process difficult reporting decisions

A clear understanding of the risks of non-reporting and the protections available to mandated reporters helps counselors engage the reporting process with greater confidence. These legal frameworks aim to balance the need to protect vulnerable adults with the recognition that reporting often involves complex professional judgments.

The legal protections for mandated reporters reflect an understanding that these professionals serve a vital public safety function. By reporting suspected abuse, counselors help ensure that vulnerable adults receive needed intervention and support. The immunity, confidentiality, and anti-retaliation provisions acknowledge the challenges inherent in this role and seek to remove barriers to reporting. At the same time, the penalties for failing to report underscore the seriousness with which California law views the protection of vulnerable adults. These consequences reflect the understanding that professionals who work with these populations have a special responsibility to recognize and respond to signs of abuse.

CHAPTER SIX

CONFIDENTIALITY AND LEGAL DUTIES

FOUNDATIONS OF CLIENT CONFIDENTIALITY

Confidentiality forms the essentials of the therapeutic relationship, creating a safe space where clients can share their most vulnerable thoughts and experiences without fear of exposure. When legal proceedings intersect with counseling practice, maintaining this confidentiality becomes both more challenging and more crucial. As a professional clinical counselor, you must navigate these situations with precision, balancing your ethical obligation to protect client privacy with your legal duty to comply with court mandates.

When responding to legal requests for information, your first consideration should always be the scope of confidentiality protection. In California, communications between licensed professional clinical counselors and their clients are protected by psychotherapist-patient privilege under Evidence Code sections 1010-1027. This privilege belongs to the client, not the counselor, meaning only the client (or their legal representative) can authorize disclosure of confidential information in most circumstances. While confidentiality refers to a counselor's professional and ethical obligation to keep client information private, privilege is a legal concept that determines whether that information may be disclosed in court. All privileged information is confidential, but not all confidential information is privileged. The distinction becomes critical when responding to legal demands, where privilege must be protected unless legally waived or overridden.

Although confidentiality and privilege are closely related, they serve different functions. Confidentiality is an ethical and professional obligation that protects client information during counseling, while privilege is a legal rule that governs whether that information can be introduced in court. As a counselor, you are ethically bound to protect client confidentiality and legally required to assert privilege on the client's behalf when appropriate. A more in-depth discussion of psychotherapist-patient privilege, including who holds it, how it can be waived, and how to respond to legal demands, is provided in Chapter 14: Understanding Legal Document Types.

California case law has repeatedly affirmed that confidentiality is central to therapeutic effectiveness. In *Ewing v. Northridge Hospital Medical Center* (2004), the court emphasized that protecting confidentiality encourages individuals to seek help without fear of stigma. In *In re Lifschultz* (1970), the court noted that clients should not be made to feel shame or guilt for what they disclose in therapy. Similarly, *People v. Stritzinger* (1983) reinforced that clients must be able to speak openly and honestly, knowing their information will remain private unless lawfully disclosed.

Before releasing any information, verify whether a valid exception to confidentiality applies. These exceptions include:

1. Client consent through a properly executed release of information
2. Mandated reporting situations (child abuse, elder abuse, etc.)
3. Danger to self or others requiring protective action
4. Court orders specifically overriding privilege
5. Client-initiated legal actions where mental health is directly at issue

When you receive a subpoena, remember that it does not automatically override the psychotherapist-patient privilege. Counselors must assess whether privilege applies, and should never release confidential information without proper client authorization or a valid court order. In most cases, you will assert privilege and notify your client of the request. A full explanation of how to respond to subpoenas, including examples and legal strategy, is provided in Chapter 14.

When redacting records for legal proceedings, follow a systematic process to ensure you protect sensitive information while complying with legal requirements:

1. Make copies of the original records, keeping originals intact and unaltered.
2. On the copies, clearly mark information for redaction using a consistent method.
3. Review all marked sections to confirm they contain privileged or irrelevant information.
4. Use proper redaction methods that permanently remove information (black marker redactions can often be reversed electronically).
5. Have a colleague review your redactions to ensure thoroughness.
6. Create a privilege log documenting what information was redacted and the legal basis for each redaction.

The redaction process requires careful judgment about what information falls outside the scope of the legal request. Generally, you should redact:

- Information about third parties not relevant to the legal matter
- Information covered by special confidentiality protections (HIV status, substance abuse treatment)
- Clinical impressions and hypotheses not directly relevant to the legal issue
- Information from time periods outside the scope of the legal request

- Personal identifying information when not directly relevant (addresses, phone numbers, etc.)

Consider this practical example: You receive a subpoena in a child custody case requesting *"all records"* for your adult client. The proper approach would be to:

1. Notify your client immediately and discuss their options.
2. If the client consents to disclosure, obtain written authorization specifying exactly what can be released.
3. Review the records to identify information relevant to parenting capacity (the legal issue at hand) versus unrelated personal history.
4. Redact information about third parties, the client's own childhood trauma unrelated to parenting, and other treatment the client received that doesn't impact parenting.
5. Prepare a cover letter explaining the scope of what you're providing and the basis for any redactions.
6. Maintain a complete copy of what was disclosed in the client's record.

Another common scenario involves responding to a subpoena in a personal injury case where your client has put their mental health at issue by claiming emotional damages. In this situation:

1. Recognize that the client has likely waived some privilege by making their mental health a legal issue.
2. Still obtain explicit written consent before disclosure.
3. Limit disclosure to the time period and conditions relevant to the claimed damages.
4. Redact information about pre-existing conditions unless directly relevant to understanding the current condition.
5. Consider providing a summary rather than raw session notes when appropriate.

When releasing records, always use secure methods that maintain confidentiality during transmission. This includes:

- Using encrypted email or secure electronic portals rather than standard email
- Sending physical records via certified mail with *"Confidential"* clearly marked
- Requiring signature confirmation for delivery
- Including cover sheets stating the confidential nature of the enclosed information
- Providing only the specific records ordered rather than entire files

While legal exceptions to confidentiality are clearly defined, counselors must also guard against everyday operational breaches. These can occur unintentionally, such as leaving confidential information visible on a computer screen, allowing other clients to overhear voicemails, using non-private appointment sign-in logs, or consulting with colleagues without a signed release. To maintain trust and uphold ethical obligations, counselors should regularly assess their administrative practices and correct any vulnerabilities that could result in accidental disclosure.

The decision to release or withhold information often requires balancing competing ethical and legal obligations. To navigate these complex situations, apply this decision-making framework:

Step 1: Identify the specific legal request and its authority

- Is it a subpoena, court order, or search warrant?
- What specific information does it request?
- Who issued it and under what authority?

Step 2: Determine if privilege applies

- Is the information protected by psychotherapist-patient privilege?
- Has the client waived privilege through legal action or consent?
- Does the information fall under special protection categories?

Step 3: Consult appropriate resources

- Speak with the client about their preferences
- Consult with an attorney familiar with mental health law

- Review relevant ethical guidelines and state regulations
- Discuss with a supervisor or colleague (without revealing identifying information)

Step 4: Document your decision-making process

- Record consultations, client discussions, and rationale
- Maintain copies of all legal documents received
- Create a timeline of actions taken in response

Step 5: Implement the appropriate response

- Release only what is legally required
- Redact appropriately
- Use secure transmission methods
- Include explanatory documentation

This framework helps ensure that your response to legal requests is thoughtful, consistent, and defensible, regardless of the specific circumstances.

When testifying in court, additional confidentiality challenges arise. Unlike written records where you can carefully review and redact information, verbal testimony requires in-the-moment decisions about what information to share. Prepare by:

1. Reviewing exactly what the subpoena or court order permits you to discuss
2. Preparing concise answers that address only what is asked
3. Practicing responses to questions that might lead to privileged areas
4. Being prepared to respectfully inform the court when a question ventures into privileged territory

During testimony, if asked about information you believe remains privileged, state clearly: *"I believe that information is protected by psychotherapist-patient privilege, and I don't have authorization to disclose it."* The judge will then determine whether to compel an answer.

Remember that different settings have different confidentiality standards. For example, information shared in a therapy session has stronger protection than information gathered during a court-ordered evaluation. Be clear about your role in each situation and the corresponding confidentiality limitations.

Electronic records present unique confidentiality challenges in legal proceedings. When electronic health records (EHRs) are subpoenaed, you must ensure that:

1. Only authorized portions are extracted from the system
2. Metadata (creation dates, modification history, etc.) is handled appropriately
3. Audit trails showing who accessed records are considered for relevance
4. System-generated templates and auto-populated fields are reviewed for accuracy

For counselors working with particularly sensitive populations, additional protections may apply. Substance use disorder treatment records protected under 42 CFR Part 2 require specific court orders for disclosure that meet heightened requirements. Records related to HIV status have special protections in many states. Military and Veterans Affairs records may have additional federal protections.

When in doubt about your legal obligations regarding confidentiality, seek legal consultation before disclosing information. Many professional liability insurance policies include legal consultation benefits specifically for these situations. The cost of consultation is minimal compared to the potential harm of improper disclosure or the legal consequences of improperly refusing to disclose.

Applying a consistent decision-making framework helps counselors navigate legal complexities while safeguarding client confidentiality. Your careful attention to these matters not only protects your clients' privacy but also maintains the integrity of the therapeutic relationship and your professional practice.

LEGAL EXCEPTIONS TO CONFIDENTIALITY

While confidentiality serves as the foundation of therapeutic relationships, California law recognizes specific circumstances where this protection must yield to other compelling interests. As a Licensed Professional Clinical Counselor (LPCC) or Associate Professional Clinical Counselor (APCC) in California, understanding these exceptions is essential for legal compliance and ethical practice. These exceptions aren't merely suggestions, they represent legal mandates that override the general duty of confidentiality.

The most well-known exception stems from the landmark Tarasoff v. Regents of the University of California (1976) case. This ruling established that mental health professionals have a duty to protect potential victims when a client makes threats against an identifiable person. The court famously stated that "protective privilege ends where public peril begins," creating the foundation for California's duty to warn and duty to protect laws. For a full explanation of Tarasoff, including risk factors, case law developments, and documentation protocols, see the section titled "More on Duty to Warn Requirements."

Under California Civil Code Section 43.92, this duty is triggered when a client communicates a *"serious threat of physical violence against a reasonably identifiable victim."* When this occurs, the counselor must take one or more of these actions:

1. Make reasonable efforts to communicate the threat to the potential victim
2. Notify a law enforcement agency in the vicinity of the potential victim or the client
3. Take steps reasonably necessary under the circumstances to protect the potential victim

The 2007 amendment to this law (AB 733) clarified that psychotherapists are only liable if they fail to discharge this duty when a patient has communicated a serious threat of physical violence against a reasonably identifiable victim. This amendment provides some protection for therapists who exercise their professional judgment in determining whether a threat is serious.

Another critical exception involves mandated reporting of suspected child abuse or neglect. Under California Penal Code Section 11166, PCCs must report when they have *"reasonable suspicion"* of child abuse or neglect. This reporting obligation applies even when the information is obtained during therapy sessions. The report must be made immediately by phone, followed by a written report within 36 hours.

Similarly, California Welfare and Institutions Code Section 15630 requires reporting of suspected elder or dependent adult abuse. This includes physical abuse, neglect, financial exploitation, abandonment, isolation, abduction, or other treatment resulting in harm. Reports must be made to Adult Protective Services or law enforcement depending on the circumstances.

When a client expresses suicidal intentions, confidentiality may also be breached. While California law doesn't explicitly mandate reporting suicidal ideation in the same way it does for threats to others, the standard of care and ethical guidelines generally support taking necessary steps to protect clients from self-harm. This could include involuntary hospitalization under California Welfare and Institutions Code Section 5150, which allows for a 72-hour hold for assessment and crisis intervention when a person presents a danger to themselves.

Court orders represent another significant exception to confidentiality. Under California Evidence Code Section 1015, the psychotherapist-patient privilege doesn't apply when the court orders an examination of the client. Additionally, Evidence Code Section 1024 creates an exception when the therapist believes disclosure is necessary to prevent danger to the client or others.

When clients place their mental condition at issue in legal proceedings, such as in personal injury cases claiming emotional distress or in child custody disputes, they may waive privilege regarding relevant aspects of their treatment. This is outlined in California Evidence Code Section 1016.

California Evidence Code Section 1020 provides an exception to the psychotherapist-patient privilege when the patient initiates a legal proceeding against the therapist, or when the therapist must defend against a legal claim involving their professional conduct. In such situations, the therapist may disclose information relevant to the claim or defense, but the disclosure should be strictly limited to what is necessary to address the legal issue at hand. As a best practice, such disclosures should be documented carefully and, when possible, made in consultation with legal counsel to ensure compliance with confidentiality laws and ethical obligations.

California law also requires breach of confidentiality in certain public health contexts. For example, under California Health and Safety Code Section 121022, certain communicable diseases must be reported to public health authorities, though mental health professionals are not typically the primary reporters for these conditions.

For clients involved in the criminal justice system, additional exceptions may apply. Under California Penal Code Section 1203.05, information about a client on probation might need to be shared with probation officers. Similarly, for clients in diversion programs, treatment information may be shared with the court to verify compliance.

When working with couples or families, counselors must ensure that any release of information is authorized by all individuals involved. Because each party in a family or relationship has distinct privacy rights, counselors may not disclose records pertaining to joint sessions unless every client has signed a release of information. If one party declines to authorize disclosure, the counselor must limit their response to only what can be shared without compromising the non-consenting individual's confidentiality.

When working with minors, confidentiality becomes more complex. While minors generally have confidentiality rights in therapy, parents typically retain the right to access treatment records under California Health and Safety Code Section 123115. However, exceptions exist for certain sensitive services, such as when the minor consented to their own treatment for sexual assault, drug or alcohol abuse, or certain mental health services.

When a client discloses participation in certain crimes, confidentiality protections may be limited. For instance, California Penal Code Section 11160 requires health practitioners to report injuries that may have resulted from assaultive or abusive conduct, though this primarily applies to physical healthcare providers rather than mental health professionals.

In cases involving conservatorship proceedings under the Lanterman-Petris-Short Act (California Welfare and Institutions Code Section 5000 et seq.), mental health professionals may need to provide information about a client's condition and functioning to help determine if conservatorship is appropriate.

When implementing these exceptions, counselors should follow a systematic approach to ensure both legal compliance and client care. Here's a practical checklist for navigating potential confidentiality breaches:

1. Identify the specific exception that applies
   - Is there a threat to an identifiable person?
   - Is there suspected abuse of a child, elder, or dependent adult?
   - Is the client at risk of harming themselves?
   - Has a court ordered disclosure?
   - Has the client placed their mental health at issue in legal proceedings?
2. Document the facts that trigger the exception
   - Record specific statements, behaviors, or observations
   - Note dates, times, and context

- Document your assessment of risk or danger
- Include any consultations with colleagues or supervisors

3. Take appropriate action based on the specific exception

    - For Tarasoff situations: warn the potential victim and/or notify law enforcement
    - For mandated reporting: contact the appropriate agency (Child Protective Services, Adult Protective Services)
    - For suicidal clients: implement safety planning, consider hospitalization if necessary
    - For court orders: review the scope of the order and respond accordingly

4. Inform the client when possible and appropriate

    - Explain the reason for the confidentiality breach
    - Discuss how and what information will be shared
    - Address the impact on the therapeutic relationship
    - Document this conversation

5. Limit disclosure to what is legally required

    - Share only information relevant to the specific exception
    - Maintain confidentiality for information not covered by the exception
    - Use secure methods for transmitting information

6. Follow up appropriately

    - Document all actions taken
    - Continue therapeutic support for the client
    - Monitor for any changes in risk status
    - Consult with legal counsel if questions arise about obligations

7. Review and reflect

    - Evaluate how the situation was handled

- Consider implications for the ongoing therapeutic relationship
- Identify any process improvements for future situations

Knowing these legal exceptions to confidentiality and following a structured approach when they arise, PCCs in California can fulfill their legal obligations while minimizing disruption to the therapeutic relationship. Remember that these exceptions exist not to undermine confidentiality but to balance it against other important values such as public safety and the protection of vulnerable populations.

- Explain the reason for the confidentiality breach
- Discuss how and what information will be shared
- Address the impact on the therapeutic relationship
- Document this conversation
- Limit disclosure to what is legally required
- Share only information relevant to the specific exception
- Maintain confidentiality for information not covered by the exception
- Use secure methods for transmitting information
- Follow up appropriately
- Document all actions taken
- Continue therapeutic support for the client
- Monitor for any changes in risk status
- Consult with legal counsel if questions arise about obligations
- Review and reflect
- Evaluate how the situation was handled
- Consider implications for the ongoing therapeutic relationship
- Identify any process improvements for future situations

MORE ON DUTY TO WARN REQUIREMENTS

The landmark Tarasoff v. Regents of the University of California (1976) case fundamentally changed how mental health professionals approach client confidentiality when threats of violence emerge. This California Supreme Court ruling established that mental health professionals have a duty to protect potential victims when clients make credible threats, famously declaring that *"protective privilege ends where public peril begins."* This legal principle has evolved through subsequent legislation and court decisions, creating specific obligations for Professional Clinical Counselors in California.

California Civil Code Section 43.92 codifies this duty, specifying that it applies when a client communicates a *"serious threat of physical violence against a reasonably identifiable victim."* The 2007 amendment (AB 733) clarified that psychotherapists are only liable if they fail to discharge this duty when a patient has communicated such a serious threat. This provides some protection for counselors who exercise professional judgment in determining threat credibility.

Subsequent case law has clarified how this duty may be triggered. In *Ewing v. Goldstein* (2004), the court found that threats reported by a family member, rather than the client directly, may initiate the duty to protect if the counselor has reason to take the warning seriously. In *Calderon v. Glick* (2005), the court acknowledged that nonverbal behavior and clinical observations, such as tone, affect, and body language, can also support a counselor's judgment that a threat exists. These rulings reinforce that the duty to protect is based not on prediction but on reasonable clinical judgment drawn from all available information.

For PCCs, recognizing when the duty to warn is triggered requires careful assessment. Several factors help determine if a threat meets the threshold for action:

- Specificity of the threat: Vague statements like *"someone might get hurt"* typically don't trigger the duty, while specific threats

such as *"I'm going to shoot my ex-wife when she leaves work tomorrow"* likely do.
- Identifiable victim: The potential victim must be reasonably identifiable, either as a specific individual or a clearly defined group (such as students at a particular school).
- Capability to carry out the threat: Consider whether the client has access to means (weapons, etc.) and opportunity to execute the threat.
- History of violence: Previous violent behavior increases the credibility of current threats.
- Current mental status: Factors like psychosis, substance use, or extreme emotional states may elevate risk.

When a counselor determines that a duty to warn exists, California Civil Code Section 43.92 outlines three possible actions, at least one of which must be taken:

- Make reasonable efforts to communicate the threat to the potential victim(s)
- Notify law enforcement in the area where the potential victim or the client resides
- Take steps reasonably necessary under the circumstances to protect the potential victim

The specific approach depends on the situation's urgency and particulars. Here's a practical protocol for implementing these options:

When warning potential victims:

- Contact them directly by phone when possible
- Provide enough information about the threat to enable self-protection
- Maintain client confidentiality except for information directly related to the threat
- Document the date, time, method of contact, and information shared

When notifying law enforcement:

- Contact the agency with jurisdiction where the potential victim is located
- Provide the client's name, the nature of the threat, and victim information
- Request a case number or officer name for documentation
- Follow up with a written report if requested

When taking other protective steps:

- Consider initiating involuntary hospitalization if criteria are met under California Welfare and Institutions Code Section 5150
- Increase session frequency to monitor the client's status
- Develop a safety plan with the client if appropriate
- Consult with colleagues or legal counsel about additional measures

Different scenarios require tailored responses. Consider these examples:

Scenario 1: A client experiencing a relationship breakup states, *"Sometimes I feel so angry I could hurt someone."* This vague statement without a specific target or plan likely doesn't trigger the duty to warn. The counselor might explore these feelings further, assess for risk factors, and document the assessment.

Scenario 2: A client says, *"I bought a gun yesterday, and I'm going to shoot my boss on Friday when he leaves the office."* This specific threat against an identifiable person with apparent means requires immediate action. The counselor could notify both the potential victim and local police, document these actions, and consider whether the client meets criteria for involuntary hospitalization.

Scenario 3: A client experiencing paranoid delusions states, *"The people in apartment 3B are poisoning me, and I need to stop them before they kill me."* This presents a threat to identifiable individuals based on delusional beliefs. The counselor might contact law enforcement to conduct a welfare check, consider hospitalization if criteria are met, and document the assessment and actions taken.

Documentation is essential when implementing the duty to warn. California Business and Professions Code Section 4999.20, which defines the scope of practice for LPCCs, implicitly requires appropriate record-keeping of all professional activities. Records should include:

- The exact threat as stated by the client
- Risk assessment factors considered
- Consultation with colleagues or supervisors (if applicable)
- Actions taken to discharge the duty
- Rationale for the chosen course of action
- Follow-up plans for continued monitoring

Risk management strategies when implementing the duty to warn include:

- Maintaining current knowledge of relevant laws and professional standards
- Consulting with colleagues or supervisors in ambiguous situations
- Contacting professional liability insurance carriers for guidance when needed
- Balancing the duty to warn with maintaining the therapeutic relationship
- Considering how to address the issue with the client, when clinically appropriate

The California Code of Regulations, Title 16, Division 18, Article 3 (Sections 1845-1858) provides additional guidance on professional conduct for LPCCs, including ethical standards that inform how confidentiality exceptions should be handled.

While the duty to warn represents a significant exception to confidentiality, it exists to balance client privacy with public safety. When in doubt about whether a specific situation triggers the duty to warn, counselors might consult with colleagues, supervisors, or legal counsel. The California Association of Marriage and Family Therapists and the

California Counseling Association also provide resources and consultation services to help navigate these complex situations.

MANAGING SUICIDAL IDEATION DISCLOSURE

When a client discloses suicidal thoughts, Professional Clinical Counselors in California face complex legal and ethical responsibilities. The landmark case of Bellah v. Greenson (1978) established that mental health professionals have a duty to take reasonable steps to prevent a patient's suicide when they become aware of suicidal intent. This California Court of Appeal case expanded on the Tarasoff duty, determining that therapists might be liable for failing to prevent a patient's suicide when they had knowledge of suicidal intent.

In Bellah v. Greenson, the court ruled that *"where a therapist knows that his patient is likely to attempt suicide... he incurs a legal obligation to use reasonable care to prevent the threatened harm."* This established that the duty of care extends beyond protecting third parties (as in Tarasoff) to protecting clients from self-harm.

Another relevant case is Nally v. Grace Community Church (1988), where the California Supreme Court limited the scope of liability for suicide, ruling that non-therapist counselors could not be held liable for failure to prevent suicide. However, this limitation does not apply to licensed mental health professionals, who maintain a duty of care based on their specialized training and professional standards.

For PCCs in California, the Business and Professions Code Section 4999.20 defines the scope of practice, which includes *"assessment, diagnosis, and treatment of mental disorders,"* implicitly covering suicide risk assessment and intervention. Additionally, the California Code of Regulations, Title 16, Division 18, Article 3 (Sections 1845-1858) outlines standards of practice that require competent care in crisis situations.

When a client discloses suicidal thoughts, a structured risk assessment protocol is essential. This assessment might include:

1. Direct inquiry about suicidal thoughts: *"Are you having thoughts about killing yourself?"* Avoiding euphemisms ensures clarity.
2. Assessment of specific plan: *"Do you have a plan for how you might end your life?"* Follow up with questions about access to means, timing, and preparations made.
3. Evaluation of intent: *"How strong is your desire to die?"* and *"What might stop you from acting on these thoughts?"*
4. Exploration of risk factors: Previous attempts, family history of suicide, recent losses, substance use, and mental health diagnoses like depression or bipolar disorder.
5. Identification of protective factors: Social support, future-oriented thinking, responsibility to others, and religious/spiritual beliefs.

Counselors could utilize standardized assessment tools such as:

- Columbia-Suicide Severity Rating Scale (C-SSRS)
- Beck Scale for Suicide Ideation (BSS)
- Patient Health Questionnaire-9 (PHQ-9), with particular attention to question 9 about suicidal thoughts

The level of risk determined through assessment guides the intervention approach:

Low Risk (passive ideation, no plan, few risk factors, strong protective factors):

- Safety planning
- Increase session frequency
- Connect with support systems
- Document assessment and plan

Moderate Risk (suicidal ideation with vague plan, some risk factors, some protective factors):

- Develop detailed safety plan

- Remove access to lethal means when possible
- Increase treatment intensity
- Consider voluntary hospitalization
- Consult with colleagues or supervisor
- Document thoroughly

High Risk (specific plan, access to means, strong intent, multiple risk factors, few protective factors):

- Maintain direct observation
- Arrange immediate evaluation for hospitalization
- Contact emergency services if needed
- Inform family/support persons with client consent when possible
- Document all actions taken

California law does not explicitly mandate when confidentiality must be breached for suicidal clients. However, California Civil Code Section 56.10(c)(1) permits disclosure without authorization when *"the health care provider believes in good faith that the disclosure is necessary to prevent or lessen a serious and imminent threat to the health or safety of the patient."*

Documentation requirements for suicide risk assessment include:

1. Verbatim statements from the client regarding suicidal thoughts
2. Specific questions asked and client responses
3. Risk and protective factors identified
4. Clinical reasoning for risk level determination
5. Safety plan components
6. Interventions implemented
7. Consultations sought
8. Follow-up plan
9. Rationale for decisions regarding confidentiality

When coordinating with emergency services, counselors might:

1. Call 911 or the local crisis team for immediate risk

2. Provide essential information: client name, location, nature of crisis, presence of weapons
3. Document the time of call, name of responder, and information shared
4. Remain with the client (in person or by phone) until help arrives when possible

For family involvement:
1. Obtain client consent when possible
2. Share only information necessary for safety
3. Provide general guidance on supporting someone in crisis without revealing confidential details
4. Document all communications with family members

When coordinating with other healthcare providers:
1. Obtain appropriate releases when time permits
2. Share relevant information about current risk level and treatment needs
3. Arrange for continuity of care during transitions
4. Document all coordination efforts

The California Board of Behavioral Sciences emphasizes that PCCs must practice within their scope of competence (Business and Professions Code Section 4999.90). This means counselors must recognize when a client's needs exceed their expertise and make appropriate referrals.

After immediate crisis resolution, ongoing monitoring includes:
1. Reassessing risk at each contact
2. Reviewing and updating safety plans
3. Addressing underlying factors contributing to suicidality
4. Gradually transitioning to lower levels of care as appropriate

These guidelines support legally compliant, ethically grounded care for clients struggling with suicidal thoughts. The balance between respecting client autonomy and ensuring safety remains a complex clinical judgment that must be made on a case-by-case basis, guided by professional standards and relevant California laws.

ELECTRONIC COMMUNICATION PRIVACY

Electronic communication has transformed how counselors interact with clients, creating both opportunities and challenges for maintaining confidentiality. Professional Clinical Counselors in California face specific legal obligations when using digital platforms to communicate with clients.

California's Confidentiality of Medical Information Act (CMIA), found in Civil Code §§ 56-56.37, requires healthcare providers to maintain the confidentiality of medical information and obtain patient authorization before disclosing such information. This law applies to electronic communications containing client information. Additionally, Business and Professions Code § 4999.90(c) identifies the unauthorized disclosure of confidential information as unprofessional conduct that could lead to disciplinary action by the Board of Behavioral Sciences.

For email communications, counselors need to implement several security measures. The Health Insurance Portability and Accountability Act (HIPAA), which applies to covered entities, recommends using encrypted email services that meet the Advanced Encryption Standard (AES) with 256-bit encryption. Even for non-HIPAA covered practices, similar encryption standards represent best practice for protecting client information. Counselors might use email providers that offer Transport Layer Security (TLS) encryption, which protects messages during transmission, or implement end-to-end encryption solutions that ensure only the sender and recipient can read message contents.

Text messaging presents particular challenges due to its convenience and widespread use. Standard SMS text messages are not encrypted and may be stored on telecommunication company servers. Counselors who communicate with clients via text might use HIPAA-compliant messaging applications that employ end-to-end encryption, such as specialized healthcare communication platforms. These applications often include features like automatic message expiration and remote deletion capabilities.

For video sessions, California Code of Regulations Title 16, § 1815.5 outlines standards for telehealth services, requiring counselors to assess whether telehealth is appropriate for each client and obtain informed consent. Video platforms used for therapy sessions need to incorporate encryption protocols, preferably meeting HIPAA standards with AES 256-bit encryption. Additional security features might include meeting passwords, waiting rooms to control participant access, and session locks to prevent unauthorized entry.

Electronic record storage requires particular attention. Business and Professions Code § 4999.75 mandates that counselors maintain client records consistent with sound clinical judgment, the standards of the profession, and the nature of the services provided. For electronic records, this translates to implementing password protection with strong, unique passwords; enabling multi-factor authentication; using encrypted storage solutions; and maintaining regular, secure backups stored separately from primary systems.

When communicating with clients about electronic privacy risks, counselors need to be transparent about the limitations of confidentiality in digital environments. An electronic communication policy might include language such as:

"While I take reasonable steps to protect your confidentiality in electronic communications, including [describe specific measures taken], no electronic communication method is completely secure. Emails, text messages, and video sessions may be vulnerable to hacking, accidental transmission to wrong recipients, or unauthorized access to devices. By consenting to electronic communication, you acknowledge these risks."

The informed consent process for electronic communication could include discussing:

- The types of electronic communication the counselor uses (email, text, video)
- The purposes for which each type might be used (scheduling, brief updates, therapy sessions)
- Expected response times for different communication methods
- appropriate for emergencies)
- Privacy risks specific to each communication method
- Security measures implemented by the counselor
- Client responsibilities for maintaining privacy on their end

A sample electronic communication policy section might read:

"Email Communication: I use [specific secure email service] for client communications. Emails are appropriate for scheduling appointments and brief updates but not for therapeutic content or emergencies. I typically respond to emails within [timeframe]. Please be aware that emails may become part of your clinical record.

Text Messaging: I use [secure messaging application] for text communications with clients. Texts are limited to appointment scheduling and brief logistical matters. Standard SMS text messages are not secure and are discouraged.

Video Sessions: Telehealth sessions are conducted through [HIPAA-compliant platform]. You will receive a unique link and password for each session. Please connect from a private location where conversations cannot be overheard and use a secure, private internet connection rather than public Wi-Fi.

Client Responsibilities: To protect your privacy, please secure your devices with passwords, log out of accounts after use, and avoid sharing devices used to communicate with me. Consider who might have access to your devices and accounts."

California Penal Code § 637.2 allows individuals to bring civil action against anyone who violates their privacy in communication. This highlights the importance of counselors obtaining explicit consent for electronic communications and documenting this consent in client records.

Best practices for maintaining confidentiality in digital environments include:

- Conducting regular security assessments of all electronic systems used in practice
- Implementing a *"minimum necessary"* approach to electronic communications, sharing only essential information
- Using separate professional accounts for client communications, distinct from personal accounts
- Establishing clear boundaries around response times and appropriate content for electronic communications
- Developing protocols for addressing potential security breaches
- Maintaining updated devices with current security patches and antivirus protection
- Using secure Wi-Fi networks with WPA2 or WPA3 encryption for all professional activities
- Implementing automatic log-out features on devices containing client information
- Regularly reviewing and updating electronic communication policies as technology evolves
- Documenting all substantive electronic communications in the client record

For mobile devices, additional precautions might include enabling remote wipe capabilities, using biometric authentication, and avoiding storing client contact information under real names.

When terminating the counseling relationship, counselors could establish protocols for handling electronic communications, including timeframes for responding to messages after termination, procedures for transferring relevant electronic records to new providers, and guidelines for securely deleting client information when retention periods expire.

By implementing these technical safeguards and communication practices, PCCs in California can navigate the complex landscape of electronic communication while upholding their legal and ethical obligations to protect client confidentiality. As technology continues to evolve, counselors need to stay informed about emerging security threats and solutions, regularly updating their practices to maintain the highest standards of client privacy protection.

MULTI-PARTY CONFIDENTIALITY CHALLENGES

Confidentiality in multi-party counseling settings presents unique challenges that extend beyond traditional individual therapy. When Professional Clinical Counselors work with couples, families, or groups, they navigate complex webs of relationships where information sharing and privacy expectations differ significantly from one-on-one counseling.

In couple's counseling, each partner might assume that what they share privately with the counselor will remain confidential from their partner. However, California law recognizes that the therapeutic relationship in couple's counseling typically involves both individuals as a unit. Professional clinical counseling includes *"relationship counseling,"* which by nature involves multiple parties. This creates a situation where the counselor might hold information from one partner that could be relevant to the therapeutic process for both.

To address this challenge, PCCs could establish a *"no secrets"* policy at the outset of couple's therapy. This policy clarifies that information shared privately by one partner might be brought into joint sessions if the counselor determines it's relevant to the therapeutic goals. A sample clause in the informed consent document might read:

"In couple's counseling, I maintain a 'no secrets' policy. Information shared with me in individual communications (whether in person, by phone, or electronically) may be discussed in joint sessions if I believe it's important to our work together. I will use my clinical judgment about when

and how to incorporate such information. If you're not comfortable with this policy, individual therapy might be more appropriate for your needs."

Family therapy presents even more complex confidentiality considerations. When working with families that include minors, counselors balance the parents' legal right to information about their children's treatment with the therapeutic need to build trust with younger family members. California Family Code §6924 allows minors 12 years and older to consent to mental health treatment in certain circumstances, creating potential conflicts between parental rights and adolescent confidentiality.

A practical approach involves creating age-appropriate confidentiality agreements. For younger children, parents might receive more detailed information, while for adolescents, the counselor might establish boundaries around what will be shared with parents, except in cases involving safety concerns. These agreements should be documented and reviewed periodically as children mature.

Group therapy settings require clear guidelines about confidentiality expectations among members. While the counselor is bound by legal and ethical confidentiality requirements, group members typically are not.

A sample group confidentiality agreement might include:

"While I am legally and ethically bound to maintain confidentiality about what's shared in this group, other group members are not under the same legal obligation. I ask that all members agree to keep information shared in this group confidential. However, I cannot guarantee that all members will honor this agreement. Please consider this limitation when deciding what to share in the group setting."

Documentation in multi-party counseling requires special attention. Records should clearly indicate who was present for each session, what agreements were made about confidentiality, and how information was shared between parties. When documenting sensitive disclosures made by one party, counselors might note their clinical decision-making process regarding whether and how to address this information in joint sessions.

Electronic communication adds another layer of complexity to multi-party confidentiality. When communicating with multiple family members or group participants, counselors must ensure they don't inadvertently share private information through email chains, text messages, or video sessions. The California Confidentiality of Medical Information Act (Civil Code §56 et seq.) requires protection of medical information, including mental health records, regardless of how it's stored or transmitted.

For electronic communications in multi-party contexts, counselors could implement these safeguards:

- Use separate email threads or secure messaging for communications with individual members of a couple or family
- Verify recipient information before sending sensitive communications
- Obtain written consent for electronic communications that specifies who may receive what types of information
- Use HIPAA-compliant platforms for video sessions with multiple participants

A sample electronic communication policy for multi-party counseling might state:

"For couples and families, I will communicate electronically only about scheduling and administrative matters with all parties included. For clinical matters, I prefer to discuss these during our sessions together. If you contact me individually about clinical concerns, I may need to bring this information into our joint sessions in accordance with our 'no secrets' policy."

Maintaining therapeutic alliances while managing these complex confidentiality boundaries requires transparency and consistency. When counselors need to share information between parties, they could:

- Remind clients of previously established confidentiality agreements

- Explain the therapeutic rationale for sharing information
- When possible, encourage the individual to disclose the information themselves in a joint session
- Frame disclosures in terms of the agreed-upon treatment goals
- Acknowledge the difficulty of the situation while maintaining professional boundaries

For example, if a partner in couple's therapy discloses an ongoing affair, the counselor might say: *"I understand this is difficult information that you're reluctant to share with your partner. However, as we discussed in our initial session, I maintain a 'no secrets' policy because secrets can interfere with the work we're doing together. I encourage you to bring this up in our next joint session, and I'm happy to help facilitate that conversation. If you're not ready to do that, we might need to reconsider whether couple's counseling is the right approach right now."*

PROFESSIONAL CONSULTATION PROTOCOL

Professional consultation is an essential component of ethical counseling practice, providing opportunities for growth, guidance, and support. However, these consultations create unique confidentiality challenges that require careful navigation. When seeking supervision or peer consultation, Professional Clinical Counselors in California need to balance their professional development needs with their primary obligation to protect client confidentiality.

When sharing case information during supervision or consultation, counselors could limit identifying details to those absolutely necessary for meaningful discussion. While consultation is part of professional clinical counseling service, this doesn't eliminate confidentiality obligations. Consider using client initials or pseudonyms rather than full names, altering non-essential demographic details, and focusing discussion on specific clinical issues rather than comprehensive case histories.

Prior to seeking consultation, counselors might inform clients about this practice during the informed consent process. As previously mentioned, the law requires PCCs to provide clients with accurate information about the counseling process. A statement such as *"I regularly consult with other professionals regarding clients with whom I work. However, during these consultations, I do not reveal any personally identifying information regarding my client"* could be included in informed consent documents.

In informal consultation settings, such as peer discussions or impromptu conversations, confidentiality risks often increase. California Penal Code §632.7 establishes civil liability for unauthorized disclosure of confidential communications. Even in casual professional conversations, counselors need to remain vigilant about protecting client information. Consider these practices for informal consultations:

- Hold discussions in private spaces where conversations cannot be overheard
- Avoid consultations in public settings like elevators, hallways, or restaurants
- Refrain from discussing cases on social media platforms, even in *"private"* professional groups
- Limit details to the minimum necessary for meaningful feedback

For group supervision or case conferences, additional protocols help maintain confidentiality. Participants could sign confidentiality agreements acknowledging their obligation to protect information shared during these sessions. The group leader might establish ground rules emphasizing that information discussed remains within the consultation setting.

Electronic communication introduces additional confidentiality challenges in counseling practice. The Health Insurance Portability and Accountability Act (HIPAA) and California's Confidentiality of Medical Information Act (Civil Code §56 et seq.) establish requirements for protecting health information, including mental health records and communications.

For email communications, PCCs could implement encryption that meets current industry standards. Regular email services typically don't provide adequate security for protected health information. Secure messaging platforms designed specifically for healthcare communications offer end-to-end encryption and other security features that better protect client confidentiality.

Text messaging presents particular challenges due to its inherently insecure nature. California Business and Professions Code §4999.90(m) identifies unprofessional conduct as including *"failure to maintain confidentiality, except as otherwise required or permitted by law."* Given this requirement, counselors might consider:

- Using HIPAA-compliant texting applications rather than standard SMS
- Limiting text communications to scheduling matters only
- Establishing clear policies about response times and emergency protocols
- Documenting all substantive text exchanges in the client record

For video sessions, platforms should provide encryption, secure access controls, and HIPAA-compliant features. The California Board of Behavioral Sciences has recognized telehealth as a legitimate service delivery method under Business and Professions Code §2290.5, but this recognition comes with expectations for maintaining appropriate security measures.

Client education about electronic communication risks forms an essential part of informed consent. A sample policy statement might include:

"Electronic communications cannot be guaranteed to be secure or confidential. While I take reasonable steps to protect your information, there are inherent risks in electronic communication. By consenting to electronic communication, you acknowledge these risks. I recommend

limiting electronic messages to scheduling matters and addressing clinical concerns during our sessions."

Documentation of client consent for electronic communications is particularly important. California Civil Code §56.10 requires written authorization for disclosure of medical information, and electronic transmission could constitute such disclosure if not properly secured. Counselors might obtain separate written consent for each form of electronic communication used in their practice.

Storage of electronic communications presents additional confidentiality considerations. Business and Professions Code §4999.75 requires LPCCs to retain client records for at least seven years from the date therapy is terminated. This retention requirement applies to electronic communications that contain substantive clinical information. Secure, encrypted storage systems with appropriate backup protocols help maintain confidentiality throughout the required retention period.

When using shared electronic practice management systems, access controls become essential for maintaining confidentiality. Each user should have unique login credentials, and access to client information should be limited based on legitimate need. Regular audits of system access help identify potential confidentiality breaches.

In professional development and training contexts, case material often provides valuable learning opportunities. However, California Business and Professions Code §4999.90 identifies unprofessional conduct as including breaches of confidentiality. When presenting cases for educational purposes, counselors could thoroughly disguise identifying information, obtain specific written consent from clients, or create composite cases that combine elements from multiple clients to prevent identification.

CHAPTER SEVEN

RECORD KEEPING REQUIREMENTS

LEGAL REQUIREMENTS FOR CLINICAL RECORDS

California law establishes specific requirements for clinical record keeping that Professional Clinical Counselors must follow. The California Health and Safety Code, along with regulations from the Board of Behavioral Sciences (BBS), creates a framework for maintaining proper clinical documentation.

Under California Health and Safety Code §123100-123149.5, clients have the right to access their health records, which places a legal obligation on counselors to maintain accurate and complete documentation. When we look at what needs to be contained in clinical records, you won't find one singular place in the law that gives specific guidance. However, California Health and Safety Code §123130 gives us some useful direction. This section comes up when a client requests access to their records and the counselor chooses to provide a summary instead of releasing the full record. In that context, the law outlines eight specific elements that should be included in the summary:

1. The client's chief complaint or complaints, including relevant history

2. Findings from consultations and referrals to other healthcare providers
3. Diagnosis, where one has been made
4. Treatment plan and interventions, including any medications prescribed
5. Progress of the treatment
6. Prognosis, including any significant continuing concerns or conditions
7. Pertinent reports from diagnostic procedures or discharge summaries
8. Objective findings from the most relevant clinical or physical examinations

Some of these categories are more directly applicable to medical providers, but for mental health professionals, the expectation is to include the information that reflects the clinical care being provided. Counselors may also wish to consult professional association guidelines to determine what other documentation elements are expected in their discipline.

The California Health and Safety Code requires that progress notes be completed within a reasonable timeframe after each session. While the exact timeframe isn't specified in statute, the standard of practice typically calls for documentation within 24-48 hours of service provision. This helps ensure accuracy and completeness while details remain fresh in the counselor's mind.

For accuracy standards, California Business and Professions Code §4999.90(v) states that unprofessional conduct includes *"The failure to keep records consistent with sound clinical judgment, the standards of the profession, and the nature of the services being rendered."* This means records should be:

- Factual and objective
- Free from speculation or personal bias
- Legible and understandable
- Consistent with the treatment provided

- Detailed enough to allow another professional to continue care if necessary

For example, a progress note might read: *"Client reported continued anxiety symptoms, rating them 7/10 today compared to 8/10 last session. Discussed and practiced deep breathing techniques. Client demonstrated ability to implement technique and reported temporary reduction in physical symptoms."* This note provides factual information about the client's condition, the intervention used, and the outcome.

Non-compliance with record-keeping requirements can lead to serious consequences. In a simulated scenario, a counselor who failed to document a client's suicidal ideation and the safety plan implemented could face disciplinary action from the BBS if the client later attempted suicide. The Board could determine that the counselor engaged in negligent record keeping under Business and Professions Code §4999.90.

Penalties for inadequate record keeping might include:

- Probation with the BBS
- Mandatory continuing education
- Fines up to $5,000 per violation
- License suspension or revocation in severe cases
- Increased vulnerability to malpractice claims

CLIENT ACCESS RIGHTS MANAGEMENT

California law grants clients the right to access their mental health records, with specific provisions outlined in the Health Insurance Portability and Accountability Act (HIPAA) and the California Patient Access to Health Records Act. Professional Clinical Counselors must understand these regulations to properly manage client record requests while maintaining appropriate confidentiality.

Under California Health and Safety Code §123110, clients have the right to inspect their records during business hours within five working days of a written request. If clients request copies rather than inspection, counselors must provide these within 15 days. The law permits charging reasonable clerical costs for copying records, typically not exceeding $0.25 per page for standard reproductions or $0.50 for records copied from microfilm.

Consider this scenario: Maria, a 32-year-old client, contacts your office requesting copies of her therapy records from the past year. She mentions needing them for a disability application. As her counselor, you should:

- Provide a standardized records request form
- Verify Maria's identity before releasing any information
- Process her request within the 15-day timeframe
- Calculate reasonable copying fees
- Document the request and your response in her file

A compliant records request form should include:

- Client identifying information
- Specific records being requested
- Purpose of the request (optional for client to provide)
- Preferred delivery method
- Client signature and date
- Notice of applicable fees

When responding to record requests, counselors might use this template:

"Dear [Client Name],

We have received your request dated [date] for copies of your counseling records. We are processing this request in accordance with California law and will provide the requested documents by [date within 15-day timeframe]. The estimated cost for copying these records is [amount], calculated at [rate] per page for approximately [number] pages.

Please contact our office if you have any questions about this process.

Sincerely,

[Counselor Name and Credentials]"

When records contain sensitive information, counselors must exercise careful judgment. While California law does not permit withholding entire records based on potential harm, counselors could provide a summary of treatment instead of full records if they believe disclosure would cause significant harm to the client or another person, as permitted under Health and Safety Code §123115(b).

For example: Dr. Chen, an LPCC, receives a record request from a client with a history of suicidal ideation. The notes contain detailed information about the client's methods and triggers. Dr. Chen might offer a treatment summary that outlines the therapeutic approach and progress without including potentially harmful details, while documenting his clinical rationale for this decision. In situations where access is denied based on risk of harm, counselors should document the request date and the specific clinical reasons for withholding the records. If the counselor is a HIPAA-covered entity, they may also rely on 45 CFR §164.524, which allows denial when disclosure could reasonably endanger the client or another person.

If a client is denied access to their records, California law allows them to request that the records be sent directly to another healthcare provider of their choosing. However, if the receiving provider is a registered associate, their licensed supervisor must sign for the records and assume responsibility for receiving them. The associate may not independently provide the client with access to those records if access was already denied by the original provider. This rule protects the integrity of the original denial and ensures compliance with Health and Safety Code §123115.

California Health and Safety Code §123105 provides some important definitions and limitations when it comes to what may be disclosed in a client's record. It clarifies that patient records include only information that pertains directly to the client who is requesting access. Importantly, it states that information given in confidence to the counselor by someone other than another healthcare provider. For example, a family member or concerned third party may be excluded from the records before they are released or reviewed. This is intended to protect the privacy of others and maintain the integrity of collateral communications. Counselors should review any such material carefully when preparing records for inspection or copying.

Special circumstances require additional considerations:

- Deceased clients: Under HIPAA, privacy protections extend 50 years after death. California law permits the deceased client's personal representative or next of kin to access records. Counselors should require documentation proving this relationship before releasing records.

- Legal representatives: Parents or guardians generally have access to minor clients' records, with important exceptions outlined in California Family Code §6924-6929, which grants minors aged 12 and older the right to consent to mental health treatment without parental knowledge in certain circumstances. When a court-appointed guardian or conservator requests records for an adult client, proper legal documentation must be verified.

- Subpoenas: When records are subpoenaed, counselors should notify clients when possible and consider consulting legal counsel to determine if the psychotherapist-patient privilege applies under California Evidence Code §1010-1027.

California law gives clients the right to request an addendum to their records if they believe something is incomplete or inaccurate. Under Health and Safety Code §123110, a client may submit a written statement of up to 250 words per item or statement they wish to correct. Even if the counselor disagrees with the client's position, the addendum must be included in the record and disclosed along with the relevant material.

Counselors should document that the addendum was submitted by the client and note the date it was added to the record.

Counselors who use electronic communication or store clinical records electronically must comply with both federal and California privacy laws. A full explanation of HIPAA's Privacy Rule, Security Rule, and the CMIA is provided in Chapter 8, along with practical guidance for secure email, texting, telehealth, and device management.

Risk Assessment Records

Risk assessment documentation is particularly important in California, where the Bellah v. Greenson case established that mental health professionals have a duty to prevent client suicide. Comprehensive risk assessment records include:

1. Specific risk factors identified
2. Protective factors present
3. Client's statements regarding intent (direct quotes when possible)
4. Access to means
5. History of previous attempts
6. Current plan specificity
7. Clinical judgment of risk level (low, moderate, high, imminent)
8. Rationale for risk determination
9.

A structured risk assessment template might include:

Risk Assessment Documentation Risk Level Determined: [Low/Moderate/High/Imminent] Risk Factors Present: [List specific factors] Protective Factors Present: [List specific factors] Suicidal/Homicidal Ideation: [Yes/No, with description] Plan: [Specificity, lethality, availability of means] Client Statements: [Direct quotes regarding intent] Previous Attempts: [History and nature of attempts] Current Stressors: [Factors contributing to current risk] Clinical Reasoning: [Explanation for risk level determination]

ESSENTIAL DOCUMENTATION COMPONENTS

As mentioned before, California law requires Professional Clinical Counselors to maintain client records for a minimum of seven years from the date of service termination, as specified in the California Business and Professions Code 4999.75 and Health and Safety Code 123145. This retention period represents the baseline requirement, though certain circumstances might necessitate longer retention periods. Understanding when to keep records and when to destroy them forms a key component of ethical and legal practice.

Record Retention Timeline

Different types of clinical records have varying retention requirements:

- **Adult Client Records**: Must be retained for at least seven years from the date of termination.

- **Minor Client Records**: Must be kept until the minor reaches age 18, plus an additional seven years. For example, records for a 12-year-old client would need to be maintained for 13 years (until age 25).

- **Records Involving Legal Proceedings**: When records become part of legal proceedings, they should be retained until the legal matter concludes, plus the standard seven-year period.

- **Insurance and Billing Records**: These typically follow the seven-year minimum but might need to be kept longer if required by specific insurance contracts or Medicare/Medicaid participation.

- **Supervision Records**: APCCs should maintain supervision documentation throughout their associate period and for seven years after licensure. Supervisors are required to keep records for seven.

Legal Requirements for Record Destruction

When the retention period expires, records may be destroyed, but the process should follow specific protocols to maintain confidentiality as required by California Civil Code Section 56.101:

- Paper Records: Must be shredded, pulverized, or incinerated to render information unreadable and reconstruction impossible.//
- Electronic Records: Must undergo secure deletion using specialized software that overwrites data multiple times, ensuring it cannot be recovered.
- Physical Media: Hard drives, USB drives, or other storage devices containing protected health information must be physically destroyed when decommissioned.
- Third-Party Services: If using a destruction service, a Business Associate Agreement (BAA) must be in place, and the service must provide a Certificate of Destruction.

RECORDS STORAGE AND ACCESS PROTOCOL

Physical storage of clinical records requires attention to both security and accessibility. Records containing protected health information must be stored in locked cabinets within secure areas with limited access. For example, Dr. Martinez, an LPCC with a small private practice, maintains a dedicated records room with commercial-grade filing cabinets secured with tamper-resistant locks. The room remains locked when not in use, and only Dr. Martinez and her office manager have keys. A sign-in/sign-out log tracks all record access, creating an audit trail of who accessed which files and when.

In another scenario, a group practice led by several LPCCs implements a color-coded filing system where active client files are stored in locked cabinets in a secure records room. Each counselor has access only to their own clients' records through a key card system that logs entry. Inactive records are transferred to a separate storage area with more restricted access, requiring formal check-out procedures.

For digital storage systems, California's Confidentiality of Medical Information Act (CMIA) requires implementation of appropriate technical safeguards. A compliant digital storage system includes encrypted servers or cloud storage with access controls, regular backups, and audit capabilities. For instance, XYZ Counseling Center uses a HIPAA-compliant electronic health record (EHR) system with role-based access controls. Each staff member has unique login credentials, and the system automatically logs all record access and modifications. The practice maintains encrypted backups both on-site and in a secure cloud environment, with quarterly testing of restoration procedures.

Access authorization procedures must balance security with clinical necessity. Under California law, only authorized personnel with legitimate need should access client records. A formal access policy might include:

1. Designation of specific staff roles authorized to access records
2. Documentation requirements for record access
3. Procedures for temporary access by consulting professionals
4. Protocols for access during emergencies or counselor absence

At Valley Mental Health Associates, a multi-disciplinary practice, the clinical director maintains an authorization matrix specifying which staff members can access different types of information. Administrative staff can view scheduling and billing information but not clinical notes. Clinicians can access only their own clients' records unless formal consultation is documented. The IT manager can maintain the system but has implemented technical controls preventing access to clinical content.

Client record request processes must comply with both HIPAA and California law. Under California Health and Safety Code §123110, clients have the right to access their records within 15 days of a written request. A structured process ensures compliance:

1. The client submits a written request specifying desired records
2. Staff verify the client's identity using government-issued ID
3. The counselor reviews records before release to identify any legally withholdable information
4. Records are provided in the requested format (paper or electronic)
5. A nominal fee may be charged for copying costs as permitted by law
6. The request and fulfillment are documented in the client's record

For example, when client Sarah J. requested her records from her LPCC, the practice provided a standardized request form. After verifying her identity, the counselor reviewed the file to ensure no third-party information was included. The records were provided electronically through the practice's secure patient portal within 10 days, and the entire process was documented in Sarah's file.

Electronic communication in counseling practice presents unique confidentiality challenges. Under California law, particularly the CMIA, counselors must implement appropriate security measures for various forms of electronic communication.

For email communications, counselors could use HIPAA-compliant email services with encryption. For instance, Dr. Williams configures his email system with TLS encryption and implements a secure patient portal for sharing sensitive information rather than using standard email. All emails include a confidentiality disclaimer, and staff are trained to limit the amount of protected health information included in messages.

Text messaging presents significant security concerns. If text messaging is used, counselors might utilize HIPAA-compliant secure messaging applications. At Bayside Counseling Center, therapists use a secure messaging platform integrated with their EHR system. Clients must opt-in to this communication method, and the system automatically deletes messages after 30 days. The platform also disables message previews on lock screens to prevent inadvertent disclosure.

Video sessions require particular attention to security. California-licensed counselors conducting telehealth services could use only HIPAA-compliant video platforms with signed business associate agreements. For example, Dr. Chen conducts telehealth sessions from a private office where conversations cannot be overheard. She uses a platform that provides end-to-end encryption, verifies client identity at the beginning of each session, and ensures her network connection is secured with a VPN when working remotely.

Client communication about electronic privacy risks is essential. California Business and Professions Code §4999.76 requires informed consent for treatment, which extends to electronic communications. Sample language for an electronic communication policy might include:

"Electronic communications involve some risk to your confidentiality. While we implement security measures to protect your information, no electronic system is completely secure. By consenting to electronic communications, you acknowledge these risks. We will limit the information shared electronically to what is necessary for your care. You may withdraw consent for electronic communications at any time."

Consent procedures should include written documentation of the client's consent, clear explanation of the types of electronic communication that will be used, description of security measures in place, information about alternatives to electronic communication, and a process for reporting concerns about privacy or security.

Best practices for maintaining confidentiality in an increasingly digital practice environment include conducting regular security assessments, staying informed about evolving security standards, implementing a *"minimum necessary"* approach to electronic communications, maintaining separate professional and personal electronic accounts, developing clear policies for handling potential security breaches, and providing regular training for all staff on security procedures. Effective storage and access procedures help counselors safeguard confidentiality while supporting compliant, efficient practice.

THIRD-PARTY RECORD REQUESTS

When a third party requests client records, Professional Clinical Counselors in California must navigate complex legal and ethical requirements to protect client confidentiality while responding appropriately.

Insurance companies frequently request client records to verify the necessity of treatment. When handling these requests, counselors could implement the following procedure:

1. **Verify the request**: Ensure the request includes specific information about what records are needed and the purpose.
2. **Obtain proper authorization**: California Civil Code Section 56.10 requires written authorization from the client before releasing medical information. The authorization should:
    - Be dated and signed by the client
    - Specify the information to be disclosed
    - Identify the recipient
    - State the purpose of the disclosure
    - Include an expiration date
3. **Apply the minimum necessary standard**: Release only the information specifically requested and needed for the stated purpose.
4. **Document the disclosure**: Keep a record of what information was released, when, to whom, and under what authorization.

A sample authorization form might include:
- Client name and identifying information
- Specific records authorized for release
- Insurance company name and contact information
- Purpose of disclosure (e.g., *"claims processing"*)
- Expiration date or event

- Statement of client's right to revoke authorization
- Client signature and date

Legal Representative Requests

Requests from attorneys or court orders require particular attention:

1. **Distinguish between types of legal requests**:
    - Subpoenas
    - Court orders
    - Discovery requests
    - Requests from client's attorney

2. **For subpoenas**: California Evidence Code Section 1015 establishes psychotherapist-patient privilege. When receiving a subpoena:
    - Notify the client immediately
    - Determine if the subpoena is accompanied by a valid authorization
    - Without authorization, consider filing an objection to protect privileged information
    - Consult with your own attorney if uncertain

3. **For court orders**: These typically override privilege concerns. However:
    - Review the order carefully for scope
    - Release only what is specifically ordered
    - Consider requesting clarification if the order seems overly broad

4. **Response template for legal requests**: *"In response to your request dated [DATE], I am providing the following records as authorized by [CLIENT NAME] or as ordered by the court. Please note that these records contain confidential information protected under California law and should be maintained accordingly. This*

disclosure consists of [SPECIFIC DOCUMENTS] covering the treatment period from [DATE] to [DATE]."

Healthcare Provider Requests

Coordination of care often necessitates sharing information with other providers:

1. **Verify the requesting provider**: Confirm the identity and credentials of the requesting healthcare professional.
2. **Obtain specific authorization**: California Civil Code Section 56.11 outlines requirements for medical information authorizations. The authorization should specify:
   - The other provider's name and contact information
   - Exactly what information can be shared
   - The purpose of sharing (e.g., coordination of care)
3. **Focus on relevant clinical information**: Share only what's necessary for continuity of care.
4. **Establish secure transmission methods**: Use encrypted email, secure fax, or other HIPAA-compliant methods.
5. **Document the exchange**: Record what was shared, when, with whom, and why.

Government Agency Requests

Government agencies, including the Board of Behavioral Sciences (BBS), may request records for various purposes:

1. **Identify the specific agency and purpose**: Different agencies have different authority to access records.
2. **Review legal requirements**: For BBS investigations, California Code of Regulations (CCR), Title 16, Section 1803, along with

BPC § 4990.20 grants authority to examine records related to alleged violations.
3. **Determine if client authorization is required**: Some government requests (like those related to abuse investigations) might not require client authorization under California Penal Code Section 11167.
4. **Maintain documentation**: Keep detailed records of all government requests and your responses.
5. **Response template**: *"This response addresses your request dated [DATE] regarding [CLIENT/MATTER]. As a licensed professional bound by confidentiality laws, I am providing the enclosed information [WITH CLIENT AUTHORIZATION/AS REQUIRED BY LAW]. Please note the confidential nature of these records and maintain them accordingly."*

CHAPTER EIGHT

HIPAA COMPLIANCE

UNDERSTANDING HIPAA'S CORE COMPONENTS

The Health Insurance Portability and Accountability Act (HIPAA) establishes a comprehensive framework for protecting client health information in clinical counseling practice. For Professional Clinical Counselors in California, understanding HIPAA's structure is essential for maintaining legal compliance while providing effective care. HIPAA consists of three fundamental components: the Privacy Rule, the Security Rule, and the Enforcement Rule, each addressing different aspects of protected health information (PHI) management.

The Privacy Rule establishes the foundation for protecting individually identifiable health information. Under this rule, counselors may only use or disclose PHI with client authorization or for specific permitted purposes outlined in the law. For example, when an LPCC receives a request from a client's insurance company for treatment information, the Privacy Rule permits disclosure for payment purposes, but limits it to the minimum necessary information. California's Confidentiality of Medical Information Act (CMIA) in Civil Code §56 et seq. provides even stronger protections than HIPAA in many cases, requiring counselors to obtain written authorization before sharing information in situations where HIPAA might permit disclosure without authorization.

In practice, the Privacy Rule requires counselors to provide clients with a Notice of Privacy Practices (NPP) at the first session. This document explains how the counselor might use and disclose their information and outlines client rights regarding their PHI. California Business and Professions Code §4999.74 reinforces this requirement by mandating that PCCs inform clients about the limits of confidentiality (counseling process disclosure). The NPP must be written in plain language, acknowledging both HIPAA and California-specific requirements.

The Security Rule specifically addresses electronic protected health information (ePHI), requiring appropriate administrative, physical, and technical safeguards. For counselors using electronic health records (EHRs), this means implementing access controls such as unique user identification, emergency access procedures, and automatic logoff features. Physical safeguards include workstation security and device and media controls, while technical safeguards encompass encryption, audit controls, and integrity mechanisms.

Consider a counseling practice that uses an EHR system. The Security Rule requires the practice to conduct a risk analysis identifying potential vulnerabilities in their electronic systems. Based on this analysis, the practice might implement measures such as encrypted devices, secure backup systems, and role-based access controls limiting which staff members can view specific client information. California Civil Code §1798.81.5 adds another layer of protection by requiring businesses that maintain personal information to implement *"reasonable security procedures and practices"* to protect that information.

The Enforcement Rule provides mechanisms for investigating violations and imposing penalties for HIPAA non-compliance. Penalties vary based on the level of negligence and can range from $100 to $50,000 per violation, with a maximum annual penalty of $1.5 million for identical violations. Beyond federal penalties, California counselors face additional consequences under state law. The California Board of Behavioral Sciences (BBS) can take disciplinary action against PCCs for confidentiality breaches under Business and Professions Code §4999.90.

Electronic communication presents unique challenges for maintaining HIPAA compliance in counseling practice. Email, text messaging, and video sessions have become increasingly common, especially following the COVID-19 pandemic, but each requires specific security measures to protect client confidentiality.

For email communication, HIPAA requires encryption both in transit and at rest. Regular email services like Gmail or Yahoo Mail typically don't provide the necessary level of security for PHI. Instead, counselors could use HIPAA-compliant email services that offer end-to-end encryption, access controls, and audit capabilities. When sending emails containing PHI, counselors might implement additional safeguards such as password-protected attachments and secure patient portals for communication.

Text messaging presents even greater challenges due to its inherently less secure nature. Standard SMS texts are not encrypted and might be stored on multiple servers during transmission. For counselors who use text messaging with clients, HIPAA-compliant secure messaging platforms that encrypt messages and require authentication for access represent a safer alternative. These platforms often include features like message expiration and remote deletion capabilities if a device is lost or stolen.

Video sessions, which became essential during the pandemic, require platforms specifically designed for healthcare. While temporary enforcement discretion was granted during the public health emergency, California counselors should now use HIPAA-compliant telehealth platforms that offer encryption, secure connections, and business associate agreements (BAAs). The California Telehealth Advancement Act (Business and Professions Code §2290.5) requires that telehealth providers inform patients about the potential risks of using electronic communication.

Client communication about electronic privacy risks forms an essential component of HIPAA compliance. Before engaging in any electronic communication, counselors must obtain informed consent from clients, clearly explaining the potential risks and limitations. This consent should be documented in writing and maintained in the client's record. California Business and Professions Code §4999.76 emphasizes the importance of informed consent in counseling relationships, which extends to electronic communication methods.

A sample electronic communication policy might include language such as:

"While I take reasonable steps to protect your confidentiality in electronic communications, please be aware that no electronic communication method is completely secure. Email and text messages could potentially be accessed by unauthorized people, compromising your privacy. By consenting to these forms of communication, you acknowledge and accept these risks. I recommend limiting electronic communications to non-clinical matters such as scheduling. For sensitive clinical information, please use our secure patient portal or discuss during sessions."

The policy should also address response times, emergency protocols, and storage practices for electronic communications. Clients should understand that while counselors strive to respond promptly, electronic communications might not be monitored continuously, and emergency situations require immediate contact with emergency services rather than electronic messages to the counselor.

Best practices for maintaining confidentiality in digital practice environments include implementing a layered security approach. This starts with strong authentication measures such as complex passwords and multi-factor authentication for all systems containing PHI. Regular security assessments help identify and address vulnerabilities before they lead to breaches. Staff training represents another crucial element, ensuring that everyone in the practice understands HIPAA requirements and follows established protocols.

Device management policies could address the use of personal devices for work purposes, requiring encryption, remote wiping capabilities, and automatic screen locks. When selecting technology vendors, counselors should verify HIPAA compliance and obtain BAAs from all business associates who might access PHI. These agreements legally bind the vendor to protect PHI according to HIPAA standards.

Documentation plays a key role in demonstrating HIPAA compliance. California counselors should maintain records of their security measures, risk assessments, staff training, and client consent forms. In the event of an audit or breach investigation, this documentation provides evidence of good-faith efforts to comply with regulations.

For breach notification, HIPAA requires covered entities to notify affected individuals, the Department of Health and Human Services, and in some cases, the media when unsecured PHI is breached. California's data breach notification law (Civil Code §1798.82) adds state-specific requirements, including notifying the California Attorney General for breaches affecting more than 500 California residents.

The integration of HIPAA's core components, Privacy, Security, and Enforcement, creates a comprehensive framework for protecting client information in mental health practice. Keeping in mind how these rules apply specifically to counseling operations and implementing appropriate safeguards for electronic communications, California PCCs can maintain compliance while providing effective care in an increasingly digital environment. This balanced approach respects both the letter of the law and the spirit of the counselor-client relationship, ensuring that technological advances enhance rather than compromise client confidentiality.

PROTECTED HEALTH INFORMATION GUIDELINES

Protected Health Information (PHI) encompasses any individually identifiable health information that is created, received, maintained, or transmitted by healthcare providers, including Professional Clinical Counselors in California. Under HIPAA regulations, there are 18 specific identifiers that transform health information into PHI when linked to a client's health status, treatment, or payment information.

The 18 identifiers that constitute PHI include:

1. Names (both full and partial)
2. Geographic identifiers smaller than a state (street addresses, city, county, zip code)
3. Dates directly related to the client (birth date, admission date, discharge date, date of death)
4. Telephone numbers
5. Fax numbers
6. Email addresses
7. Social Security numbers
8. Medical record numbers
9. Health plan beneficiary numbers
10. Account numbers
11. Certificate/license numbers
12. Vehicle identifiers and serial numbers, including license plate numbers
13. Device identifiers and serial numbers
14. Web Universal Resource Locators (URLs)
15. Internet Protocol (IP) address numbers
16. Biometric identifiers, including finger and voice prints
17. Full face photographic images and any comparable images
18. Any other unique identifying number, characteristic, or code

In clinical counseling practice, these identifiers appear throughout documentation and communications. For example, intake forms typically contain multiple identifiers including the client's name, address, phone number, email, date of birth, and potentially insurance information. Progress notes might reference a client's name, dates of service, and unique identifiers like medical record numbers. Even appointment scheduling systems contain PHI when they link a client's name or contact information with the fact that they're receiving mental health services.

Consider a scenario where an LPCC documents a therapy session in an electronic health record (EHR). The note might begin with *"Jane Doe (DOB: 01/15/1985) attended her weekly therapy session on 06/10/2024 to address anxiety symptoms."* This single sentence contains multiple PHI identifiers: the client's name, date of birth, and the date of service, all connected to information about her mental health condition.

In another common scenario, a counselor might receive an email from a client that states, *"Hi Dr. Smith, I've been feeling more depressed since our last session and wanted to discuss increasing my medication at our appointment tomorrow."* This email contains the client's name (in the email address and possibly signature), references to mental health status, and treatment information, all constituting PHI under HIPAA.

Verbal exchanges also frequently contain PHI. When an APCC consults with a supervisor about a challenging case, mentioning the client's name or specific identifying details transforms the clinical information into PHI. Similarly, when discussing appointment scheduling with a client over the phone, the conversation links the client's identity with the fact that they're receiving mental health services, creating PHI that requires protection.

To properly identify and protect PHI in physical formats, California counselors could implement several practical measures. Paper records containing PHI should be stored in locked cabinets within secured areas with restricted access. When not in active use, files should be returned to secure storage rather than left on desks or in unsecured areas. The California Confidentiality of Medical Information Act (CMIA), Civil Code §56 et seq., reinforces these protections by establishing strict requirements for maintaining the confidentiality of medical information, including mental health records.

For transporting physical PHI, counselors might use opaque, sealed envelopes or locked briefcases, and maintain a chain of custody documentation. When disposing of physical PHI, physical records should be shredded, pulped, or otherwise destroyed in a manner that renders the information unreadable and reconstruction impossible.

In digital formats, PHI protection becomes more complex. Electronic PHI should be stored on encrypted devices with strong access controls. California Civil Code §1798.81.5 requires businesses that own or license personal information about California residents to *"implement and maintain reasonable security procedures and practices"* to protect that information. For counselors, this means implementing measures such as:

- Password protection with complex passwords that are regularly updated
- Encryption of devices containing PHI
- Automatic logoff features on computers and devices
- Secure backup systems with encryption
- Regular software updates and security patches
- Audit trails that track who accesses electronic PHI and when

ELECTRONIC SECURITY MEASURES

Electronic security for mental health records requires robust safeguards that go beyond basic protection measures. California law, particularly the Confidentiality of Medical Information Act (CMIA) and HIPAA regulations, establishes specific requirements for Professional Clinical Counselors regarding the protection of electronic health information. These requirements address not only the storage of records but also their transmission and access.

Encryption serves as the foundation of electronic security for counseling records. California Business and Professions Code §4999.75 requires counselors to maintain client records in a manner that preserves confidentiality, which in electronic formats means implementing encryption that meets current standards. For data at rest (stored information), counselors could implement AES-256 bit encryption, the current industry standard recognized by the National Institute of Standards and Technology (NIST). This encryption strength makes unauthorized access mathematically impractical even with advanced computing resources.

For data in transit (information being sent electronically), Transport Layer Security (TLS) protocols provide encryption that protects information as it moves between systems. When selecting electronic health record (EHR) systems or communication platforms, counselors might verify that these use TLS 1.2 or higher, as older protocols contain known vulnerabilities. This verification helps ensure compliance with HIPAA's Security Rule, which requires appropriate technical safeguards for electronic protected health information (ePHI).

Access controls represent another critical security component. These controls determine who can view, modify, or transmit client information. A multi-layered approach to access control includes:

1. User authentication requiring unique identifiers for each person accessing the system
2. Role-based access limiting information availability based on job function
3. Automatic logoff features that terminate sessions after periods of inactivity
4. Emergency access procedures for situations requiring immediate information access

The California Code of Regulations Title 22 §77921 emphasizes the importance of limiting access to confidential patient information to authorized individuals with a legitimate need. In practice, this means counselors might assign specific access permissions to different staff members based on their roles. For example, administrative staff might access scheduling and billing information but not clinical notes, while clinical supervisors might have broader access rights.

Audit trails provide accountability by recording who accesses information and when. These electronic logs document every interaction with protected health information, creating a verifiable record of system activity. California Civil Code §56.101 requires health care providers to preserve the integrity of electronic medical information against unauthorized access, tampering, or loss. Audit trails support this requirement by enabling the detection of unauthorized access attempts or unusual patterns that might indicate security breaches.

A comprehensive audit trail might include:

- User identification
- Date and time of access
- Actions performed (viewing, editing, printing)
- Specific records accessed
- Location or device used for access

Awareness of security breaches highlight the importance of these measures. In 2021, Scripps Health experienced a ransomware attack that compromised the personal and health information of over 147,000 patients. This incident was a wake up call for others to look at their own systems to prevent such an incident through regular security updates, stronger access controls, and network monitoring to detect unusual activity.

In another case, Lifespan Health faced HIPAA penalties after a stolen laptop containing unencrypted client information led to a data breach. The practice had failed to implement device encryption and remote wiping capabilities. This breach illustrates the importance of device-level security measures, particularly for portable devices that might leave secure office environments.

Password management forms a fundamental aspect of electronic security. Weak passwords represent one of the most common vulnerabilities in healthcare systems. Counselors might implement password policies that require:

- Minimum length (at least 12 characters)
- Complexity (combination of uppercase, lowercase, numbers, and special characters)
- Regular changes (every 60-90 days)
- Prohibition of password reuse
- Multi-factor authentication when possible

Data backup procedures ensure continuity of care and protect against data loss from system failures, natural disasters, or cyberattacks. The HIPAA Security Rule requires covered entities to create retrievable exact copies of electronic protected health information. California counselors might implement a 3-2-1 backup strategy: three copies of data, on two different media types, with one copy stored off-site or in the cloud.

Cloud storage presents both opportunities and challenges for counseling practices. While it offers convenient off-site backup, not all cloud services meet HIPAA requirements. Counselors could select HIPAA-compliant cloud providers that offer:

- End-to-end encryption
- Business Associate Agreements (BAAs)
- Server locations within the United States
- Transparent security practices
- Regular security audits

Device security extends beyond office computers to include all devices that might access or store client information. Mobile devices, laptops, and tablets require particular attention due to their portability and higher risk of loss or theft. California counselors might implement mobile device management (MDM) solutions that enable:

- Remote wiping of lost or stolen devices
- Encryption of all stored data
- Automatic screen locks after brief periods of inactivity
- Application controls limiting which programs can access sensitive information

- Location tracking for lost devices

Electronic communication presents unique confidentiality challenges in counseling practice. Email, text messaging, and video sessions have become increasingly common methods of client interaction, especially following the COVID-19 pandemic. However, each requires specific security measures to protect client confidentiality.

For email communication, regular email services typically don't provide the level of security required for PHI. Instead, counselors could use HIPAA-compliant email services that offer end-to-end encryption, access controls, and audit capabilities. These services encrypt messages both in transit and at rest, meaning the information is protected while being sent and while stored on servers. California counselors might also implement additional safeguards such as password-protected attachments and secure patient portals for communication.

Text messaging presents even greater challenges due to its inherently less secure nature. Standard SMS texts are not encrypted and might be stored on multiple servers during transmission. For counselors who use text messaging with clients, HIPAA-compliant secure messaging platforms represent a safer alternative. These platforms encrypt messages and require authentication for access, often including features like message expiration and remote deletion capabilities if a device is lost or stolen.

Video sessions require platforms specifically designed for healthcare use. While temporary enforcement discretion was granted during the public health emergency, California counselors should now use HIPAA-compliant telehealth platforms that offer encryption, secure connections, and business associate agreements (BAAs). The California Telehealth Advancement Act (Business and Professions Code §2290.5) defines telehealth as *"the mode of delivering health care services and public health via information and communication technologies to facilitate the diagnosis, consultation, treatment, education, care management, and self-management of a patient's health care."*

Client communication about electronic privacy risks forms an essential component of HIPAA compliance. Before engaging in any electronic communication, counselors might obtain informed consent from clients, clearly explaining the potential risks and limitations. This consent could be documented in writing and maintained in the client's record. California Business and Professions Code §4999.76 emphasizes the importance of informed consent in counseling relationships, which extends to electronic communication methods.

A sample electronic communication policy might include language such as:

"While I take reasonable steps to protect your confidentiality in electronic communications, please be aware that no electronic communication method is completely secure. Email and text messages could potentially be accessed by unauthorized people, compromising your privacy. By consenting to these forms of communication, you acknowledge and accept these risks. I recommend limiting electronic communications to non-clinical matters such as scheduling. For sensitive clinical information, please use our secure patient portal or discuss during sessions."

Essential security measures checklist for California counselors:

1. Implement encryption for all electronic protected health information (both at rest and in transit)
2. Establish role-based access controls with unique user identification
3. Enable automatic logoff features on all devices accessing PHI
4. Maintain comprehensive audit trails of system access and activity
5. Create and test regular data backup procedures
6. Develop and enforce strong password policies
7. Implement device-level security for all equipment accessing PHI
8. Use only HIPAA-compliant platforms for electronic communication
9. Obtain and document informed consent for electronic communication

10. Conduct regular security risk assessments
11. Develop and maintain a breach notification protocol
12. Provide regular security awareness training for all staff
13. Establish business associate agreements with all vendors accessing PHI
14. Document all security measures and policies
15. Stay informed about evolving security threats and standards

Security protocols help protect client privacy while enabling ethical use of electronic tools and telehealth services. This balanced approach allows for the integration of technology into counseling practice while maintaining compliance with state and federal regulations.

CLIENT RIGHTS AND ACCESS

Under HIPAA and California law, clients possess specific rights regarding their health information that Professional Clinical Counselors must honor. The Health Insurance Portability and Accountability Act (HIPAA) establishes a foundation of patient rights that California law often expands upon through statutes like the Confidentiality of Medical Information Act (CMIA) and the Patient Access to Health Records Act (PAHRA).

Clients have the right to access their health records, as established in 45 CFR §164.524 of HIPAA and reinforced by California Health and Safety Code §123110. When a client requests access to their records, counselors might follow a structured process that begins with verifying the client's identity through photo identification or other secure methods. California law specifies that healthcare providers must make records available during business hours within five working days after receiving a written request (Health and Safety Code §123110(a)). Counselors could provide this access through inspection of records at the office or by providing copies.

For copy requests, California law permits charging reasonable fees not exceeding $0.25 per page for paper records or $0.50 for records from microfilm (Health and Safety Code §123110(b)). Electronic records might be provided at a cost that reflects the actual labor involved in preparing the electronic copy. The law requires that records be provided within 15 days of the request.

Clients also have the right to request amendments to their health information under HIPAA (45 CFR §164.526) when they believe information is inaccurate or incomplete. The process for handling amendment requests might include:

1. Receiving the written amendment request from the client
2. Acknowledging receipt within 10 days as required by California law
3. Reviewing the request and the original record
4. Making a determination within 60 days (with a possible 30-day extension if needed)
5. Notifying the client of the decision in writing

If the counselor accepts the amendment, they would update the record and inform the client and any relevant parties who received the original information. If denying the request, the counselor might provide a written explanation of the reasons, which could include:

- The record is accurate and complete
- The record was not created by this provider
- The record is not available for inspection under federal law
- The requested amendment pertains to information the client has no right to access

Even when denying an amendment, counselors must inform clients of their right to submit a statement of disagreement, which would be included in future disclosures of the record. This process aligns with both HIPAA requirements and California's emphasis on patient rights.

Another key right is the accounting of disclosures, outlined in HIPAA regulation 45 CFR §164.528. Clients can request information about how their health information has been shared outside the practice for purposes other than treatment, payment, or healthcare operations. When processing these requests, counselors might:

1. Verify the client's identity
2. Determine the time period requested (limited to six years prior to the request)
3. Compile a list of applicable disclosures including:

- Date of disclosure
- Name and address of the recipient
- Brief description of information disclosed
- Brief statement of purpose

1. Provide the accounting within 60 days (with a possible 30-day extension if needed)
2. Document the request and response

Certain disclosures are exempt from this accounting requirement, including those made for treatment, payment, or healthcare operations, disclosures authorized by the client, and certain disclosures to law enforcement or national security agencies.

For example, if a client named Maria requests an accounting of disclosures, a counselor might respond with a letter stating:

"Dear Maria,

In response to your request dated [date], I am providing an accounting of disclosures of your protected health information made between [start date] and [end date]. During this period, the following disclosures were made:

1. Date: 03/15/2024

Recipient: County Mental Health Services

Information: Assessment summary

Purpose: Coordination of care as authorized by you on 03/10/2024

2. Date: 04/22/2024

Recipient: Superior Court of California, County of [County]

Information: Treatment summary

Purpose: Response to court order dated 04/15/2024

No other disclosures requiring accounting were made during this period. If you have questions about this information, please contact our office.

Sincerely,

[Counselor name]"

Clients also have the right to request restrictions on how their information is used or disclosed (45 CFR §164.522). While counselors are not always required to agree to these restrictions, they must have a process for considering such requests. If a restriction is agreed upon, it must be documented and honored.

Additionally, clients have the right to request confidential communications through alternative means or at alternative locations. For example, a client might request that appointment reminders be sent to a specific email address rather than by phone. California Business and Professions Code §4999.75 requires LPCCs to maintain client confidentiality, which includes respecting these communication preferences when reasonable.

California Business and Professions Code §4999.75 requires counselors to ensure the confidentiality of electronic client information. Counselors may also implement the following specific technical safeguards to further protect client information in electronic practice environments::

- Firewalls and antivirus software
- Automatic screen locks after periods of inactivity
- Secure Wi-Fi networks with strong encryption
- Regular security assessments
- Backup systems for data recovery

In the event of a security breach involving client information, California Civil Code §1798.82 requires notification to affected individuals. Counselors could develop a breach response plan that includes:

- Immediate steps to contain the breach
- Assessment of what information was compromised
- Notification to affected clients without unreasonable delay
- Documentation of the incident and response
- Evaluation of security measures to prevent future breaches

Understanding and applying these client rights protocols allows counselors to maintain both legal compliance and ethical transparency in digital practice. This balanced approach respects client autonomy while protecting confidentiality in an increasingly digital practice environment.

SPECIAL CIRCUMSTANCES AND EXCEPTIONS

HIPAA regulations include specific provisions for exceptional circumstances where the standard privacy protections may be modified. Professional Clinical Counselors in California need to understand these exceptions to navigate situations involving emergencies, law enforcement, and public health concerns while maintaining appropriate confidentiality.

Emergency situations represent one of the most common exceptions to standard HIPAA requirements. Under 45 CFR §164.510(b), healthcare providers may share protected health information (PHI) with family members, friends, or others involved in a patient's care if the patient is incapacitated or in an emergency situation. For example, if a client experiences a severe mental health crisis during a session and becomes unable to make healthcare decisions, a counselor could share relevant information with emergency responders or family members to facilitate immediate treatment.

The California Confidentiality of Medical Information Act (CMIA) aligns with HIPAA in this regard, allowing disclosure without authorization when necessary to prevent or lessen a serious and imminent threat to the health or safety of a person or the public. This exception is particularly relevant for counselors dealing with clients in crisis.

When applying this exception, counselors could consider the following factors:

1. Is there an immediate threat to the client's health or safety?
2. Is the client capable of providing consent for disclosure?
3. Is the disclosure limited to information necessary for emergency treatment?
4. Is the disclosure being made to individuals who can help address the emergency?

For example, if a client loses consciousness during a session and requires immediate medical attention, a counselor might share information about the client's current medications or recent psychological symptoms with paramedics. However, this disclosure should be limited to information relevant to the emergency situation.

Law enforcement requests represent another important exception category. Under 45 CFR §164.512(f), HIPAA permits disclosure of PHI to law enforcement in specific circumstances, including:

1. In response to a court order, warrant, subpoena, or summons
2. To identify or locate a suspect, fugitive, material witness, or missing person
3. In response to a request about a crime victim
4. To alert law enforcement about a death that might have resulted from criminal conduct
5. When the counselor believes the PHI constitutes evidence of criminal conduct on the premises
6. In a medical emergency, to alert law enforcement about the commission of a crime

California law provides additional guidance through the California Penal Code §11160, which requires healthcare practitioners to report certain injuries and conditions to law enforcement, including injuries resulting from assaultive or abusive conduct.

When responding to law enforcement requests, counselors might follow this decision-making framework:

1. Verify the identity of the requesting law enforcement official
2. Determine which specific exception applies to the request
3. Limit disclosure to the minimum necessary information
4. Document the request and the information disclosed
5. Inform the client when possible and appropriate

For instance, if a counselor receives a court order requiring disclosure of a client's records in a criminal investigation, they could review the order with legal counsel, provide only the specific records requested, document the disclosure, and inform the client about the disclosure unless doing so would interfere with the investigation or place someone at risk.

Public health reporting represents a third category of exceptions. Under 45 CFR §164.512(b), HIPAA permits disclosure of PHI to public health authorities authorized by law to collect information for preventing or controlling disease, injury, or disability. While mental health professionals may not frequently encounter traditional public health reporting situations like infectious disease outbreaks, they might still face scenarios requiring disclosure for public health purposes.

In California, the Health and Safety Code §120130 authorizes the State Department of Public Health to take measures necessary to prevent the spread of communicable diseases. While counselors are not typically primary reporters for communicable diseases, they might need to report certain conditions if they become aware of them in the course of their practice.

For public health reporting, counselors could consider:

1. Is the disclosure required by law?
2. Is the disclosure being made to an authorized public health authority?
3. Is the disclosure limited to the minimum necessary information?
4. Has the client been informed about mandatory reporting requirements?

Documentation requirements for these special circumstances are substantial. Under both HIPAA and California law, counselors should maintain detailed records of any disclosures made under these exceptions. This documentation could include:

1. Date and time of the disclosure
2. Name and position of the person or entity receiving the information
3. Description of the information disclosed
4. Purpose of the disclosure
5. Legal basis for the disclosure (specific exception applied)
6. Efforts made to inform the client, if applicable
7. Measures taken to limit the disclosure to the minimum necessary

For risk management in these situations, counselors could:

1. Develop written policies and procedures for handling exception situations
2. Consult with colleagues or legal counsel when uncertain about applying an exception
3. Regularly review and update policies to reflect changes in law or regulation
4. Include information about these exceptions in informed consent documents
5. Document decision-making processes when applying exceptions

Electronic communication presents unique confidentiality challenges in counseling practice. California Business and Professions Code §4999.75 requires LPCCs to ensure the confidentiality of electronic client information. This extends to various forms of communication including email, text messaging, and video sessions.

For email communication, security requirements might include:

1. End-to-end encryption that meets current standards (minimum of 128-bit encryption)
2. Secure transmission protocols (TLS 1.2 or higher)
3. Authentication measures to verify sender and recipient identities
4. Secure storage of message content
5. Automatic logoff features for webmail access
6. Confidentiality disclaimers on all messages

Text messaging presents even greater security concerns due to the typically limited encryption of standard SMS. If used in practice, counselors might:

1. Utilize HIPAA-compliant secure messaging applications rather than standard SMS
2. Implement applications with message expiration features
3. Ensure messages are encrypted both in transit and at rest
4. Use platforms that allow for remote wiping of messages if a device is lost
5. Limit text content to non-clinical information like appointment reminders

For video sessions, California Business and Professions Code §2290.5 defines telehealth as a mode of delivering healthcare services via information and communication technologies. Security measures for video platforms might include:

1. End-to-end encryption of all session content
2. Password protection for session access
3. Waiting room features to control participant admission
4. No recording of sessions without explicit consent
5. Secure storage of any session notes or documentation
6. Verification of client identity at the beginning of each session

BUSINESS ASSOCIATE AGREEMENTS

Business Associate Agreements (BAAs) form a key aspect of HIPAA compliance for Professional Clinical Counselors in California. These legally binding contracts establish the responsibilities of third-party service providers who handle protected health information (PHI) on behalf of counselors. Under the HIPAA Privacy Rule, specifically 45 CFR §164.502(e), counselors are required to obtain written assurances from their business associates that they will appropriately safeguard any PHI they receive or create.

California law reinforces these federal requirements through the Confidentiality of Medical Information Act (CMIA), California Civil Code §56 et seq., which provides additional protections for medical information and applies to all providers of health care, including mental health professionals. The CMIA works alongside HIPAA to create a comprehensive framework for protecting client information in California.

A business associate is defined as a person or entity that performs certain functions or activities involving the use or disclosure of PHI on behalf of a covered entity. For counseling practices, common business associates might include:

1. Electronic Health Record (EHR) system providers
2. Billing and collection services
3. Practice management software companies
4. Email or messaging platform providers used for client communication
5. Cloud storage services where client records are kept
6. Answering services that receive client information
7. IT consultants who may have access to systems containing PHI
8. Attorneys who review client records for legal purposes
9. Accountants who have access to billing records
10. Telehealth platform providers

Not all service providers require BAAs. The determining factor is whether the vendor creates, receives, maintains, or transmits PHI on behalf of the counselor. For example, a janitorial service typically would not need a BAA if they don't have access to PHI, while an electronic health records provider would definitely require one.

The California Board of Behavioral Sciences, which regulates PCCs under Business and Professions Code §4999.12, emphasizes the importance of maintaining confidentiality in all aspects of practice. While the Board doesn't specifically mandate BAAs, compliance with HIPAA and the CMIA effectively requires them for California counselors who use business associates.

A compliant BAA contains several essential elements as outlined in 45 CFR §164.504(e). These include:

1. Description of permitted and required PHI uses by the business associate
2. Prohibition on uses or disclosures of PHI other than as permitted by the agreement or required by law
3. Requirement that the business associate implement appropriate safeguards to prevent unauthorized use or disclosure
4. Requirement to report to the covered entity any use or disclosure not provided for by the agreement
5. Requirement to report security incidents and breaches of unsecured PHI
6. Agreement to make PHI available for access, amendment, and accounting of disclosures
7. Agreement to make its internal practices, books, and records relating to PHI available to the Secretary of HHS for compliance determination
8. Provision that, upon termination of the agreement, the business associate will return or destroy all PHI
9. Authorization for termination of the agreement if the covered entity determines the business associate has violated a material term

For example, a BAA with an EHR provider might include language such as:

"Business Associate may only use or disclose Protected Health Information as necessary to perform the services set forth in the Service Agreement, or as required by law, and shall not use or disclose Protected Health Information for any other purpose without Covered Entity's prior written consent."

When implementing BAAs in practice, counselors could follow these steps:

1. Identify all vendors who qualify as business associates
2. Request a BAA from each vendor, or provide your own template
3. Review the agreement carefully, possibly with legal counsel
4. Ensure all required elements are included
5. Sign and maintain copies of all agreements
6. Document the implementation of BAAs in your HIPAA compliance program

Many service providers, particularly those familiar with healthcare clients, offer their own BAA templates. However, counselors might want to review these carefully or have them examined by an attorney familiar with healthcare privacy law to ensure they meet all requirements.

For maintaining and updating BAAs, counselors could establish a system that includes:

1. A master list of all business associates with contract renewal dates
2. Annual review of existing BAAs to ensure they remain current with changing regulations
3. Procedures for terminating relationships with business associates who fail to comply with privacy requirements
4. Documentation of any reported breaches or security incidents
5. Processes for obtaining new BAAs when engaging new service providers

BREACH NOTIFICATION PROTOCOLS

A breach of Protected Health Information (PHI) under HIPAA occurs when there is an unauthorized acquisition, access, use, or disclosure of unsecured PHI that compromises the security or privacy of the information. For Professional Clinical Counselors in California, understanding breach notification protocols is essential for maintaining compliance with both federal HIPAA regulations and California state laws, particularly the California Confidentiality of Medical Information Act (CMIA) as outlined in California Civil Code §56-56.37.

Not all privacy incidents qualify as breaches. Under 45 CFR §164.402, a breach is presumed unless the covered entity or business associate demonstrates a low probability that PHI has been compromised based on a risk assessment. This assessment examines factors including the nature of the PHI involved, the unauthorized person who accessed the information, whether the PHI was actually acquired or viewed, and the extent to which risk has been mitigated.

California law provides additional protections through the CMIA, which applies to all providers of health care, including PCCs as defined in Business and Professions Code §4999.12. The CMIA requires notification when unencrypted computerized data containing personal information is acquired by an unauthorized person, as specified in California Civil Code §1798.82.

When a potential breach is discovered, counselors could follow a structured timeline of actions:

Within 24 hours of discovery:

- Document the incident details, including date, time, nature of the breach, and PHI involved
- Initiate a preliminary investigation to determine the scope of the breach
- Implement immediate measures to contain the breach and prevent further unauthorized access

- Notify the practice's privacy officer (if applicable)
- Begin the risk assessment process to determine if the incident constitutes a reportable breach

Within 72 hours:

- Complete the risk assessment using the four-factor analysis outlined in 45 CFR §164.402
- Consult with legal counsel if necessary to determine reporting obligations
- Document the risk assessment findings and decision-making process
- Begin preparing notification materials if the incident is determined to be a reportable breach

For breaches affecting fewer than 500 individuals:

- Provide notification to affected individuals within 60 calendar days of discovery
- Submit notification to the Department of Health and Human Services (HHS) within 60 days of the end of the calendar year in which the breach was discovered

For breaches affecting 500 or more individuals:

- Provide notification to affected individuals within 60 calendar days of discovery
- Notify HHS concurrently with individual notifications
- Notify prominent media outlets serving the state or jurisdiction if the breach affects more than 500 residents of a state or jurisdiction

California law imposes additional requirements through Civil Code §1798.82, which mandates notification *"in the most expedient time possible and without unreasonable delay."*

The content of breach notifications could include:

1. A description of the breach
2. The types of information involved

3. Steps individuals should take to protect themselves
4. What the practice is doing to investigate, mitigate, and prevent future breaches
5. Contact procedures for questions or additional information

Different types of breaches require tailored responses. For example:

Scenario 1: Lost or stolen device

An LPCC's laptop containing unencrypted session notes is stolen from their car. This represents a reportable breach under both HIPAA and California law. The counselor might:

- File a police report
- Determine which clients' information was on the device
- Notify all affected clients within the required timeframe
- Implement encryption on all devices going forward
- Review and enhance physical security protocols

Scenario 2: Misdirected email

A counselor accidentally sends a client's treatment summary to the wrong email address. The counselor might:

- Attempt to recall the email if possible
- Contact the recipient and request deletion of the information
- Conduct a risk assessment to determine if this constitutes a reportable breach
- Notify the client of the incident regardless of reporting requirements
- Implement an email verification protocol for future communications

Scenario 3: Unauthorized access by staff

A receptionist accesses client records without authorization out of curiosity. The counselor might:

- Document the unauthorized access
- Take appropriate disciplinary action
- Assess whether the incident constitutes a reportable breach
- Implement additional access controls and staff training
- Review audit logs to determine the extent of unauthorized access

Documentation of breach incidents could include:

1. Discovery date and time
2. Description of the breach
3. Types of PHI involved
4. Individuals affected
5. Risk assessment findings
6. Notification decisions and justifications
7. Mitigation actions taken
8. Preventive measures implemented

To minimize breach occurrence, counselors might implement preventive measures including:

- Regular risk assessments as required by the HIPAA Security Rule
- Encryption of all devices containing PHI
- Implementation of access controls based on the principle of least privilege
- Regular staff training on privacy and security practices
- Development and testing of an incident response plan
- Audit procedures to detect unauthorized access

CHAPTER NINE

PROFESSIONAL CONDUCT AND ETHICS

DEFINING UNPROFESSIONAL CONDUCT

Unprofessional conduct in clinical counseling encompasses a range of behaviors that violate ethical standards, legal requirements, and professional expectations. The California Board of Behavioral Sciences (BBS) defines unprofessional conduct as actions that breach the established standards of practice, potentially causing harm to clients or undermining public trust in the profession. These violations can range from minor lapses in judgment to serious ethical breaches that may result in license revocation.

At its core, unprofessional conduct involves any behavior that compromises client welfare, violates boundaries, demonstrates incompetence, or breaches confidentiality. For Licensed Professional Clinical Counselors (LPCCs), understanding these boundaries is essential not only for maintaining licensure but for providing ethical care that truly serves clients' best interests.

Sexual misconduct represents one of the most serious forms of unprofessional conduct. This includes any sexual contact, sexual suggestions, or romantic relationships with current clients. Even seemingly minor behaviors like flirtatious comments, unnecessary physical contact, or sharing personal sexual information cross professional boundaries. The power differential between counselor and client makes any sexual or romantic involvement inherently exploitative, regardless of who initiates it.

Consider the case of a counselor who began treating a client for relationship issues. Over time, sessions shifted to include personal disclosures from the counselor about their own marriage difficulties. The counselor eventually suggested meeting for coffee outside the office to *"continue their conversation in a more relaxed setting."* This gradual boundary erosion, moving from appropriate therapeutic conversation to personal disclosure to suggesting out-of-office contact, represents the typical pattern of boundary violations that often precede more serious misconduct.

Dual relationships constitute another common area of unprofessional conduct. These occur when counselors maintain multiple roles with clients beyond the therapeutic relationship. Examples include hiring clients for services, entering business partnerships, or developing close friendships. While some dual relationships may be unavoidable in small communities, counselors must carefully evaluate potential harm and document their decision-making process.

A counselor in a rural community faced disciplinary action after referring multiple clients to a financial planning business she co-owned without disclosing her financial interest. The counselor rationalized this behavior by believing she was helping clients access needed services while maintaining separate professional roles. However, this arrangement created conflicts of interest that compromised therapeutic relationships and violated disclosure requirements.

Financial impropriety represents another category of unprofessional conduct. This includes insurance fraud, improper billing practices, fee splitting, and exploitation of clients for financial gain. Examples include billing for services not provided, misrepresenting services to insurance companies, or pressuring clients to continue unnecessary treatment for financial benefit.

In one case, a counselor was disciplined for routinely billing insurance for 50-minute sessions while providing only 30-minute appointments. The counselor also encouraged clients to attend more frequent sessions than clinically indicated, justifying this by telling clients they needed *"intensive treatment"* when documentation showed minimal clinical necessity.

Breach of confidentiality remains one of the most common forms of unprofessional conduct. This includes unauthorized disclosure of client information, failure to secure records properly, discussing clients in public settings, or posting about clients on social media (even without identifying information). The duty to maintain confidentiality extends beyond active treatment and continues after the therapeutic relationship ends.

A counselor lost their license after discussing a high-profile client's treatment in a social setting, believing that not mentioning the client's name protected confidentiality. However, the details provided were sufficient for others to identify the client, resulting in significant harm to the client's reputation and a subsequent lawsuit against the counselor.

Practicing outside one's scope of competence constitutes unprofessional conduct that can cause significant harm. This includes providing services without adequate training, failing to refer when appropriate, or misrepresenting qualifications. Counselors must recognize their limitations and seek appropriate supervision, consultation, or additional training when working with unfamiliar populations or conditions.

One counselor faced disciplinary action after attempting to provide specialized trauma treatment without proper training. The counselor had attended a weekend workshop on the technique but lacked the supervised experience necessary for competent implementation. The improper application of the technique resulted in client decompensation and hospitalization.

Documentation failures represent a form of unprofessional conduct that may seem administrative but can have serious clinical and legal consequences. Inadequate documentation includes missing or incomplete records, failure to document risk assessments, backdating notes, or falsifying records. Proper documentation serves as both a clinical tool and legal protection.

A counselor received a formal reprimand after failing to document suicidal ideation discussed in session. When the client later attempted suicide, the lack of documentation made it impossible to demonstrate that the counselor had conducted an appropriate risk assessment or developed a safety plan, raising questions about the standard of care provided.

Impairment while providing services constitutes clear unprofessional conduct. This includes practicing while under the influence of substances, working while experiencing acute mental health symptoms that impair judgment, or continuing to practice despite physical conditions that affect clinical performance. Counselors have an ethical obligation to monitor their own fitness to practice and take appropriate steps when impairment occurs.

In one case, a counselor continued seeing clients while experiencing severe depression and sleep deprivation. The counselor fell asleep during sessions, forgot important client information, and made inappropriate self-disclosures. Colleagues noticed the impairment but hesitated to intervene, allowing the situation to continue until a client filed a formal complaint.

Unprofessional conduct often develops gradually through a process called *"boundary drift."* This occurs when small boundary crossings accumulate over time, eventually leading to more serious violations. Warning signs include making exceptions for specific clients, keeping secrets about interactions, looking forward to seeing certain clients more than others, thinking about clients outside of professional contexts, or feeling defensive about relationships with particular clients.

The path to unprofessional conduct frequently begins with good intentions. A counselor might extend session time, offer special fee arrangements, or share personal information in an attempt to be helpful or build rapport. Without regular self-reflection and supervision, these minor boundary crossings can evolve into more problematic behavior.

Prevention requires ongoing vigilance and self-assessment. Counselors should regularly evaluate their practice using the following checklist:

1. Boundary Maintenance

- Do I maintain consistent session times and lengths for all clients?
- Do I avoid personal disclosures that don't serve a clear therapeutic purpose?
- Do I refrain from physical contact beyond a professional handshake?
- Do I maintain clear financial boundaries and consistent fee practices?
- Do I avoid socializing with current or recent clients?

2. Competence Assessment

- Do I practice only within areas where I have adequate training and experience?
- Do I seek consultation when faced with unfamiliar clinical situations?
- Do I maintain current knowledge through continuing education?
- Do I recognize when clients need services beyond my expertise and refer appropriately?
- Do I regularly evaluate outcomes to ensure effectiveness?

3. Documentation Practices

- Do I maintain timely, accurate, and complete records for all client interactions?
- Do I document risk assessments, referrals, and consultations?
- Do I avoid altering records after the fact?
- Do I document the rationale for clinical decisions, especially when deviating from standard practice?

- Do I maintain secure storage systems for all client information?

4. **Confidentiality Safeguards**

- Do I discuss clients only in appropriate professional contexts?
- Do I obtain proper authorization before disclosing information?
- Do I avoid identifying information when seeking consultation?
- Do I maintain appropriate privacy in electronic communications?
- Do I properly secure all client records and information?

5. **Self-Care and Impairment Prevention**

- Do I monitor my own physical and mental health?
- Do I have a plan for client coverage during personal emergencies?
- Do I maintain appropriate work-life balance?
- Do I seek help when experiencing personal difficulties?
- Do I recognize signs of burnout or compassion fatigue?

6. **Red Flags in Client Relationships**

- Do I find myself making exceptions to policies for certain clients?
- Do I look forward to sessions with some clients more than others for personal reasons?
- Do I think about specific clients outside of professional contexts?
- Do I share details about my personal life with certain clients?
- Do I feel defensive or secretive about my relationship with any clients?

Unprofessional conduct rarely begins with an intention to violate ethical standards. Instead, it typically develops through a series of small decisions that gradually erode professional boundaries. By maintaining awareness of these potential pitfalls and regularly engaging in self-assessment, supervision, and consultation, counselors can maintain the high standards of practice that protect both clients and the integrity of the profession.

SEXUAL MISCONDUCT AND BOUNDARY VIOLATIONS

Sexual misconduct in the counseling profession represents one of the most serious ethical violations a practitioner can commit. The California Board of Behavioral Sciences (BBS) explicitly prohibits sexual contact between counselors and their clients under Business and Professions Code Section 4999.90, which defines unprofessional conduct to include *"engaging in sexual relations with a client, or a former client within two years following termination of therapy."* This prohibition exists because the therapeutic relationship inherently involves a power imbalance that makes truly consensual intimate relationships impossible, regardless of who initiates the contact.

Sexual misconduct encompasses a broad spectrum of behaviors beyond obvious physical contact. At its most explicit, it includes sexual intercourse, touching of intimate areas, kissing, or other overtly sexual physical contact with current clients. However, the definition extends to verbal behaviors such as sexual comments, flirtation, discussions of the counselor's personal sexual experiences, or inappropriate inquiries into a client's sexual history beyond what is clinically relevant. Even non-verbal behaviors like lingering gazes, suggestive facial expressions, or sharing sexually explicit materials can constitute misconduct.

Sexual misconduct fundamentally compromises this ability by replacing the therapeutic focus with the counselor's personal gratification. Consider the case of a counselor who began treating a 28-year-old female client for relationship difficulties. During the fourth session, the counselor commented on the client's appearance, saying, *"You look particularly beautiful today. I can't imagine why anyone would have relationship problems with someone as attractive as you."* In subsequent sessions, the counselor shared details about his own marriage problems, positioned his chair increasingly closer to the client, and eventually suggested they continue their conversations *"in a more comfortable setting"* outside the office. This progression from inappropriate compliments to personal disclosures to suggestions of meeting outside therapy represents the typical pattern of boundary erosion that often precedes more serious violations.

Boundary violations often begin subtly and progress along a continuum. The concept of the *"slippery slope"* applies here, minor boundary crossings can gradually lead to more serious violations if left unchecked. Early warning signs might include:

1. Session boundary violations: Extending sessions consistently for a particular client, scheduling appointments during off-hours, or meeting in unusual locations
2. Self-disclosure: Sharing excessive personal information not relevant to therapeutic goals
3. Special treatment: Waiving fees, giving gifts, or making exceptions to policies for specific clients
4. Role blending: Developing social relationships, business arrangements, or other dual relationships with clients
5. Contact outside sessions: Unnecessary phone calls, texts, emails, or social media interactions beyond what is clinically indicated

A particularly insidious aspect of boundary violations is that they often begin with seemingly benign intentions. A counselor might extend a session because they believe a client needs extra support, share personal experiences to normalize a client's struggles, or offer special fee arrangements to help a client in financial difficulty. Without regular self-reflection and supervision, these minor boundary crossings can evolve into more problematic behavior.

The power differential inherent in the therapeutic relationship makes clients particularly vulnerable to boundary violations. Clients often enter therapy during periods of emotional distress, seeking guidance and support. They typically view their counselor as an authority figure and may be eager to please them. This dynamic creates a situation where clients may be reluctant to question a counselor's behavior, even when it makes them uncomfortable.

The prohibition against sexual relationships extends beyond the active treatment period. Business and Professions Code Section 4999.90

prohibits sexual contact with former clients for at least two years following the termination of therapy. Even after this two-year period, sexual contact is only permissible if it can be demonstrated that there has been no exploitation of the former client. Given the lasting impact of the therapeutic relationship, many ethical experts argue that sexual relationships with former clients remain problematic regardless of the time elapsed.

Consider the following case example: A counselor terminated therapy with a client after six months of treatment for anxiety. Fourteen months later, they encountered each other at a community event and began dating. Despite the counselor's belief that enough time had passed to change the nature of their relationship, the BBS determined this constituted unprofessional conduct because the two-year prohibition period had not elapsed. Additionally, the board found evidence that the counselor had begun to view the client romantically during therapy, which influenced the decision to terminate treatment.

California law places specific requirements on counselors who learn that a client has had sexual contact with another therapist. Business and Professions Code Section 728 mandates that when a psychotherapist becomes aware through a patient that the patient had alleged sexual intercourse or sexual contact with a previous therapist during the course of treatment, the current therapist has specific legal obligations:

1. The therapist must provide the client with the brochure *"Professional Therapy Never Includes Sex"* published by the Department of Consumer Affairs

2. The therapist must discuss the contents of the brochure with the client

3. If the client indicates they would like to report the previous therapist, the current therapist must provide the client with information about how to file a complaint with the appropriate licensing board

Maintaining appropriate boundaries requires ongoing vigilance and self-assessment. Counselors should implement the following practices to prevent boundary violations:

1. Establish clear policies: Develop and communicate consistent policies regarding session length, fees, contact between sessions, and termination procedures.

2. Limit self-disclosure: Share personal information only when it directly serves the client's therapeutic goals, not to meet the counselor's emotional needs.

3. Maintain physical boundaries: Avoid unnecessary physical contact beyond a professional handshake or culturally appropriate greeting.

4. Recognize warning signs: Be alert to feelings of special connection with particular clients, looking forward to sessions for personal reasons, or thinking about clients outside of professional contexts.

5. Seek regular supervision: Engage in ongoing consultation with colleagues or formal supervisors, particularly when feeling drawn to cross boundaries with specific clients.

6. Document boundary decisions: When therapeutic reasons necessitate boundary crossings (such as attending a client's graduation in specific contexts), document the rationale, expected benefit to the client, and measures taken to minimize harm.

7. Maintain clear separation between personal and professional life: Avoid socializing in settings where clients might be present, establish clear policies about social media connections, and consider how personal actions might impact professional relationships.

When boundary issues arise, counselors should:

1. Recognize the potential problem immediately
2. Consult with colleagues or supervisors
3. Document concerns and consultations
4. Take corrective action, which may include discussing the issue with the client when appropriate, referring the client if necessary, or seeking additional supervision
5. Implement preventive measures to avoid similar situations in the future

The consequences of sexual misconduct and serious boundary violations extend beyond potential disciplinary action by the BBS. They include psychological harm to clients, damage to the counselor's career and reputation, erosion of public trust in the profession, and potential civil liability. Under Business and Professions Code Section 4999.90, the BBS has the authority to revoke or suspend licenses, place licensees on probation, or take other disciplinary action against counselors who engage in sexual misconduct.

MANAGING DUAL RELATIONSHIPS

Dual relationships in counseling occur when a Licensed Professional Clinical Counselor (LPCC) or Associate Professional Clinical Counselor (APCC) maintains both a professional and another type of relationship with a client. These relationships take various forms, including business connections, social interactions, familial ties, or romantic involvements. Under California Business and Professions Code Section 4999.90, engaging in inappropriate dual relationships may constitute unprofessional conduct, potentially resulting in disciplinary action by the Board of Behavioral Sciences (BBS).

When counselors engage in dual relationships that compromise their professional judgment or exploit clients, they violate this regulation. The law recognizes that dual relationships can create conflicts of interest that interfere with the counselor's ability to provide objective, client-centered care. Different types of dual relationships present varying levels of risk. Business relationships, such as hiring a client for services or entering into financial arrangements, create conflicts between the counselor's financial interests and therapeutic responsibilities. For example, an LPCC who hires a current client to redesign their website places both parties in a problematic position where the power dynamics of therapy complicate the business relationship.

Social relationships, including friendships or community connections, blur the boundaries necessary for effective therapy. Consider an APCC who regularly attends the same small church as a client. They may encounter each other at social events, share mutual friends, and have access to personal information outside the therapeutic context. This situation compromises confidentiality and may inhibit the client's willingness to disclose sensitive information in therapy.

Familial relationships present particularly complex challenges. The California Business and Professions Code does not explicitly prohibit treating family members, but Section 4999.90 addresses unprofessional conduct that could result from such arrangements. When an LPCC provides therapy to a relative, pre-existing emotional attachments and family dynamics inevitably influence the therapeutic process, potentially compromising clinical objectivity.

Dual relationships often arise unavoidably in specific contexts. In rural or small communities, counselors and clients frequently encounter each other outside the therapeutic setting. An LPCC practicing in a town of 2,000 people might shop at the same grocery store as clients, have children attending the same school, or participate in the same community events. These overlapping connections require careful management rather than complete avoidance.

Specialized practice areas also present unique challenges. An APCC specializing in treating first responders in a small county might find that many potential clients are colleagues within the same emergency response network. Similarly, counselors working with specific cultural or linguistic communities might share social spaces, religious institutions, or community organizations with clients.

The case of an LPCC practicing in a rural mountain community illustrates these complexities. The counselor, one of only two mental health providers in the area, encountered a situation where a potential client was also the owner of the only pharmacy in town. Recognizing the inevitable dual relationship that would develop through regular interactions at the pharmacy, the counselor needed to carefully evaluate whether effective therapy could be provided despite these overlapping roles.

Dual relationships can lead to serious clinical and therapeutic complications. When boundaries become blurred, clients may hesitate to share certain information, fearing it might affect the secondary relationship. For instance, a client who is also a counselor's landlord might withhold details about relationship problems, concerned that the counselor might view them differently in their landlord capacity.

The therapeutic alliance can also suffer when role confusion develops. A client who interacts with their counselor in multiple contexts may struggle to engage fully in the therapeutic process, uncertain about which *"version"* of the relationship takes precedence. This confusion undermines the clear structure and boundaries that facilitate effective therapy.

Consider the case of an APCC who joined a local business networking group and later discovered that a potential client was a long-standing member of the same group. After careful consideration and consultation, the APCC determined that the ongoing business relationship would compromise therapy and appropriately referred the individual to another provider. This decision aligned with Business and Professions Code Section 4999.90, which addresses unprofessional conduct that could result from conflicting relationships.

In another situation, an LPCC in a small town discovered that a client was the parent of their child's close friend. As the children's friendship developed, the families began to socialize regularly. The counselor recognized the emerging dual relationship and discussed the situation with the client, ultimately facilitating a referral to another provider to prevent boundary complications. This action demonstrated compliance with California Code of Regulations, Title 16, Section 1881, which requires licensees to perform their duties with appropriate care and competence.

When evaluating potential dual relationships, PCCs should consider several key factors. First, they must assess the risk of exploitation or harm to the client. The potential impact on clinical objectivity represents another crucial consideration. Counselors might ask themselves: *"Could this secondary relationship affect my ability to make sound clinical judgments?"* If personal feelings or interests from the non-therapeutic relationship might influence professional decisions, the dual relationship could compromise care quality.

The power differential inherent in the therapeutic relationship requires special attention. Even seemingly equal secondary relationships exist in the context of the counselor's professional authority and the client's vulnerability. This imbalance increases the risk that clients might feel unable to set appropriate boundaries or decline requests related to the secondary relationship.

When faced with potential dual relationships, counselors could implement a structured decision-making process. This might include:

1. Identifying the specific nature of the existing or potential dual relationship
2. Assessing the necessity of the therapeutic relationship (considering factors like the availability of alternative providers)
3. Evaluating the potential benefits and risks to the client
4. Consulting with colleagues or supervisors
5. Documenting the decision-making process and rationale

In some situations, particularly in small communities with limited mental health resources, dual relationships might be unavoidable. When this occurs, counselors might implement several strategies to maintain appropriate professional boundaries.

Clear communication about roles and boundaries forms the foundation for managing unavoidable dual relationships. At the outset of therapy, counselors should discuss the nature of the dual relationship, how they will handle encounters outside the therapeutic setting, and protocols for addressing concerns that arise. This conversation should be documented in the client's record to demonstrate compliance with professional standards.

Establishing explicit parameters for each relationship helps minimize confusion. For example, an LPCC who attends the same religious congregation as a client might agree to acknowledge each other with a simple greeting but avoid extended conversations in that setting. These parameters should be revisited periodically as the therapeutic relationship evolves.

Maintaining heightened awareness of potential conflicts represents an ongoing responsibility. Counselors should regularly reflect on how the dual relationship might be affecting therapy and be prepared to address emerging concerns. This self-monitoring aligns with the professional responsibility established in California Code of Regulations, Title 16, Section 1881.

Regular consultation with colleagues or supervisors provides valuable perspective when navigating dual relationships. When discussing specific situations (while maintaining client confidentiality), counselors can identify potential blind spots and develop appropriate strategies. This consultation should be documented to demonstrate due diligence in managing complex professional situations.

In some cases, the most appropriate action might be referring the client to another provider. When the risks of a dual relationship outweigh the benefits of continuing therapy, facilitating a thoughtful transition to another qualified professional protects both the client's interests and the counselor's professional standing.

MAINTAINING PROFESSIONAL BOUNDARIES

Professional boundaries serve as the invisible framework that defines the therapeutic relationship, creating a safe space for clients while protecting both the client and counselor. Establishing clear boundaries begins with the first client contact and continues throughout the therapeutic relationship. The California Board of Behavioral Sciences emphasizes boundary maintenance as a requirement of ethical practice, with the Business and Professions Code Section 4999.90 specifically identifying violations of professional boundaries as potential grounds for disciplinary action.

When meeting a client for the first time, setting the foundation for appropriate boundaries starts with clear communication about the therapeutic relationship. This includes explaining your role as a counselor, the purpose of counseling, and the parameters within which you'll work together. The initial paperwork and informed consent process provide an excellent opportunity to outline boundaries regarding session length, cancellation policies, between-session contact, and emergency procedures. This clear communication establishes expectations from the beginning, reducing the likelihood of misunderstandings later.

For example, your informed consent document might state: *"Sessions are scheduled for 50 minutes. If you need to cancel, please provide 24 hours' notice to avoid being charged for the missed appointment. Between sessions, I check messages once daily during business hours and will return your call within 24 hours. For emergencies requiring immediate attention, please contact the crisis line at [number] or go to your nearest emergency room."*

Physical boundaries in the therapeutic space require thoughtful consideration. The counseling office should be arranged to provide comfort while maintaining appropriate distance. Some counselors prefer a desk between themselves and clients, while others opt for chairs positioned at a comfortable angle. Whatever arrangement you choose, ensure it allows for eye contact and communication while preserving personal space.

Self-disclosure represents another boundary area requiring careful navigation. Limited self-disclosure might build rapport in some circumstances, but excessive sharing shifts the focus from the client to the counselor. When considering self-disclosure, ask yourself:

- Does this disclosure serve the client's therapeutic goals?
- Am I sharing to benefit the client or to meet my own needs?
- How might this disclosure affect the therapeutic relationship?
- Could this information be harmful or confusing to the client?

For example, briefly mentioning that you've experienced anxiety when working with an anxious client might normalize their experience. However, sharing details about your personal relationships or current struggles would likely cross appropriate boundaries.

Digital boundaries have become increasingly important as technology permeates professional relationships. California counselors should establish clear policies regarding:

- Social media connections (generally avoided with current clients)
- Email communication (including response timeframes and privacy limitations)
- Text messaging (typically limited to scheduling matters)
- Online searches (avoiding researching clients online)

Your informed consent might include language such as: *"To maintain professional boundaries, I do not accept friend or connection requests from clients on social media platforms. Email communication is not completely secure and should be limited to scheduling matters. I do not engage in therapy via email or text message."*

The Business and Professions Code Section 4999.90 could be interpreted to include digital boundary violations as unprofessional conduct, particularly when they compromise client confidentiality or create dual relationships. Common boundary challenges arise in various contexts, each requiring thoughtful response:

Gift-giving often presents boundary dilemmas. Small tokens of appreciation at termination might be appropriate, while expensive gifts or those with personal significance could create boundary confusion. When a client offers a gift, consider:

- The monetary and symbolic value of the gift

- The timing and context of the offering
- The client's cultural background and gift-giving norms
- The potential impact on the therapeutic relationship

You might respond to an inappropriate gift by saying: *"I appreciate your thoughtfulness, but accepting this gift would change our professional relationship in ways that might interfere with our work together. I value our therapeutic relationship as it is."*

Cultural differences significantly impact boundary expectations and interpretations. What constitutes appropriate distance, eye contact, or self-disclosure varies across cultures. For example, in some Latino cultures, personalismo (warm, personal interaction) might lead clients to expect more personal engagement than typical Western therapeutic boundaries suggest. Similarly, some Asian cultures might view direct eye contact as disrespectful rather than attentive.

When working with clients from diverse cultural backgrounds:

- Educate yourself about cultural norms and expectations
- Discuss boundary expectations explicitly, acknowledging potential cultural differences
- Remain flexible while maintaining core ethical principles
- Consult with culturally knowledgeable colleagues when uncertain

Special circumstances might require boundary adaptations. When working with children, appropriate boundaries might include sitting on the floor during play therapy while maintaining professional demeanor. With clients experiencing severe trauma, boundaries regarding session length or between-session contact might require flexibility while still maintaining the therapeutic frame.

Self-assessment represents a crucial component of boundary maintenance. Regular reflection on the following questions helps identify potential boundary concerns:

- Do I look forward to or dread sessions with particular clients?

- Do I find myself thinking about certain clients outside work hours?
- Have I shared information with a client that I haven't shared with others?
- Do I make exceptions to my policies for specific clients?
- Do I feel defensive about my relationship with any client?

Affirmative answers to these questions warrant further reflection and possibly consultation with a supervisor or colleague.

Ongoing monitoring strategies help maintain boundaries throughout the therapeutic relationship. These include:

- Regular supervision or consultation, particularly for complex cases
- Documentation of boundary-related decisions and rationales
- Periodic review of policies and procedures
- Attention to countertransference reactions that might signal boundary issues
- Self-care practices that maintain personal well-being and professional perspective

For example, if you notice feeling unusually invested in a client's outcomes or irritated by their behaviors, these countertransference reactions might signal potential boundary issues requiring attention. Documentation provides both protection and guidance in boundary management. When making boundary-related decisions, document:

INVESTIGATION AND ENFORCEMENT PROCEDURES

When a complaint is filed against a Licensed Professional Clinical Counselor (LPCC) or Associate Professional Clinical Counselor (APCC) in California, it triggers a structured investigation process governed by the California Business and Professions Code and overseen by the Board of Behavioral Sciences (BBS). Understanding this process is essential for counselors to protect their professional standing and respond appropriately if they face allegations of misconduct.

The investigation process typically begins when the BBS receives a complaint from a client, colleague, employer, or member of the public. Complaints may allege various violations, including unprofessional conduct, scope of practice violations, documentation failures, or boundary violations.

For example, a client might file a complaint alleging that their counselor breached confidentiality by discussing their case with unauthorized individuals. Alternatively, an employer might report a counselor for practicing while impaired by substance use, or a colleague might report concerns about sexual misconduct with clients.

Upon receiving a complaint, BBS staff conduct an initial review to determine if the allegations fall within the Board's jurisdiction and warrant investigation. This screening process helps filter out complaints that don't involve actual violations or that should be addressed by other agencies. If the complaint appears to involve potential violations of the LPCC Practice Act (Business and Professions Code Sections 4999.10-4999.129), it advances to formal investigation.

The formal investigation is typically conducted by the Board's enforcement unit or, in more complex cases, by investigators from the Department of Consumer Affairs' Division of Investigation. These investigators have significant authority under Business and Professions Code Section 4990.16, which states that the Board may *"employ personnel as it deems necessary"* to enforce the provisions of the chapter.

During this phase, investigators gather evidence through various means. They may:

1. Interview the complainant to clarify allegations and obtain additional information
2. Request and review client records (with appropriate releases or subpoenas)
3. Interview the accused counselor

4. Speak with witnesses, including other clients, colleagues, or supervisors
5. Collect documentary evidence such as emails, text messages, or billing records
6. Consult with subject matter experts to evaluate standard of care issues

The investigation process is confidential until formal accusations are filed. For counselors under investigation, the process can be lengthy and stressful. Investigations may take several months to over a year, depending on case complexity, investigator caseloads, and the availability of witnesses and evidence. Throughout this period, the counselor may continue practicing unless the Board determines that temporary suspension is necessary to protect public safety.

After completing the investigation, the enforcement analyst and legal counsel review the evidence to determine if violations occurred and what action is warranted. The possible outcomes include:

1. Closure without action if evidence doesn't support the allegations
2. Issuance of a citation and fine for minor violations
3. Filing of a formal accusation for more serious violations

Citations and fines represent an intermediate level of discipline for violations that don't warrant license restriction or revocation. Business and Professions Code Section 125.9 authorizes the Board to establish a system for issuing citations, which may include fines up to $5,000 per violation. Citations are public records but don't restrict the counselor's ability to practice.

For more serious violations, the Board may file a formal accusation, which is the first public document in the disciplinary process. The accusation details the alleged violations and the laws or regulations breached. Once an accusation is filed, the case enters the administrative hearing process governed by the Administrative Procedure Act.

The counselor has the right to contest the accusation by filing a Notice of Defense within 15 days of receiving the accusation. This initiates the right to an administrative hearing before an Administrative Law Judge (ALJ) from the Office of Administrative Hearings.

Administrative hearings resemble court trials but with somewhat relaxed rules of evidence. Both sides present testimony and documentary evidence, and witnesses may be cross-examined. The counselor has the right to legal representation, though this is not provided by the state. The ALJ evaluates the evidence according to the *"clear and convincing"* standard, which is higher than the *"preponderance of evidence"* standard used in civil cases but lower than the *"beyond reasonable doubt"* standard used in criminal cases.

After the hearing, the ALJ issues a proposed decision, including findings of fact, conclusions of law, and a recommended discipline if violations are found. The full Board then reviews this proposed decision and may adopt it, reduce the penalty, or increase the penalty with certain limitations.

Disciplinary options available to the Board include:

1. Revocation of license
2. Suspension of license
3. Probation with specific terms and conditions
4. Public reprimand
5. Restrictions on practice

For example, in cases involving boundary violations that don't include sexual misconduct, the Board might impose probation with conditions such as additional ethics training, supervised practice, and psychotherapy for the counselor. For documentation violations, probation might include record-keeping courses and periodic audits of client files.

For counselors facing investigation, several key principles can guide an appropriate response:

First, take all complaints seriously, regardless of perceived merit. Even allegations that seem unfounded require careful attention and response. Dismissing or minimizing complaints can worsen the situation and create an impression of indifference to ethical concerns.

Second, obtain legal counsel experienced in professional licensing matters. While general practice attorneys may have broad legal knowledge, specialists in administrative law and professional licensing understand the nuances of Board proceedings and can provide targeted guidance.

Third, maintain thorough documentation of all interactions related to the investigation. This includes keeping copies of all correspondence with the Board, notes from conversations with investigators, and records of any materials provided. This documentation helps ensure accurate recall of events and demonstrates cooperation with the process.

Fourth, respond promptly and honestly to investigator requests. Delays or evasiveness can create negative impressions and potentially worsen outcomes. However, counselors should consult with legal counsel before providing statements or records to ensure their rights are protected.

Fifth, continue maintaining appropriate clinical records for all clients. Investigators may review records beyond those directly related to the complaint, so all documentation should meet professional standards.

Throughout the investigation and potential disciplinary process, counselors should maintain confidentiality about the proceedings. Discussing the case with colleagues, supervisees, or clients could compromise the investigation and potentially create additional ethical issues.

If a counselor believes they may have committed a violation, early consultation with an attorney about potential self-reporting could be advisable. In some cases, voluntary disclosure and remedial action may result in more favorable outcomes than waiting for complaints to be filed. The investigation and enforcement process serves the essential function of protecting public safety while providing due process for accused counselors.

CHAPTER TEN

MENTAL HEALTH HOLDS

UNDERSTANDING 5150 HOLD CRITERIA

California's involuntary psychiatric hold system, commonly known as a *"5150 hold,"* provides a legal mechanism for mental health professionals to temporarily detain individuals experiencing severe mental health crises. The name derives from Section 5150 of the California Welfare and Institutions Code, which authorizes a qualified professional to place a person in a psychiatric facility for up to 72 hours for assessment, evaluation, and crisis intervention when certain criteria are met.

The three primary criteria for initiating a 5150 hold are danger to self, danger to others, and grave disability. Each criterion has specific definitions, behavioral indicators, and assessment considerations that Professional Clinical Counselors must understand to fulfill their professional responsibilities.

Danger to Self

Danger to self refers to a situation where an individual, as a result of a mental health disorder, presents a substantial risk of physical harm to themselves. This criterion encompasses both active suicidal behavior and passive self-harm through neglect.

The California Welfare and Institutions Code §5150(a) defines this as a situation where *"a person, as a result of a mental health disorder, is a danger to others, or to themselves, or gravely disabled."* Behavioral indicators that might suggest danger to self include:

- Explicit verbal statements about suicide plans or intentions
- Recent suicide attempts or self-harming behaviors
- Specific, detailed suicide plans with access to means
- Significant preparation activities such as giving away possessions
- Extreme hopelessness coupled with statements of wanting to die
- Sudden calmness after a period of agitation (which could indicate a decision has been made)

For example, a client who arrives at a session intoxicated, reveals they have purchased a firearm specifically for suicide, and states they *"won't be around by tomorrow"* presents clear danger to self. Their behavior demonstrates intent, plan, and means, all critical factors in assessing suicide risk.

Documentation for danger to self should include direct quotes from the client about suicidal thoughts, observations of relevant behaviors, assessment of risk factors (previous attempts, access to means, impulsivity), and protective factors (social support, future orientation, engagement in treatment). California Business and Professions Code requires PCCs to be trained in suicide risk assessment and intervention, emphasizing the importance of thorough documentation in these situations.

Danger to Others

Danger to others refers to a situation where an individual, due to a mental health disorder, presents a substantial risk of physical harm to another person or persons. Behavioral indicators that might suggest danger to others include:

- Specific threats to harm identifiable individuals
- Recent acts of violence or aggression

- Detailed plans to harm others with access to means
- Command hallucinations directing violence toward others
- Paranoid delusions focused on specific individuals
- Escalating patterns of aggression or threatening behavior
- Impulsivity combined with homicidal ideation

Consider a composite scenario: A client with paranoid schizophrenia stops taking medication and becomes convinced his neighbor is poisoning him through the ventilation system. He describes detailed plans to *"eliminate the threat"* and has purchased weapons. This situation presents clear danger to others, requiring immediate intervention. Documentation for danger to others should include direct quotes regarding threats, observations of aggressive behaviors, assessment of risk factors (history of violence, substance use, command hallucinations), and contextual factors (access to potential victims, ability to carry out threats).

The California Supreme Court decision in Tarasoff v. Regents of University of California (1976) established the duty to warn and protect potential victims when a client makes specific threats. This duty was later codified in California Civil Code §43.92, which requires therapists to make reasonable efforts to communicate threats to potential victims and law enforcement when a client presents a serious danger of violence to a reasonably identifiable victim.

Grave Disability

Grave disability refers to a condition where an individual, as a result of a mental health disorder, is unable to provide for their basic personal needs for food, clothing, or shelter.

California Welfare and Institutions Code §5008(h)(1)(a), expanded by SB43, defines grave disability as *"a condition in which a person, as a result of a mental health disorder, a severe substance use disorder, or a co-occurring mental health disorder and a severe substance use disorder, is unable to provide for their basic personal needs for food, clothing, shelter, personal safety, or necessary medical care."* Behavioral indicators that might suggest grave disability include:

- Severe malnutrition or dehydration due to inability to obtain or prepare food
- Inappropriate clothing for weather conditions (e.g., minimal clothing in freezing temperatures)
- Homelessness due to inability to maintain shelter because of mental illness
- Severe disorganization preventing self-care
- Inability to manage basic hygiene resulting in medical complications
- Delusions or hallucinations that prevent eating or seeking shelter

For example, a client with severe depression who has stopped eating, lost significant weight, and whose apartment has no utilities because they cannot organize themselves to pay bills might meet the criteria for grave disability. Their mental health condition has directly impaired their ability to meet basic needs for food and shelter. Documentation for grave disability should include observations of self-care deficits, weight loss, living conditions, cognitive functioning, and the direct connection between the mental health disorder and the inability to provide for basic needs.

5585 Holds for Minors

It's important to note that minors (under 18 years of age) are not placed on 5150 holds but instead are placed on 5585 holds, as specified in the California Welfare and Institutions Code §5585. The criteria for 5585 holds mirror those for adults: danger to self, danger to others, and grave disability. However, the assessment process takes into account developmental factors and the minor's dependence on caregivers. When evaluating minors, PCCs must consider the family context, including the capacity of parents or guardians to provide supervision and support.

Common Assessment Pitfalls and How to Avoid Them

Several common pitfalls can complicate the assessment process for 5150/5585 holds:

1. **Overreliance on client self-report**: Clients in crisis might minimize symptoms or deny suicidal/homicidal ideation. Collateral information from family members, previous treatment records, and observable behaviors could provide a more complete picture.
2. **Failure to distinguish between chronic and acute risk**: Some clients present with chronic suicidal ideation but low acute risk. Assessment should focus on changes from baseline and specific triggers that increase imminent risk.
3. **Cultural misinterpretation**: Cultural factors might influence how distress is expressed. California Business and Professions Code requires training in cultural factors relevant to assessment, emphasizing the importance of culturally informed evaluations.
4. **Inadequate documentation**: Vague documentation (e.g., *"client appears suicidal"*) fails to support the legal criteria for a hold. Specific behaviors, statements, and observations should be documented.
5. **Overlooking less restrictive alternatives**: A 5150/5585 hold represents a significant restriction of liberty and should be used only when less restrictive options (e.g., crisis residential treatment, intensive outpatient programs) cannot adequately address the risk.

To avoid these pitfalls, PCCs could:

- Use structured assessment tools like the Columbia-Suicide Severity Rating Scale (C-SSRS) to supplement clinical judgment
- Consult with colleagues or supervisors in ambiguous cases
- Document specific behaviors and statements rather than conclusions
- Consider cultural factors that might influence symptom presentation
- Explore all less restrictive alternatives before recommending a hold

- Maintain current knowledge of local resources and referral options

EMERGENCY RESPONSE PROTOCOLS

When a psychiatric emergency unfolds in a clinical setting, the counselor's immediate response can determine the outcome for the client and others present. The first priority is always safety, both for the client in crisis and for everyone in the vicinity. Professional Clinical Counselors need a structured approach to these high-stakes situations, beginning with a rapid but thorough safety assessment.

Immediate Safety Assessment

The initial safety assessment focuses on identifying immediate threats. This includes scanning for:

- Potential weapons or objects that could be used to inflict harm
- Positioning relative to exits (ensure you maintain access to the door)
- Signs of escalating agitation (pacing, clenched fists, raised voice)
- Indications of imminent self-harm or harm to others

California Business and Professions Code requires LPCCs to be trained in suicide risk assessment and intervention, which forms the foundation for these emergency evaluations. The assessment might begin with direct questions:

"I'm concerned about your safety right now. Are you having thoughts about harming yourself?"

"You seem very upset. Are you having thoughts about hurting someone else?"

"I notice you're holding your bag tightly. Do you have anything in there that could be used to hurt yourself or someone else?"

Office Security Protocols

Every counseling practice should establish office security protocols before emergencies arise. These protocols might include:

1. **Panic button or alert system**: A discreet way to signal colleagues that assistance is needed
2. **Clear evacuation routes**: Marked and accessible exits for staff and clients
3. **Designated safe rooms**: Spaces where other clients can be directed during an emergency
4. **Emergency contact list**: Readily available phone numbers for emergency services, building security, and crisis response teams
5. **De-escalation kit**: Items that might help calm a client (stress balls, weighted blankets)

CULTURAL CONSIDERATIONS IN CRISIS

Cultural factors significantly influence how individuals express psychological distress and how they perceive mental health interventions. When Professional Clinical Counselors in California assess clients for potential psychiatric holds, understanding these cultural variations becomes essential for accurate evaluation and appropriate intervention.

Different cultural groups express mental health crises in vastly different ways. For example, some East Asian cultures might emphasize somatic complaints like headaches or stomach pain rather than emotional distress when experiencing depression or anxiety. Latino clients might describe experiences of *"nervios"* or *"ataque de nervios,"* which can include symptoms that overlap with panic attacks but have distinct cultural meanings. Middle Eastern clients might express psychological distress through metaphorical language related to the heart or spirit rather than using Western psychological terminology.

These variations in expression can complicate the assessment process for 5150 holds. California Welfare and Institutions Code §5150 authorizes involuntary psychiatric holds when an individual presents a danger to self, danger to others, or grave disability due to a mental disorder. However, determining whether someone meets these criteria requires understanding how distress manifests within their cultural context.

Language barriers present a primary challenge in crisis assessment. When evaluating a client who speaks limited or no English, PCCs could utilize professional interpreters rather than family members to ensure accurate communication. Family interpreters might filter information based on their own perspectives or cultural stigma, potentially compromising assessment accuracy.

The California Department of Health Care Services emphasizes that interpreters should be trained in mental health terminology and concepts. During crisis situations, counselors might access language services through county mental health departments, hospital language lines, or community-based organizations. Documentation should include the interpreter's name, their relationship to the client (professional or personal), and any challenges encountered during the interpretation process.

For example, a Mandarin-speaking client might use the term *"心病"* (xīn bìng or *"heart disease"*) to describe emotional distress rather than using terminology that translates directly to depression or anxiety. Without cultural context, this could be misinterpreted as a physical complaint rather than a psychological one, potentially affecting the assessment of dangerousness or grave disability.

Religious beliefs also influence how individuals understand and respond to mental health crises. Some clients might attribute psychological symptoms to spiritual causes, such as divine punishment, demonic influence, or karma. Others might view suffering as a test of faith or an opportunity for spiritual growth. These perspectives affect how clients perceive the need for intervention and their willingness to accept treatment. When working with clients whose religious beliefs shape their understanding of mental health, counselors might integrate spiritually sensitive approaches while still fulfilling their professional obligations to assess risk.

For instance, a devout Catholic client experiencing command hallucinations might interpret these as communications from God rather than symptoms of psychosis. Rather than dismissing this belief, a culturally competent counselor might explore whether the content of these *"communications"* poses a safety risk while respecting the client's religious framework. If the client reports hearing commands to harm themselves as a form of religious sacrifice, this would warrant consideration of a hold regardless of the religious attribution.

Cultural stigma surrounding mental illness and treatment presents another significant barrier. In many communities, mental health problems carry shame that extends beyond the individual to the entire family. This stigma might prevent individuals from seeking help until crises become severe and might lead to resistance when intervention is offered.

When considering a psychiatric hold for a client from a highly stigmatized community, counselors might anticipate and address concerns about shame and family reputation. This could include explaining confidentiality protections and discussing how treatment might be framed in ways that minimize stigma.

A case example illustrates this challenge: A 22-year-old Vietnamese American woman presents with severe depression and suicidal ideation but begs the counselor not to hospitalize her because it would bring shame to her family. The counselor acknowledges her concern about family honor while explaining that safety must take priority. The counselor offers to meet with family members (with the client's permission) to provide education about depression as a medical condition rather than a personal or family failing, potentially reducing stigma while still ensuring the client receives needed care.

Family dynamics vary significantly across cultures and influence both the expression of mental health crises and appropriate intervention strategies. In collectivist cultures, family involvement in healthcare decisions is often expected, while in individualist cultures, adult autonomy is typically prioritized. California law recognizes both the importance of confidentiality and the potential value of family support in mental health treatment.

California Welfare and Institutions Code §5328 protects the confidentiality of mental health information but allows disclosure to family members in certain circumstances, such as when the client consents or when necessary for the client's care. When considering a psychiatric hold, counselors might evaluate the potential benefits and risks of family involvement based on the client's cultural context and individual family dynamics.

For example, in many Latino families, the concept of *"familismo"* emphasizes strong family bonds and collective decision-making. A Latino client in crisis might benefit from family involvement in safety planning as an alternative to hospitalization if appropriate. Conversely, in situations where family dynamics contribute to the crisis, such as in cases of family conflict or abuse, more careful boundaries might be needed.

The following case study demonstrates culturally competent crisis intervention:

An LPCC receives an urgent referral for Mohammad, a 35-year-old Iraqi refugee with limited English proficiency who is experiencing severe PTSD symptoms, including flashbacks, hypervigilance, and what his wife describes as *"angry outbursts."* The local emergency department is considering a 5150 hold based on potential dangerousness to others, but staff are uncertain due to communication difficulties.

The counselor arranges for a professional Arabic interpreter and learns that Mohammad's *"angry outbursts"* involve yelling and breaking objects when triggered by flashbacks, but he has never threatened or harmed anyone. The counselor recognizes that Mohammad's behavior, while concerning, might not meet the legal threshold for *"danger to others"* under California Welfare and Institutions Code §5150.

Through the interpreter, the counselor learns that Mohammad views his symptoms as a normal response to the trauma he experienced and fears that hospitalization would separate him from his family, his primary source of support. The counselor also discovers that Mohammad's religious leader has been a trusted source of guidance.

Rather than proceeding with a hold, the counselor develops a safety plan that incorporates cultural and religious resources. This includes:

1. Arranging for Mohammad to stay with his brother temporarily while acute symptoms stabilize
2. Involving his imam in support and spiritual guidance
3. Connecting the family with an Arabic-speaking psychiatrist for medication evaluation
4. Providing psychoeducation about PTSD to both Mohammad and his family
5. Scheduling follow-up appointments with an Arabic-speaking therapist trained in trauma treatment

This intervention respects Mohammad's cultural and religious context while still addressing safety concerns. The counselor documents the assessment process, the rationale for not pursuing a hold, and the alternative safety measures implemented.

When cultural factors complicate crisis assessment, consultation becomes invaluable. Resources for cultural consultation during emergencies might include:

1. County mental health cultural competence coordinators
2. Community-based organizations serving specific cultural groups
3. University-based cultural psychology or psychiatry programs
4. Religious leaders from various traditions
5. The National Center for Cultural Competence's emergency preparedness resources

6. The DSM-5 TR Cultural Formulation Interview, which provides a structured approach to gathering culturally relevant information

The California Pan-Ethnic Health Network offers resources specific to California's diverse communities, including guidance on culturally appropriate crisis intervention. County mental health departments typically maintain lists of culturally and linguistically appropriate service providers who might be available for consultation.

When time permits, a cultural formulation might enhance assessment accuracy. This approach, outlined in the DSM-5, examines:

1. Cultural identity of the individual
2. Cultural conceptualizations of distress
3. Cultural stressors and supports
4. Cultural elements of the relationship between the individual and the clinician
5. Overall cultural assessment

Even in emergency situations, brief attention to these elements might improve assessment accuracy and intervention effectiveness.

Documentation of cultural considerations in crisis assessment demonstrates due diligence and culturally competent care. When cultural factors influence hold decisions, counselors might document:

1. Cultural identity factors relevant to the assessment
2. Language used during the assessment and interpreter information if applicable
3. Cultural expressions of distress observed
4. Cultural or religious resources incorporated into safety planning
5. Consultations with cultural experts
6. How cultural factors influenced the decision to pursue or not pursue a hold

This documentation supports clinical decision-making and demonstrates compliance with legal and ethical standards for culturally competent care.

CHAPTER ELEVEN

WORKING WITH MINOR CLIENTS

LEGAL FOUNDATIONS OF MINOR CONSENT

The legal framework governing consent for minors in counseling represents a complex balance between parental rights and the minor's need for accessible mental health services. The general rule under California Family Code Section 6500 defines a minor as an individual under 18 years of age, with parents or legal guardians typically holding the legal authority to consent to their child's medical and mental health treatment. However, California law recognizes several important exceptions that allow minors to independently consent to certain types of counseling services.

The *"mature minor doctrine"* serves as a foundational concept in California's approach to minor consent. While not explicitly codified in California statutes, this doctrine acknowledges that some minors possess sufficient maturity to make informed decisions about their own healthcare, including mental health services. Courts might consider factors such as the minor's age, intelligence, emotional development, and ability to understand the nature and consequences of the proposed treatment when determining if a minor can provide informed consent.

California Family Code Section 6924 establishes one of the most significant exceptions to the general consent rule. Under this provision, minors who are 12 years of age or older may consent to mental health treatment or counseling on an outpatient basis without parental consent under specific circumstances. These circumstances include when the mental health professional believes the minor is mature enough to participate intelligently in the services and when the minor would present a danger to themselves or others without the treatment, or is the alleged victim of incest or child abuse.

It's important to note that this provision includes limitations. The treatment is restricted to outpatient or residential services, and the mental health professional would involve the minor's parent or guardian unless they determine that such involvement would be inappropriate.

For substance abuse treatment, California Family Code Section 6929 permits minors who are 12 years of age or older to consent to medical care and counseling related to the diagnosis and treatment of a drug or alcohol-related problem. The provider could notify the parent or guardian if they determine that notification would be appropriate. However, parental involvement is not required for the minor to receive these services.

The California Health and Safety Code Section 124260 further expands minor consent rights, allowing minors who are 12 years of age or older to consent to outpatient mental health services if the attending professional believes the minor is mature enough to participate intelligently. When working with minor clients, these professionals must determine whether the minor can legally consent to treatment independently or whether parental consent is required.

Consider the following example: A 15-year-old experiencing depression and anxiety seeks counseling services from an LPCC. The adolescent expresses concern about parental notification, fearing family conflict. Under California Family Code Section 6924, the LPCC could provide counseling without parental consent if they determine the minor is mature enough to participate intelligently in treatment and that involving the parents might be inappropriate or detrimental to the therapeutic process.

In another scenario, a 13-year-old struggling with substance abuse approaches an APCC for help. According to California Family Code Section 6929, the minor can consent to counseling for substance abuse treatment without parental involvement. The APCC could notify the parents if they believe it would be beneficial, but parental consent is not legally required to provide these services.

The concept of confidentiality intersects with consent in important ways. California Health and Safety Code Section 123115(a)(2) allows parents to access their minor child's medical records unless the minor lawfully consented to the treatment or the healthcare provider determines that parental access would have a detrimental effect on the provider's professional relationship with the minor or the minor's physical safety or psychological well-being.

In practice, this means that when a minor has legally consented to mental health services under one of the exceptions discussed above, the LPCC or APCC might withhold information from parents to protect the therapeutic relationship and the minor's well-being. However, there are limits to confidentiality, particularly in situations involving risk of harm to self or others.

The California Supreme Court case American Academy of Pediatrics v. Lungren (1997) provides additional context for understanding minor consent rights. While this case focused on abortion rights, it established important principles regarding minors' privacy interests in healthcare decisions. The court recognized that minors have privacy rights under the California Constitution, though these rights might be subject to greater limitations than those of adults.

When working with minors who have experienced trauma, PCCs should be aware of additional considerations. California Evidence Code Section 1010 defines psychotherapist-patient privilege, which protects confidential communications between a patient and their therapist. This privilege applies to communications with minors, though there are exceptions for situations involving danger to self or others, or when the minor has consented to disclosure.

PCCs working with minor clients should maintain thorough documentation of their consent procedures. This includes documenting the legal basis for providing services without parental consent when applicable, the minor's capacity to consent, and any discussions regarding the limits of confidentiality. Such documentation helps protect both the provider and the minor client in case of legal challenges.

DIVORCED PARENTS AND TREATMENT DECISIONS

Navigating the therapeutic landscape when working with children of divorced or separated parents presents unique challenges for Professional Clinical Counselors in California. The intersection of legal custody arrangements, parental rights, and the child's therapeutic needs creates a complex environment that requires careful consideration and documentation.

California Family Code Section 3003 defines joint legal custody as a situation where *"both parents shall share the right and the responsibility to make the decisions relating to the health, education, and welfare of a child."* This arrangement is common following divorce or separation and directly impacts how counselors obtain consent for treatment. When parents share joint legal custody, both generally have equal rights to make decisions about their child's mental health treatment.

In contrast, California Family Code Section 3006 defines sole legal custody as a situation where *" one parent shall have the right and the responsibility to make the decisions relating to the health, education, and welfare of a child."* In these cases, the parent with sole legal custody typically has the exclusive right to consent to mental health treatment for the child, though exceptions exist.

The first step in providing counseling to a minor with divorced or separated parents is to verify the custody arrangement. This verification process might include:

1. Requesting a copy of the most recent court order outlining custody arrangements
2. Documenting the date and specific provisions related to healthcare decisions
3. Clarifying which parent has authority to make mental health treatment decisions

For example, a court order might specify that parents share joint legal custody but that one parent has *"tie-breaking"* authority for mental health decisions if the parents cannot agree. Alternatively, the order might grant one parent sole decision-making authority for healthcare while sharing other aspects of legal custody.

When parents share joint legal custody, some California custody orders require consent from both parents for non-emergency medical treatment, including mental health services. However, obtaining consent from both parents can be challenging when conflict exists. PCCs might encounter several scenarios:

Scenario 1: Both parents support counseling but disagree on goals

A 10-year-old child is referred for anxiety following her parents' divorce. Both parents consent to treatment, but the mother wants therapy to focus on the child's adjustment to the divorce, while the father wants therapy to address school performance issues.

In this situation, the counselor could:

- Document each parent's stated goals for therapy
- Conduct a thorough assessment to determine the child's clinical needs
- Develop a treatment plan that addresses the child's needs while acknowledging both parents' concerns

- Schedule a joint parent session (if appropriate) to discuss treatment goals
- Obtain written consent from both parents for the agreed-upon treatment plan

Scenario 2: One parent consents to treatment, the other refuses

A 14-year-old boy is struggling with depression after his parents' separation. His mother schedules an appointment and provides consent, but the father, who shares joint legal custody, explicitly refuses to authorize treatment.

In this case, California law presents a challenge. Without a court order specifying that one parent has decision-making authority for mental health treatment, the counselor might not be able to proceed with treatment over one parent's objection when parents share joint legal custody. Options include:

- Suggesting family mediation to resolve the disagreement
- Recommending that the consenting parent seek a court order specifically addressing mental health treatment
- Providing referrals to legal resources that might help resolve the impasse
- Documenting all communications with both parents regarding consent

Again, California Family Code Section 6924 allows minors 12 years or older to consent to mental health treatment without parental consent, so the minor could opt to do just that.

Scenario 3: Parents with joint custody disagree about sharing information

A 9-year-old girl is in therapy with both parents' consent, but the father requests that no information be shared with the mother, despite their joint legal custody arrangement.

In this situation, the California Health and Safety Code Section 123110 generally grants both parents with legal custody the right to access their child's medical records. The counselor could:

- Clarify to both parents that under joint legal custody, both typically have equal rights to information about their child's treatment
- Explain the limits of confidentiality and the counselor's legal obligations
- Document the discussion and any agreements reached
- Consider whether limited information sharing might be clinically appropriate while complying with legal requirements
- Consult with a colleague or attorney if the situation remains unresolved

Documentation becomes particularly important when working with divorced or separated parents. When working with minors of divorced parents, this documentation might include:

1. Copies of court orders establishing custody arrangements
2. Signed consent forms from the appropriate parent(s)
3. Records of all communications with both parents
4. Notes on any disagreements regarding treatment and how they were addressed
5. Documentation of consultations with colleagues or legal counsel regarding complex consent issues

For conflicting parental directives, a structured documentation approach is essential. This might include:

- Creating a specific section in the client file for parental communications
- Maintaining a chronological log of all directives received from each parent
- Recording the counselor's response to each directive and the rationale
- Documenting efforts to resolve conflicts between parents

- Noting any impact on the therapeutic process

Maintaining therapeutic neutrality presents another challenge when working with children of divorced or separated parents. Strategies for maintaining neutrality include:

1. Establishing clear boundaries regarding the counselor's role
2. Focusing communications on the child's needs rather than parental conflicts
3. Using separate parent sessions when appropriate to address concerns
4. Avoiding taking sides in custody disputes or other legal matters
5. Consulting regularly with colleagues or supervisors

FOSTER CARE CLIENT PROTOCOLS

When counseling minors in the foster care system, Professional Clinical Counselors face a complex web of legal requirements, ethical considerations, and multiple stakeholders. Unlike traditional counseling relationships with minors, where parental consent typically forms the foundation of treatment authorization, foster care cases involve a layered decision-making structure established by California law.

Under California Welfare and Institutions Code Section 16010(a), children in foster care have the right to receive medical, dental, vision, and mental health services. However, determining who can authorize these services requires understanding the hierarchy of decision-making authority established by law.

The legal hierarchy for mental health treatment decisions for foster youth typically follows this order:

1. The juvenile court judge
2. The child welfare agency (county social services)
3. The biological parents (if parental rights have not been terminated)

4. The foster parents or resource family
5. Court-appointed advocates

County social workers, acting as representatives of the child welfare agency, typically hold the next level of authority. California Welfare and Institutions Code Section 16501.1 requires social workers to develop case plans that include *"health and education"* provisions. For mental health services, social workers often serve as the primary point of contact for authorizing treatment, especially for routine outpatient counseling.

Biological parents retain certain rights regarding their children's mental health care unless their parental rights have been terminated. Under California Welfare and Institutions Code Section 361, even when a child is removed from parental custody, the court may still allow parents to make decisions regarding the child's developmental services or medical treatment. This creates a situation where PCCs might need to obtain consent from biological parents in addition to the social worker's authorization.

Foster parents (resource families) have limited authority to consent to routine mental health services. According to California Health and Safety Code Section 1530.6, a foster parent may consent to *"medical and dental care"* for a foster child if the care is *"routine"* or *"minor."* However, for significant mental health interventions, foster parents typically need authorization from the social worker or court.

For PCCs, navigating this hierarchy requires careful documentation and communication. A structured intake process for foster youth might include:

1. Verification of current placement status
2. Identification of the social worker assigned to the case
3. Determination of biological parents' legal status and rights
4. Documentation of court orders related to mental health treatment
5. Identification of other involved parties (CASA, attorney, etc.)

EMANCIPATED MINOR TREATMENT GUIDELINES

Emancipated minors occupy a unique legal position in California's mental health landscape, existing in a space between childhood and adulthood that requires careful navigation by Professional Clinical Counselors. Under California Family Code Section 7002, a minor can become legally emancipated through marriage, active military service, or a court declaration. This status grants them many of the legal rights of adults while they are still chronologically minors, creating distinctive considerations for mental health treatment.

When an emancipated minor seeks counseling services, they possess the legal authority to consent to their own mental health treatment without parental involvement. California Family Code Section 7050(e) specifically states that an emancipated minor *"may consent to medical, dental, or psychiatric care, without parental consent, knowledge, or liability."* This provision places decision-making authority squarely with the emancipated minor, allowing them to initiate therapy, determine treatment goals, and make decisions about medication management when appropriate.

The verification of emancipation status represents a critical first step in the intake process. PCCs might request documentation such as a Declaration of Emancipation issued by a California Superior Court, marriage certificate, or military identification. According to California Family Code Section 7122, this Declaration serves as legal proof of emancipation status and *"is conclusive evidence"* of the minor's right to be treated as an adult for specified purposes, including healthcare decision (emancipated).

A sample verification protocol might include:
1. Requesting the original Declaration of Emancipation or other qualifying document
2. Making a copy for the client's file
3. Documenting the verification in the intake notes

4. Returning the original document to the client

For example, when 17-year-old Miguel presented for therapy after experiencing anxiety related to his new job, he provided his Declaration of Emancipation obtained six months earlier. The counselor made a copy for his file, noted the verification in the intake documentation, and proceeded with treatment planning directly with Miguel, without parental involvement.

The informed consent process with emancipated minors follows the same requirements as with adult clients. With emancipated minors, this process acknowledges their legal autonomy while potentially adapting the explanation to their developmental level.

A comprehensive informed consent document for an emancipated minor might include:

1. Clear explanation of confidentiality and its limits
2. Description of the counselor's qualifications and approach
3. Fee structure and payment expectations
4. Emergency protocols
5. Client rights and responsibilities
6. Acknowledgment of the client's emancipated status

The confidentiality rights of emancipated minors mirror those of adult clients. Under California Civil Code Section 56.10 and the Health Insurance Portability and Accountability Act (HIPAA), their health information receives the same protections as adult clients. This means that, absent specific exceptions like mandated reporting situations or imminent danger, the content of therapy sessions remains confidential.

CAREGIVER AUTHORIZATION PROCEDURES

Caregiver authorization in counseling settings presents unique challenges for Professional Clinical Counselors in California. When working with minor clients or dependent adults who are under the care of someone other than their legal parent or guardian, counselors need to navigate complex legal requirements to ensure proper consent for treatment. The California Family Code provides specific guidelines for caregiver authorization affidavits that allow certain individuals to make healthcare decisions for minors in their care.

Under California Family Code Sections 6550-6552, a caregiver who is not the legal parent or guardian may authorize medical and dental care, including mental health services, for a minor living in their home through a properly executed Caregiver's Authorization Affidavit. This provision helps ensure that children can receive necessary care even when parents are unavailable or unable to provide consent.

For a Caregiver's Authorization Affidavit to be valid in California, it must contain several key elements. The affidavit needs to include the minor's name and birth date, the caregiver's name and address, the caregiver's relationship to the minor, and a statement affirming that the minor lives with the caregiver. Additionally, the caregiver must declare under penalty of perjury that they have informed the parents or legal guardians about their intention to authorize medical care, or that they are unable to contact the parents or legal guardians.

The California Family Code specifies two types of caregivers who can use this affidavit:

1. Qualified relatives (grandparents, aunts, uncles, siblings, step-relatives, or first cousins) who can authorize any medical care, including mental health treatment.
2. Non-relative caregivers who can authorize school-related medical care only, which might include school-based counseling but could limit other mental health services.

When presented with a Caregiver's Authorization Affidavit, PCCs could implement a verification protocol that includes:

1. Examining the affidavit for completeness, including all required information and signatures

2. Verifying the caregiver's identity through government-issued photo identification
3. Confirming the relationship between the caregiver and minor
4. Documenting the verification process in the client's record

It's important to note that the scope of a caregiver's decision-making authority has specific limitations under California law. According to Family Code Section 6550(a), the Caregiver's Authorization Affidavit does not affect the rights of the minor's parents or legal guardians regarding the care, custody, and control of the minor. The parents retain the right to revoke the authorization at any time.

For qualified relatives serving as caregivers, the authorization allows them to consent to:

- Medical and dental care, including mental health treatment
- Psychological testing related to treatment
- Release of relevant medical information
- Participation in the minor's treatment planning

For non-relative caregivers, the authorization is more limited, allowing them to consent only to:

- School-related medical care
- Basic first aid and emergency care

When working with caregivers who have limited authorization, counselors might need to seek additional consent from legal parents or guardians for certain types of treatment or assessment.

The Caregiver's Authorization Affidavit remains valid until the minor no longer lives with the caregiver or the caregiver revokes it. However, healthcare providers, including mental health professionals, might establish protocols for periodically updating and confirming the continued validity of the authorization. A reasonable approach could include:

1. Reviewing the authorization status at least annually

2. Requesting written confirmation from the caregiver that the minor continues to reside with them
3. Updating contact information for both the caregiver and, when possible, the legal parents or guardians
4. Documenting these verification efforts in the client record

When working with caregivers who are not legal parents or guardians, PCCs might encounter situations where the legal parents disagree with the caregiver's decisions regarding mental health treatment. In these cases, the counselor could:

1. Review the court orders or custody agreements, if available
2. Consult with legal counsel regarding the hierarchy of decision-making authority
3. Document all communication with caregivers and legal parents
4. Consider the best interests of the minor client while navigating the conflict

The California Code of Regulations, Title 16, Section 1815.5, which addresses telehealth services by PCCs, requires proper documentation of consent for treatment. When providing telehealth services to minors under caregiver authorization, counselors might need additional verification steps, such as:

1. Confirming the caregiver's identity visually during video sessions
2. Obtaining electronic signatures on consent forms
3. Documenting the verification process specifically for telehealth services

RECORDS MANAGEMENT FOR MINOR CLIENTS

Records management for minor clients presents unique challenges for Professional Clinical Counselors in California. The intersection of parental rights, minor privacy, and legal requirements creates a complex landscape that requires careful navigation. Understanding the specific legal parameters that govern record-keeping for minors helps counselors maintain ethical practice while protecting the therapeutic relationship.

California law establishes distinct frameworks for record access based on who authorized the minor's treatment. Under California Health and Safety Code Section 123110, parents and legal guardians generally have the right to access their child's health records. However, this right is not absolute and contains several important exceptions that counselors must understand to properly manage minor client records.

When a minor consents to their own treatment under California Family Code Section 6924 and Health and Safety Code Section 124260, which permits minors 12 and older to consent to mental health treatment, the minor maintains control over their records. In these cases, the minor client, not the parent or guardian, holds the authority to access or release those records. Additionally California Health and Safety Code Section 123115(a)(1) specifically states that a representative of a minor shall not be entitled to inspect or obtain copies of the minor's patient records where the minor has the right to consent to care.

For example, if a 15-year-old client self-refers for counseling related to suicidal thoughts under the previously specified codes, the records generated from these sessions remain under the minor's control. The counselor could not release these records to parents without the minor's written authorization. Record access becomes more nuanced in cases of divorced or separated parents. As previously mentioned, California Family Code Section 3025 establishes that both parents have equal access to records and information pertaining to their minor children, including medical and dental records, unless a court order specifically limits this access. This applies regardless of which parent has physical custody of the child.

A sample protocol for verifying parental access rights might include:

1. Requesting and copying court custody documents
2. Documenting the verification in the client file

3. Creating an access log that notes who has requested and received information
4. Establishing a system to flag records with special access restrictions

Storage and security requirements for minor client records parallel those for adult clients but with additional considerations. California Business and Professions Code Section 4999.75 requires PCCs to retain patient records for at least seven years from the date therapy is terminated. For minor clients, records must be maintained for at least seven years after the minor reaches 18 years of age.

Physical records require secure storage in locked cabinets with restricted access, while electronic records necessitate password protection, encryption, and secure backup systems. As with adult records, the California Confidentiality of Medical Information Act (CMIA) establishes penalties for the unauthorized disclosure of medical information, making proper security measures not just ethical practice but a legal requirement.

Electronic health records (EHRs) for minor clients require particular attention to access controls. Systems should allow for segmentation of sensitive information that might be protected under minor consent laws. For instance, an EHR might need to restrict parental access to portions of the record related to treatment the minor consented to independently, while allowing access to other parts of the record.

A comprehensive security protocol for minor client records might include:

1. Role-based access controls that limit who can view specific types of information
2. Audit trails that track who has accessed records and when
3. Secure messaging systems for communication about minor clients
4. Regular security assessments and updates
5. Staff training on minor confidentiality laws

The release of information to schools or other providers presents another area requiring careful consideration. Under the Family

Educational Rights and Privacy Act (FERPA), schools generally need parental consent to release student information. However, when coordinating care between a counselor and school personnel, California law provides specific guidance.

California Education Code Section 49602 allows for limited information sharing between health providers and school personnel when necessary for a student's welfare. However, this does not override the confidentiality protections for minors who have consented to their own treatment under Family Code or Health and Safety Code..

A protocol for information release might include:
1. Determining who holds the legal right to authorize release (parent/guardian or minor)
2. Obtaining written authorization specifying exactly what information can be shared
3. Limiting disclosure to the minimum necessary information
4. Documenting all releases in the client record
5. Providing a copy of the authorization to the client and/or parent/guardian

For example, when coordinating care for 14-year-old Sophia between her school counselor and private therapist, the LPCC might obtain a detailed authorization specifying that information about her anxiety management strategies can be shared, while keeping details about family dynamics confidential.

Handling sensitive information within minor client records requires particular attention. California law recognizes certain categories of information that receive heightened protection, including substance use treatment, sexual health, and mental health information obtained through self-consent.

Under California Health and Safety Code Section 121020, information related to HIV testing receives special protection. Similarly, California Health and Safety Code Section 11845.5 protects the confidentiality of records related to substance use disorder treatment.

When these sensitive topics arise in therapy with minors, counselors might consider maintaining separate records or clearly segregating this information within the client file.

A system for managing sensitive information could include:

1. Clear labeling of protected information within the record
2. Separate storage systems for highly sensitive material
3. Specific protocols for responding to record requests that might include protected information
4. Regular audits to ensure compliance with confidentiality requirements

Documentation methods for minor client records should capture essential clinical information while respecting legal parameters around confidentiality. Progress notes should focus on clinical observations, interventions used, and client response, avoiding unnecessary details about sensitive disclosures that might not be legally accessible to parents. For a discussion about other documentation, see Chapter 7.

CRISIS INTERVENTION WITH MINORS

Crisis intervention with minor clients requires a structured approach that balances immediate safety concerns with legal requirements and therapeutic considerations. California law establishes specific parameters for Professional Clinical Counselors when responding to crises involving minors. When assessing suicide risk and self-harm in minor clients, counselors could implement a multi-tiered approach. The initial assessment might begin with direct questioning about suicidal thoughts, plans, means, and intent.

California Welfare and Institutions Code Section 5585 recognizes that minors experiencing a mental health crisis may require immediate intervention. Questions should be age-appropriate but direct: *"Have you been thinking about hurting yourself?"* or *"Have you thought about ending your life?"* Avoiding these questions due to discomfort might constitute negligence under California's standard of care.

A structured assessment tool appropriate for the minor's developmental level could enhance this process. For adolescents, the Columbia-Suicide Severity Rating Scale (C-SSRS) provides a validated framework, while younger children might respond better to tools like the Ask Suicide-Screening Questions (ASQ). Documentation of the specific tool used and the minor's responses is essential, as noted in California Code of Regulations Title 16, Section 1815.5, which addresses standards of practice for telehealth services, including crisis intervention.

Risk factors that might elevate concern include:

1. Previous suicide attempts
2. Family history of suicide
3. History of non-suicidal self-injury
4. Recent loss or trauma
5. Access to lethal means
6. Substance use
7. Social isolation or bullying
8. Exposure to suicide of peers

Protective factors that might mitigate risk include:

1. Strong family connections
2. Engagement in school or activities
3. Cultural or religious beliefs that discourage suicide
4. Effective coping skills
5. Access to mental health services
6. Sense of purpose or future orientation

MULTI-STAKEHOLDER COMMUNICATION PROTOCOLS

When working with minor clients, Professional Clinical Counselors in California often find themselves at the center of a complex communication network involving multiple stakeholders. Effective coordination with schools, medical providers, child protective services, and families requires careful navigation of legal requirements, ethical boundaries, and the therapeutic relationship. This work frequently necessitates collaboration with other professionals while maintaining appropriate confidentiality.

Coordinating with school personnel presents particular challenges. Under the Family Educational Rights and Privacy Act (FERPA) and California Education Code Section 49076, schools have specific limitations on sharing student information. Similarly, counselors must adhere to the Health Insurance Portability and Accountability Act (HIPAA) and California's Confidentiality of Medical Information Act (CMIA) when sharing client information with schools. A balanced approach might include:

1. Obtaining specific written authorization from parents/guardians before initiating communication with school personnel
2. Limiting information shared to what is directly relevant to the student's educational needs
3. Documenting all communications with school staff in the client record
4. Establishing regular check-in protocols with designated school contacts

Communication with medical providers requires similar care. California Health and Safety Code Section 123110 addresses patient access to health records and the coordination of care among providers. When communicating with physicians, psychiatrists, or other healthcare providers, PCCs could implement a structured approach:

1. Obtain specific authorization for communication with each medical provider
2. Clarify the purpose and scope of information exchange
3. Use secure communication methods that comply with HIPAA and CMIA

4. Maintain a communication log documenting all provider interactions

Throughout all stakeholder communications, PCCs must maintain awareness of their ethical and legal obligations. The California Business and Professions Code outlines core content areas for counselor education, including professional ethics and law, which encompasses appropriate management of multi-stakeholder communications. Regular consultation and supervision regarding complex communication situations could help counselors navigate these challenges while maintaining appropriate boundaries and protecting client confidentiality.

CHAPTER TWELVE

TELEHEALTH PRACTICE REQUIREMENTS

TELEHEALTH FOR THE PROFESSIONAL COUNSELOR

California law defines telehealth as the use of technology to deliver health care services when the provider and client are in different physical locations. As outlined in Business and Professions Code § 2290.5, telehealth includes the use of real-time or near real-time communication tools such as video conferencing, telephone, and other electronic means to facilitate diagnosis, consultation, treatment, and care management. Although previously referred to as "telemedicine," the term telehealth now encompasses a broader range of behavioral health services. In California, only individuals who are licensed, registered as associates, or serving as trainees under proper supervision may provide therapy via telehealth.

Before initiating telehealth, counselors must inform clients that services will be delivered remotely, obtain verbal or written consent, and document that consent in the client's record. Although written consent was previously required, Assembly Bill 415 eliminated that requirement, and verbal consent is now considered sufficient under the law if properly documented. The therapist must also provide the client with their license or registration number and type, and make reasonable efforts to identify emergency services or local resources in the client's geographic area. Clients should be clearly informed of the potential risks and benefits of telehealth, including concerns about privacy, technology failures, and the possibility that telehealth may not be appropriate for every clinical situation. This discussion should be revisited periodically and integrated into the informed consent process.

Jurisdictional issues require careful attention. If the client is located in California and the therapist is temporarily out of state, telehealth may proceed as long as the license or registration is active and the care provided aligns with professional standards. However, if the client is located in another state, the California therapist must comply with the laws of that jurisdiction. California Code of Regulations § 1815.5(e) makes clear that a licensee or registrant may only provide telehealth services across state lines if the other state allows it and the therapist meets that state's legal requirements for practice. It is the California clinician's responsibility to confirm whether such services are lawful in the client's state. Providing therapy to a client located in a jurisdiction that does not allow it, or without meeting licensure requirements there, constitutes unlicensed practice and is subject to disciplinary action. It is both illegal and unprofessional.

California's regulations also apply to out-of-state therapists seeking to provide telehealth to clients who are temporarily within California. As of January 1, 2024, a temporary practice allowance permits qualifying mental health professionals licensed in other U.S. jurisdictions to continue serving established clients for up to 30 days per calendar year while the client is physically present in California. This provision is limited to existing treatment relationships and is contingent on meeting all eligibility requirements. More information about this allowance and the application process is available on the Board of Behavioral Sciences website.

Each time a therapist provides telehealth services, they are required to take specific steps. At the beginning of every session, the counselor must verbally confirm and document the client's full name and physical location. They must evaluate whether telehealth remains clinically appropriate for the client, taking into account the individual's psychosocial context, presenting issues, and ongoing progress. The provider must also use secure, industry-standard practices for maintaining confidentiality and safeguarding the communication medium, such as using encrypted video platforms, private workspaces, and secure internet connections. These are not optional considerations, they are legal requirements that protect the client, the provider, and the therapeutic relationship.

VIRTUAL SESSION SECURITY PROTOCOLS

As discussed in prior chapters, encryption serves as a basic requirement of secure telehealth counseling sessions, creating a protective barrier around sensitive client information. California's Confidentiality of Medical Information Act (CMIA) requires Professional Clinical Counselors to implement reasonable security measures to protect client data. For telehealth sessions, this means using platforms with end-to-end encryption, which scrambles data during transmission so only authorized participants can access it.

Selecting a telehealth platform with at least AES 256-bit encryption ensures the privacy of client communications. This level of encryption is currently considered industry standard for healthcare communications. The platform's encryption should cover all aspects of the session, including video, audio, chat features, and any shared documents or screen sharing functions.

Consider the case of a mental health provider who used a non-encrypted video conferencing platform for client sessions. During one session, an unauthorized third party gained access to the video stream, exposing sensitive client information. This breach resulted in a complaint to the licensing board and potential HIPAA violations. The incident could have been prevented by using a properly encrypted, HIPAA-compliant platform.

Beyond the platform itself, counselors need to ensure encryption extends to all devices used for telehealth. This includes:

- Enabling full-disk encryption on computers (FileVault for Mac, BitLocker for Windows)
- Setting up encrypted backups
- Using encrypted connections (HTTPS websites, secure Wi-Fi with WPA3)
- Implementing encrypted messaging for any client communications

Secure waiting room protocols form the next layer of telehealth security. Virtual waiting rooms function similarly to physical waiting areas but require specific security configurations. California Code of Regulations Title 16, Section 1815.5 addresses telehealth standards of practice, emphasizing that the standard of care for telehealth is the same as in-person services, which includes maintaining privacy and security.

A secure waiting room setup could include:

1. Enabling the waiting room feature in your telehealth platform
2. Customizing waiting room settings to prevent participants from joining before the host
3. Requiring a password or meeting ID for entry
4. Disabling *"join before host"* options
5. Setting up notifications when someone enters the waiting room

When managing the waiting room, counselors could follow this protocol:

1. Schedule sessions with buffer time between clients to prevent overlap
2. Admit clients from the waiting room only after verifying their identity
3. Lock the session once the client has joined to prevent unauthorized access
4. Monitor the waiting room throughout the session in case of disconnection and reconnection

A notable security incident occurred when a counselor failed to enable waiting room features and had back-to-back sessions scheduled.

When one session ended early, the next client joined automatically and overheard confidential information about the previous client. This breach of confidentiality violated California Civil Code Section 56.10, which prohibits unauthorized disclosure of medical information. Proper waiting room protocols would have prevented this incident.

Authentication procedures ensure that only the intended client participates in the telehealth session. The California Board of Behavioral Sciences emphasizes the importance of verifying client identity in telehealth settings. A multi-layered authentication approach provides the strongest security.

For initial sessions, counselors could implement this authentication protocol:

1. Request government-issued photo identification to be shown via video at the first session
2. Document the type of ID verified and date of verification in the client record
3. Establish a unique identifier or password known only to the client for future sessions
4. Create challenge questions based on information in the client's record

For ongoing sessions, a streamlined authentication process might include:

1. Visual verification (recognizing the client by sight)
2. Verbal confirmation using the established unique identifier or password
3. Conducting sessions from consistent locations to help identify unusual circumstances

When working with new clients who haven't been seen in person, additional verification steps could include:

1. Collecting and verifying insurance information prior to the first session
2. Sending verification codes to the client's phone or email

3. Using multi-factor authentication features if available on the telehealth platform

A security breach example related to authentication involved a counselor who relied solely on visual recognition for client authentication. During one session, the client's family member with similar appearance used the client's device to join the session, gaining access to confidential information. This incident could have been prevented with proper authentication protocols.

Session recording guidelines address another potential security vulnerability in telehealth. Under California law, specifically Penal Code Section 632, all parties must consent to the recording of confidential communications. For telehealth sessions, this means explicit client consent is required before any recording occurs.

A comprehensive recording protocol could include:

1. Obtaining written consent before recording any session
2. Explaining the purpose of the recording, how it will be stored, who will have access, and when it will be deleted
3. Confirming verbal consent at the start of any recorded session
4. Using only the secure recording features built into HIPAA-compliant platforms
5. Never recording sessions using third-party software or external devices
6. Storing recordings with the same level of security as written clinical notes
7. Establishing a retention policy for recordings that aligns with record-keeping requirements

The consent form for recording could include:

- Purpose of recording (supervision, training, client review)
- Storage location and security measures
- Access limitations (who can view the recording)
- Retention period and deletion procedure
- Client's right to revoke consent at any time

- Confirmation that refusing recording won't affect quality of care

A security incident involving recordings occurred when a counselor used a personal device to record sessions for supervision purposes. The device was later stolen, potentially exposing multiple clients' sessions. The counselor faced disciplinary action for failing to maintain appropriate security measures as required by Business and Professions Code.

Environmental security considerations extend beyond digital measures to the physical spaces where telehealth occurs. Both counselor and client environments need attention to maintain confidentiality.

For the counselor's environment, these measures could be implemented:

1. Conducting sessions in a private room with a closed door
2. Using noise machines or white noise generators outside the door
3. Positioning the camera so that no confidential information is visible in the background
4. Using a virtual background if a private space isn't available
5. Wearing headphones to prevent others from overhearing the client
6. Ensuring no smart devices with voice activation are nearby
7. Locking computer screens when stepping away, even briefly

Counselors could also provide guidance to clients about creating secure environments:

1. Finding a private location for the session
2. Using headphones to maintain privacy
3. Informing household members about session times and privacy needs
4. Considering the use of white noise machines if privacy is limited
5. Being aware of smart devices that might be listening
6. Closing other applications on their device during the session

REMOTE CRISIS MANAGEMENT PROCEDURES

Telehealth counseling presents distinct challenges during crisis situations that require careful preparation. The physical distance between counselor and client creates additional complexities that require careful planning and preparation. California law, particularly Business and Professions Code requires counselors to maintain the same standard of care in telehealth as they would in person, including during crisis situations.

Before initiating telehealth services, counselors need to establish a basis for effective crisis management through emergency contact verification. This process begins during the intake session, where counselors collect and verify essential information. Again, as mentioned before, California Code of Regulations Title 16, Section 1815.5, counselors must obtain appropriate consent for telehealth services, which includes emergency protocols.

A comprehensive emergency contact form might include:

- Client's full legal name and date of birth
- Current physical address where sessions typically occur
- Alternative locations where client might attend sessions
- Primary phone number and backup contact methods
- Emergency contact person's name, relationship, and phone number
- Secondary emergency contact information
- Permission to contact these individuals in case of emergency
- Client's primary care physician contact information
- Local emergency services information (nearest hospital, crisis center)
- Current medications and allergies
- Existing mental health diagnoses relevant to crisis situations

Verification of this information could follow a structured protocol:

1. Request the client to verbally confirm their current location at the beginning of each session
2. Periodically review and update emergency contact information
3. Test emergency contact numbers during the intake process (with client permission)
4. Document verification procedures in the client record

The following scenario illustrates the importance of this verification: A counselor was conducting a telehealth session when the client began experiencing severe chest pain and shortness of breath. Because the counselor had verified the client's exact location at the beginning of the session, emergency services were dispatched promptly to the correct address, potentially saving the client's life.

Local resource identification forms another critical component of telehealth crisis management. For telehealth providers, this includes identifying resources in the client's geographic area.

Counselors could develop a resource database for each client's location including:

- Local crisis hotlines and warmlines
- Nearest emergency departments equipped for psychiatric emergencies
- Mobile crisis response teams in the client's county
- Walk-in crisis centers and their hours of operation
- Local law enforcement non-emergency numbers
- County mental health services contact information
- Substance use treatment resources for dual-diagnosis situations

This information might be organized by client location and updated regularly, as services and contact information can change. A practical approach involves creating a digital resource document for each client's geographic area that can be quickly accessed during a session.

For example, a counselor working with a client in Alameda County would maintain a resource list specific to that area, including the Alameda

County Crisis Support Services (800-309-2131), local emergency departments, and the county's mobile crisis team contact information.

Crisis intervention protocols for telehealth require adaptation from in-person approaches. The California Board of Behavioral Sciences emphasizes that telehealth providers must be prepared to manage crises effectively despite the physical distance from clients.

A structured telehealth crisis intervention protocol might include:

1. Assessment Phase

When a client presents in crisis during a telehealth session, the counselor could:

- Maintain visual contact if possible
- Assess for immediate danger using direct questions
- Determine the client's current location
- Evaluate support resources currently available to the client
- Assess the client's ability to collaborate in safety planning

2. Stabilization Strategies

Depending on the assessment, the counselor might:

- Implement grounding techniques appropriate for virtual delivery
- Guide the client through breathing exercises while maintaining visual contact
- Help the client identify immediate coping resources in their environment
- Engage support persons present in the client's location if appropriate

3. Resource Activation

Based on the severity of the crisis, the counselor could:

- Connect the client with local crisis services via conference call
- Contact emergency services if there is imminent risk
- Activate the client's predetermined support system

- Remain on the video call until additional support arrives

4. Documentation Procedures

Following the crisis, thorough documentation is essential:

- Record the nature of the crisis and presenting symptoms
- Document assessment procedures and results
- Detail interventions implemented and client response
- Note all resources contacted and their responses
- Plan for follow-up care

This scenario demonstrates this protocol in action: During a telehealth session, a client revealed active suicidal ideation with a specific plan and intent. The counselor maintained visual contact while asking direct questions about safety, determined the client's exact location, and contacted local emergency services while keeping the client engaged on the video call. The counselor stayed connected until emergency personnel arrived, then documented the entire interaction and arranged for immediate follow-up care.

VIRTUAL SESSION BEST PRACTICES

Effective telehealth counseling begins with thorough preparation before the client ever logs in. Professional Clinical Counselors in California could establish a pre-session routine that includes testing all equipment at least 15 minutes before the scheduled appointment. This preparation time allows for troubleshooting any technical issues that might arise and creates a buffer to ensure the session starts promptly.

Pre-session preparation might include verifying that the camera is positioned at eye level to create a natural sense of eye contact. Lighting should illuminate the counselor's face clearly without creating shadows or glare. The background should be professional and free from distractions, with personal items removed from view to maintain appropriate boundaries. Some counselors find that a bookshelf with professional texts or a plain wall with minimal decorations works well.

Before the session begins, counselors could prepare all necessary materials, including assessment tools, worksheets, or resources that might be shared during the session. Having these materials readily accessible in digital format allows for seamless screen sharing when appropriate. Additionally, keeping a physical notepad nearby for taking notes can be helpful in case of technical difficulties with electronic documentation systems.

During the session itself, establishing and maintaining a therapeutic presence requires intentional effort in a virtual environment. The session might begin with a brief check-in about the client's physical space, ensuring they have privacy and feel comfortable discussing sensitive topics. Counselors could ask, *"Are you in a private space where you feel comfortable talking freely?"* This simple question acknowledges the unique aspects of telehealth and demonstrates care for the client's confidentiality.

Maintaining eye contact in virtual sessions presents a unique challenge. Looking directly at the camera, rather than at the client's image on the screen, creates the appearance of eye contact for the client. However, this means the counselor cannot simultaneously observe the client's facial expressions. A practical approach might be to position the client's video window as close to the camera as possible and alternate between looking at the camera and the client's image.

Non-verbal communication takes on heightened importance in telehealth. Counselors could consider using slightly more pronounced facial expressions and head nods to convey active listening, as subtle expressions might not translate well through video. Verbal acknowledgments like *"I hear you"* or *"I'm following what you're saying"* can replace the subtle non-verbal cues that might be missed in virtual settings.

Technical interruptions can disrupt the therapeutic flow, so having a pre-established protocol for handling these situations is valuable. At the beginning of the therapeutic relationship, counselors might discuss with clients how to proceed if the connection is lost. For example, *"If we get disconnected, I'll try to reconnect through the platform. If that doesn't work within two minutes, I'll call you at the phone number you provided."*

For clients who struggle with focus during virtual sessions, counselors might implement structured grounding techniques at the beginning of each session. A simple exercise like having the client identify five things they can see, four things they can touch, three things they can hear, two things they can smell, and one thing they can taste can help center them in the present moment and prepare them for therapeutic work.

Screen sharing can be a powerful tool in telehealth sessions when used intentionally. Sharing worksheets, educational materials, or even collaborative documents where both the counselor and client can write can enhance engagement. However, counselors should practice using these features before implementing them in sessions to ensure smooth execution.

Post-session procedures are equally important for maintaining the quality and continuity of care. Immediately after the session ends, counselors could take a few minutes to complete their documentation while the details are fresh. Additionally, documentation should include the client's location during the session, the platform used, any technical difficulties encountered, and how they were addressed.

A brief period of reflection after each session allows counselors to assess what worked well and what might be adjusted for future sessions. This reflection might include considerations about the technical aspects of the session, the therapeutic interventions used, and how well the virtual format supported the therapeutic goals.

Following up with clients between sessions can help maintain connection and continuity, especially in telehealth where the physical separation might create a sense of distance. A secure message through the telehealth platform or patient portal with a brief reminder about the next appointment or a link to resources discussed during the session can bridge the gap between meetings.

Regular assessment of the telehealth process itself can improve the quality of care. Periodically asking clients about their experience with the virtual format allows for adjustments that enhance the therapeutic relationship. Questions might include: *"How is the telehealth format working for you?" "Is there anything about our virtual sessions that could be improved?" "Are there any technical aspects that have been challenging for you?"*

Common challenges in telehealth sessions include audio delays, video freezing, distractions in the client's environment, and difficulty reading non-verbal cues. Strategies for addressing these challenges might include:

1. For audio delays: Speaking in complete thoughts and pausing slightly longer than usual before responding to allow for transmission delays.
2. For video freezing: Having a backup plan for continuing the session by phone if video quality becomes problematic.
3. For environmental distractions: Helping clients problem-solve ways to create a more private and quiet space, such as using headphones, placing a *"do not disturb"* sign on their door, or scheduling sessions when others are less likely to be home.
4. For non-verbal cues: Explicitly checking in about emotions more frequently than in in-person sessions, asking questions like *"How did that land with you?"* or *"What emotions are coming up for you right now?"*

A session quality assessment tool could help counselors systematically evaluate and improve their telehealth practice. This tool might include ratings on a scale of 1-5 for factors such as:

- Technical quality (audio clarity, video stability, connection reliability)

- Therapeutic presence (ability to convey empathy, maintain engagement)
- Client engagement (participation, focus, openness)
- Session structure (clear beginning, middle, and end; accomplishment of session goals)
- Environmental factors (privacy, comfort, freedom from distractions)
- Overall effectiveness (progress toward therapeutic goals)

For each category, counselors could note specific strengths and areas for improvement, along with action steps for enhancing future sessions. Effective telehealth counseling requires intentional adaptation of traditional counseling skills to the virtual environment. By establishing thorough pre-session, during-session, and post-session protocols, PCCs in California can provide high-quality care while complying with all relevant legal and ethical standards. Regular assessment and refinement of telehealth practices ensure that the virtual format enhances rather than hinders the therapeutic relationship, ultimately supporting client growth and well-being in this increasingly important mode of service delivery.

INTERSTATE PRACTICE REGULATIONS

Interstate practice for telehealth services presents a complex legal landscape that Professional Clinical Counselors must navigate carefully. The fundamental principle governing telehealth across state lines is that the counselor must comply with the licensing requirements in both the state where they are located and the state where the client is located at the time of service.

California Code of Regulations, Title 16, 1815.5.explicitly states that *"All persons engaging in the practice of marriage and family therapy, educational psychology, clinical social work, or professional clinical counseling via telehealth, as defined in Section 2290.5 of the Code, with a client who is physically located in this State must have a valid and current license or registration issued by the Board."* This statute further states "All psychotherapy services offered by board licensees and registrants via telehealth fall within the jurisdiction of the board just as traditional face-to-face services do. Therefore, all psychotherapy services offered via telehealth are subject to the board's statutes and regulations". This has been taken to mean that California-licensed counselors remain bound by California regulations even when providing services to clients in other states via telehealth.

However, this does not exempt counselors from meeting the requirements of the client's state of residence. Most states consider the practice of counseling to occur where the client is physically located, not where the counselor is situated. This creates a jurisdictional framework where counselors may need multiple state licenses to practice legally across state lines.

The California Board of Behavioral Sciences (BBS) has not entered into any reciprocity agreements or interstate compacts with other states regarding telehealth practice. This is a critical point for California PCCs to understand: unlike some other mental health professions that have established interstate practice agreements, professional clinical counselors must independently verify and comply with each state's requirements.

State licensing requirements vary substantially across the United States. Some states offer temporary practice provisions, while others require full licensure regardless of how briefly or occasionally a counselor might work with a client in their jurisdiction. For example, New York requires full licensure for any counselor providing services to clients physically located in New York, even for a single session. In contrast, some states like Arizona may offer temporary practice allowances under specific circumstances.

When considering whether to accept an out-of-state client, California PCCs could follow this decision-making framework:
1. Verify the client's physical location during sessions
2. Research the specific licensing requirements in the client's state

3. Determine if you meet those requirements or can reasonably obtain necessary credentials
4. Assess whether the client's needs can be appropriately met via telehealth
5. Consider whether local referrals in the client's area might better serve their needs
6. Document your decision-making process and compliance efforts

The COVID-19 pandemic temporarily altered this landscape when many states issued emergency orders allowing out-of-state providers to practice telehealth without obtaining local licenses. However, most of these emergency provisions have expired or are set to expire. California's emergency telehealth provisions under Executive Order N-43-20 have ended, returning the state to pre-pandemic requirements.

A compliant interstate practice arrangement might look like this example: A California-licensed LPCC who also holds a license in Nevada provides telehealth services to a client who lives in Reno but occasionally travels to California. The counselor maintains documentation of where the client is physically located during each session. When the client is in Nevada, the counselor practices under their Nevada license and follows Nevada regulations. When the client is in California, the counselor practices under their California license and follows California regulations.

Another example involves a California LPCC who obtains a limited telehealth registration in Florida (which offers such an option) to work with a specific client who has relocated there but wishes to continue therapy. The counselor maintains both credentials, documents the client's location for each session, and follows the regulations of the state where the client is located during the session.

The risks of non-compliance with interstate practice regulations are substantial. California Business and Professions Code Section 4999.90(d) identifies practicing outside the scope of the license or in a manner that violates the statute or regulations as unprofessional conduct subject to disciplinary action. Additionally, practicing without a license in another state could potentially result in:

- Disciplinary action by the California BBS
- Disciplinary action by the other state's licensing board
- Civil liability
- Insurance coverage issues
- Ethical violations

For California PCCs who frequently work with clients who travel or who serve populations across multiple states, developing a state-specific compliance protocol is advisable. This might include:

1. Creating a database of state requirements
2. Establishing relationships with legal counsel familiar with interstate practice
3. Developing state-specific informed consent addendums
4. Implementing systems to track and verify client location
5. Maintaining a list of emergency resources for each state where clients might be located

In conclusion, while telehealth technology has made crossing geographic boundaries easier than ever, the legal boundaries remain firmly in place. California PCCs must approach interstate practice with careful attention to the legal requirements of each jurisdiction, thorough documentation, and a commitment to obtaining appropriate credentials before providing services across state lines. The absence of interstate compacts or reciprocity agreements for California counselors means that each state's requirements must be addressed individually, creating a complex but navigable pathway to compliant interstate practice.

CHAPTER THIRTEEN

LEGAL PROCEEDINGS

UNDERSTANDING LEGAL DOCUMENT TYPES

Legal documents can significantly impact a counselor's practice, requiring careful attention to their specific requirements and implications. Professional Clinical Counselors in California might encounter various legal documents throughout their careers, each with distinct characteristics and response protocols.

Subpoenas

A subpoena is a legal document issued by a court or attorney that compels the recipient to provide testimony or produce documents in connection with a legal proceeding. For counselors, subpoenas typically fall into two categories:

1. **Subpoena ad Testificandum**: Requires the counselor to appear and give testimony, either in court or at a deposition.
1. **Subpoena Duces Tecum**: Requires the counselor to produce specific client records or documents.

According to California Code of Civil Procedure Section 1985, a valid subpoena must contain:

- The name of the court

- The title of the action
- A command to appear at a specified time and place
- A description of records to be produced (for subpoena duces tecum)
- The signature of the issuing authority

When receiving a subpoena, California PCCs could follow these validation steps:

- Verify the subpoena is properly issued and served
- Check that it contains all required elements
- Confirm it was served by an authorized individual
- Ensure it provides reasonable time to respond (generally at least 15 days for records)

An example might be that a counselor receives a subpoena duces tecum requesting therapy records for a client involved in a custody dispute. Before responding, the counselor should verify the document's validity and consider whether the psychotherapist-patient privilege applies. For comprehensive, step-by-step guidance on how to validate, object to, or respond to subpoenas, see the section titled Responding to Subpoenas later in this chapter.

Court Orders

A court order is a directive issued by a judge that requires specific actions. Unlike subpoenas, which can be issued by attorneys, court orders come directly from the court and carry greater authority.

Court orders affecting counselors might include:

- Orders to release confidential information
- Orders to appear as an expert witness
- Orders related to child custody evaluations
- Orders for involuntary treatment

When receiving a court order, counselors could:

- Verify it bears an original or electronic judicial signature
- Confirm it was issued by a court with proper jurisdiction
- Review the scope of information requested
- Note any deadlines for compliance

Search Warrants

A search warrant is a court order authorizing law enforcement to search specific premises and seize particular items. While less common in counseling settings, search warrants might be issued in cases involving serious crimes.

If presented with a search warrant, counselors could:

- Ask to see the officer's identification
- Carefully read the warrant to understand its scope
- Cooperate with the search within the warrant's parameters
- Document everything that occurs during the search

If the search warrant identifies one of your clients as the subject of a criminal investigation, you must proceed with caution. Under California Penal Code Section 1524(c), a special master, typically a court-appointed attorney, must be present to execute a search involving privileged materials such as mental health records. The warrant should specifically indicate that a special master will review any seized materials before they are disclosed to law enforcement.

Should the warrant not include a special master and the client is the subject of the search, you should assert psychotherapist-patient privilege under California Evidence Code Section 1015. Politely request that any seized documents be sealed and delivered directly to the court for review. Ask the officer to document that you are asserting privilege and to confirm this in writing or in the search inventory. Then, document the interaction, including the name of the officer, badge number, and details of the warrant. As with all legal encounters involving search and seizure, therapists are advised to consult with legal counsel as soon as possible to ensure compliance without compromising client confidentiality.

Responding to Legal Documents

When responding to legal documents, counselors could balance legal compliance with ethical obligations. For subpoenas, California Evidence Code Section 1015 recognizes the psychotherapist-patient privilege, which might provide grounds for objection. However, this privilege has exceptions, including:

- When the client has initiated legal proceedings related to their mental condition
- In child custody evaluations
- When mandated reporting laws apply

Therapists practicing in California should not assume such subpoenas are valid without verification. Specific jurisdictional requirements must be met for an out-of-state subpoena to be enforceable within California. If you receive a subpoena from another state, it is prudent to consult with an attorney to determine whether you are legally obligated to respond. For court orders, compliance is generally required, but counselors might seek clarification if the order seems overly broad or potentially harmful to the client. For search warrants, immediate compliance is required, but counselors could document any concerns about the search's scope or execution.

Common Pitfalls to Avoid

1. **Ignoring the subpoena**: This could result in contempt charges. Always respond, even if only to object.
2. **Over-disclosure**: Provide only what is specifically requested and legally required. Redact information not covered by the subpoena.
3. **Failing to assert privilege**: Remember that as the holder of the privilege, you have a duty to assert it on your client's behalf when applicable.
4. **Missing deadlines**: Calendar all response dates and allow sufficient time to prepare objections if needed.

5. **Releasing original records**: Always provide copies and maintain your originals.
6. **Informal responses**: Avoid discussing subpoenaed information over the phone with attorneys or others.

Documentation Best Practices

Maintain a *"legal issues"* section in each client file that includes:
1. Copies of all subpoenas received
2. Records of all communications about the subpoena (with client, attorneys, court)
3. Copies of any objections filed
4. Detailed logs of what was disclosed, when, and to whom
5. Copies of any court orders received
6. Notes from any testimony given

This documentation serves both as protection for you and as a record of how you maintained client confidentiality while complying with legal obligations. PCCs in California can navigate the complex intersection of therapeutic confidentiality and legal demands, maintaining professional integrity while fulfilling their legal responsibilities.

MANAGING ATTORNEY COMMUNICATIONS

Professional Clinical Counselors in California frequently interact with attorneys in various contexts, from providing client records to offering expert testimony. These interactions require careful navigation of legal, ethical, and professional boundaries to protect client confidentiality while fulfilling legal obligations.

When an attorney contacts a counselor, the first step is to verify their identity and authority. This verification process includes requesting the attorney's bar number, confirming their identity through the California State Bar website, and documenting this verification in your records.

Upon receiving a request from an attorney, counselors could respond with an acknowledgment that includes:

- Confirmation of receipt of the request
- Timeline for response
- Any clarifying questions
- Request for proper documentation (if needed)

For example:

"Thank you for your request dated June 15, 2024. I have received your inquiry regarding Jane Doe. At this time I cannot confirm (assuming the client did not tell you they would have their attorney contact you) that Jane Doe is a client in this practice. Before proceeding, I will need a properly executed authorization for release of information signed by the reported client or a valid subpoena. Once received, I can respond to your request within 15 business days. Please note that my professional obligations under California Business and Professions Code and the California Code of Regulations Title 16, require me to protect client confidentiality."

When communicating with attorneys, maintaining appropriate boundaries protects both the therapeutic relationship and the counselor's professional role. Communication boundaries might include:

1. Limiting discussion to factual information rather than opinions unless specifically serving as an expert witness
2. Avoiding informal conversations about clients
3. Directing all communication through formal channels (written correspondence, scheduled calls)
4. Maintaining a neutral, professional tone in all interactions

For example, if an attorney attempts to engage in an impromptu phone conversation about a client, a counselor might respond:

"I appreciate your call regarding this matter. To ensure accuracy and maintain appropriate professional boundaries, I would prefer to address your questions in writing after reviewing my records. This also

allows me to ensure I have proper authorization from my client before discussing their case. Could you please email your specific questions, and I'll respond once I've confirmed I have the necessary authorization?"

When attorneys request counselors to perform services beyond standard record provision, such as writing reports, attending depositions, or testifying in court, billing considerations come into play. For legal-related services, counselors might establish a separate fee schedule that includes:

1. Record review and preparation: $X per hour
2. Report writing: $X per hour
3. Phone consultations: $X per hour (minimum X minutes)
4. Deposition testimony: $X per hour (minimum X hours)
5. Court testimony: $X per hour (minimum X hours)
6. Travel time: $X per hour
7. Cancellation fees: Full fee if less than 48 hours' notice

Before providing these services, counselors could send a professional services agreement to the requesting attorney that outlines:

- Scope of services
- Fee structure
- Payment terms
- Cancellation policy
- Limitations (e.g., factual testimony only unless retained as an expert)

For example:

"This letter confirms my agreement to review records and provide a written summary regarding my treatment of John Smith from January to June 2024. My professional fee for this service is $200 per hour, with an estimated 3 hours required for review and report preparation. Payment is due upon receipt of the report. Please note that I can only address factual information regarding my direct treatment of Mr. Smith and cannot offer opinions on matters outside my scope of practice as defined in California Business and Professions Code Section 4999.20."

When interacting with attorneys representing opposing parties in legal proceedings, additional caution is warranted. The California Evidence Code Sections 1010-1027 establish the psychotherapist-patient privilege, which protects confidential communications between counselors and clients. However, this privilege has exceptions and limitations in certain legal contexts.

In these situations, counselors might:

1. Inform the client about the contact from opposing counsel
2. Consult with the client's attorney before responding
3. Request that all communication go through the client's attorney
4. Respond only to properly issued subpoenas or court orders

Professional correspondence with attorneys should maintain a formal, clear tone. Here's an example of a response to an attorney's request for information:

"Re: Request for Information - Jane Doe (DOB: 01/16/1980)

Dear Attorney Johnson:

I am in receipt of your letter dated August 3, 2024, requesting information about any potential therapeutic relationship with Jane Doe. As you may know, the psychotherapist-patient privilege (California Evidence Code Section 1014) and my ethical obligations as a Licensed Professional Clinical Counselor require me to maintain client confidentiality.

Before I can provide any information about Ms. Doe, I will need one of the following:

1. *A written authorization for release of information signed by Ms. Doe that meets the requirements of HIPAA and the California Confidentiality of Medical Information Act*
2. *A valid subpoena duces tecum*
3. *A court order compelling disclosure*

If you have questions about this process, please feel free to contact me directly. I am committed to responding appropriately to legal requests while honoring my professional obligations to protect client confidentiality.

Sincerely,

[Counselor Name]

Licensed Professional Clinical Counselor #XXXXX"

SPECIAL CIRCUMSTANCES AND EXCEPTIONS

When a client discloses historical abuse during a therapy session, Professional Clinical Counselors in California face complex reporting decisions. California Penal Code Section 11166 requires mandated reporters to report suspected child abuse or neglect when they have *"reasonable suspicion,"* but historical disclosures present unique challenges that aren't always clearly addressed in standard protocols.

Historical abuse disclosures occur when an adult client reveals childhood abuse. The reporting obligation hinges on several factors, including the current age of the victim, the statute of limitations, and whether the alleged perpetrator might have continued access to vulnerable individuals.

For adult clients disclosing childhood abuse, California law generally does not require reporting if the client is now an adult and the disclosure pertains to abuse they experienced as a child. However, counselors must consider whether the alleged perpetrator might have ongoing access to children or vulnerable populations. If there's reasonable suspicion that the perpetrator continues to have access to children, reporting might be necessary despite the historical nature of the disclosure.

For example, if a 30-year-old client discloses that his uncle abused him when he was 8 years old, and that uncle now works at an elementary school, the counselor might need to report this information to protect current potential victims if the client presented a concern for those minors based on their experiences, and that is, if the counselor has reasonable suspicion. The counselor could document their decision-making process: *"Client disclosed historical abuse by uncle who currently works with children. Based on specific details provided and perpetrator's current position, I determined there is reasonable suspicion of risk to current minors."* It has been understood that the clients information (their abuse) is not being reported necessarily, but the concern to the minors at the school would be reported.

Out-of-state incidents create another layer of complexity. When a California-based counselor learns about abuse that occurred in another state, they might need to navigate multiple reporting systems. If a client discloses abuse that happened in Nevada, for example, the California-licensed counselor could report to California child protective services, who might then coordinate with Nevada authorities. Alternatively, the counselor might contact Nevada's child protective services directly. California Penal Code 11165.9 specifically identifies the agencies that a mandated report can submit such reports.

NAVIGATING DEPOSITIONS

Depositions represent a formal legal proceeding where your testimony is taken under oath outside of court, typically in an attorney's office or conference room. As a Licensed Professional Clinical Counselor (LPCC) or Associate Professional Clinical Counselor (APCC) in California, you may be called to participate in a deposition related to your clinical work with clients. Unlike court testimony, depositions occur without a judge present, but they carry the same legal weight and consequences for providing false information.

The deposition process begins when you receive a subpoena, which legally compels your participation. According to California Code of Civil Procedure Section 2025.010, a deposition is part of the discovery process, allowing attorneys to gather information before trial.

During a deposition, you'll be placed under oath by a court reporter who records everything said. Attorneys from all parties involved may question you, with the attorney who requested your deposition typically going first. Questions often focus on your professional relationship with the client, your observations, treatment provided, and documentation practices.

Depositions serve several legal purposes. They preserve testimony that might not be available at trial, allow attorneys to evaluate you as a potential witness, uncover additional information, and sometimes help facilitate settlements. For counselors, depositions frequently occur in cases involving child custody disputes, personal injury claims where emotional distress is alleged, or malpractice actions.

Next, review all relevant client records thoroughly. Create a chronological summary of your work with the client, including session dates, treatment goals, interventions used, and significant developments. Pay particular attention to documentation that might be discussed, such as:

- Initial assessment and diagnosis
- Treatment plans and updates
- Progress notes
- Risk assessments
- Consultation notes
- Correspondence with other providers
- Termination summary

The California Health and Safety Code Section 123110 grants patients the right to access their records, so assume the attorneys have reviewed everything you've documented. Your records should comply with the documentation standards outlined in California Code of Regulations, Title 16, Section 1815, which requires records to be consistent with the standard of care for the profession.

Consider consulting with your own attorney before the deposition, especially if you have concerns about confidentiality or privilege. The California Evidence Code Section 1014 establishes the psychotherapist-patient privilege, which protects confidential communications between a patient and therapist. However, there are exceptions to this privilege, such as when the patient has put their mental condition at issue in litigation (California Evidence Code Section 1016).

Notify your professional liability insurance carrier about the subpoena, as they may provide legal consultation or representation. Documentation requirements for a deposition include bringing any materials specifically requested in the subpoena. Make copies of these documents for your reference, though you'll typically need to provide the originals for inspection. Maintain a log of all communications related to the deposition, including dates of subpoena receipt, conversations with attorneys, and any legal advice received.

When answering questions during a deposition, remember these guidelines:

1. Tell the truth. You're under oath, and California Penal Code Section 118 defines perjury as a felony.
2. Listen carefully to each question before answering. Take time to understand exactly what's being asked.
3. Answer only the question asked. Don't volunteer additional information.
4. If you don't understand a question, ask for clarification.
5. If you don't know or don't remember, say so. Don't guess or speculate.
6. Be aware of questions that assume facts not in evidence or mischaracterize your previous testimony.
7. Maintain a professional demeanor throughout the proceeding.
8. Take breaks when needed to maintain your focus and composure.

In all cases and in all these situation, even with the recommended approach, you should speak with your attorney, as, I am not an attorney and cannot, will not, and have not given you legal advice!

PREPARING FOR COURT TESTIMONY AS FACT WITNESS

Testifying in court can be an intimidating experience for Professional Clinical Counselors in California. The unfamiliar environment, formal procedures, and high-stakes nature of legal proceedings create unique challenges that differ significantly from the therapeutic setting. Understanding how to prepare for court testimony helps counselors fulfill their professional obligations while maintaining ethical standards and client confidentiality as required by California law.

When preparing to testify, your professional appearance matters. Courts expect a level of formality that reflects respect for the legal process. This typically means wearing a suit or dress pants with a button-down shirt and in neutral colors like navy, gray, or black. Clothing should be clean, pressed, and fit properly. Jewelry and accessories should be minimal and not distracting.

Your demeanor in court is equally important. Maintain good posture, speak clearly and at a moderate pace, and address the judge as *"Your Honor"* and attorneys as *"Counsel"* or other title and honorific followed by their last name. Make eye contact with the person asking questions and with jurors when answering. Avoid defensive body language such as crossing arms or looking down frequently.

Before your court date, organize and review all relevant clinical records thoroughly. Begin by creating a chronological summary of your work with the client, including dates of sessions, major treatment goals, and significant events. Review your case notes, assessments, treatment plans, and any correspondence related to the case.

When reviewing records, pay particular attention to:
- Initial assessment and diagnosis
- Treatment goals and progress
- Risk assessments and safety planning
- Consultations with colleagues or supervisors
- Significant changes in treatment approach

- Termination planning or referrals

Create a separate file of the specific records requested in the subpoena or court order. Make copies of these documents for your reference during testimony, though be aware that the court might not allow you to refer to them without permission. Preparing to answer questions effectively requires understanding the different types of questions you might face. Direct examination questions from the attorney who called you to testify are typically open-ended and designed to elicit information supportive of their case. Cross-examination questions from opposing counsel are often closed-ended (yes/no) and might attempt to challenge your credibility or the reliability of your testimony.

For all questions, follow these guidelines:

- Listen carefully to the entire question before answering
- Answer only what was asked, without volunteering additional information
- If you don't understand a question, ask for clarification
- If you don't know an answer, simply state *"I don't know"* or *"I don't recall"*
- Avoid absolute statements like *"always"* or *"never"*
- Speak in plain language, avoiding clinical jargon when possible

Common court questions for counselors might include:

1. *"What is your professional background and qualifications?"*

Appropriate response: Briefly state your education, licensure status, years of experience, and relevant specialized training. For example: *"I hold a Master's degree in Counseling Psychology from California State University. I've been licensed as an LPCC in California since 2018, with specialized training in trauma treatment and cognitive-behavioral therapy."*

2. *"What was the nature of your professional relationship with the client?"*

Appropriate response: *"I provided outpatient counseling services to Mr. Smith from January 2022 to December 2022. We met weekly for individual therapy sessions focusing on depression and anxiety management."*

3. *"What was your diagnosis for this client?"*

Appropriate response: *"Based on my clinical assessment, which included a structured interview and standardized measures, I diagnosed Mr. Smith with Major Depressive Disorder, moderate, as defined in the DSM-5."*

4. *"Did the client ever express thoughts of harming themselves or others?"*

Appropriate response: *"In our session on March 15, 2022, Mr. Smith reported having fleeting thoughts about death but denied any specific plan or intent to harm himself. We completed a safety assessment, and I determined he was at low risk at that time."*

5. *"Is it possible your diagnosis was incorrect?"*

Appropriate response: *"Clinical diagnosis is based on the information available at the time. I used multiple assessment methods and followed standard diagnostic criteria. While no diagnosis is absolute, I believe my assessment was accurate based on the client's reported symptoms and my observations."*

Understanding the difference between serving as a fact witness versus an expert witness is crucial for counselors. As defined in California Evidence Code Sections 700-723, a fact witness testifies about direct observations and experiences with the client. Most counselors testifying about their own clients serve as fact witnesses. You might testify about what you observed, what the client reported, your diagnosis, and the treatment provided.

In contrast, an expert witness, as defined in California Evidence Code Section 801, offers opinions based on specialized knowledge and expertise, even without direct involvement with the individuals in the case.

If you're asked to serve as an expert witness, you might evaluate records, offer opinions about standard of care, or explain psychological concepts to the court. Expert witnesses typically require additional preparation and might need to submit detailed reports before testimony.

A preparation timeline for court appearances could look like this:

2-4 weeks before testimony:

- Receive and review subpoena or court order
- Consult with your own attorney if needed
- Begin organizing relevant records
- Notify your professional liability insurance carrier
- Block the court date in your calendar

1-2 weeks before testimony:

- Create a chronological summary of your work with the client
- Review all case notes and documentation
- Refresh your memory on relevant ethical guidelines and laws
- Practice answering potential questions
- Arrange coverage for your clients during your court appearance

1-3 days before testimony:

- Confirm the time and location of your appearance
- Prepare your professional attire
- Review your notes one final time
- Get adequate rest
- Plan your route to the courthouse, accounting for traffic and parking

Day of testimony:

- Arrive at least 30 minutes early
- Bring photo identification and any required documentation
- Bring a notepad and pen
- Turn off electronic devices before entering the courtroom

- Check in with the court clerk or bailiff upon arrival

A court appearance checklist might include:

Documentation:

☐ Subpoena or court order
☐ Photo identification
☐ Business card
☐ Chronological case summary (for personal reference)
☐ Copies of records specified in the subpoena (if permitted)
☐ Contact information for attorneys involved

Professional preparation:

☐ Professional attire selected and prepared
☐ Knowledge of courthouse location, parking, and security procedures
☐ Understanding of your role (fact witness vs. expert witness)
☐ Review of relevant laws and ethical guidelines
☐ Practice of potential testimony

Self-care:

☐ Adequate sleep the night before
☐ Meals planned around court schedule
☐ Water bottle (to be consumed outside the courtroom)
☐ Plan for managing anxiety (deep breathing, etc.)
☐ Support person to debrief with after testimony (while maintaining confidentiality)

Remember that while testifying, you represent not only yourself but the counseling profession. Your professional conduct in court upholds the integrity of the field and contributes to the court's understanding of mental health issues. Thoughtful preparation for testimony helps ensure compliance with legal expectations and supports ethical practice throughout the court process.

EXPERT WITNESS GUIDELINES

Professional Clinical Counselors in California may be called upon to serve as expert witnesses in legal proceedings. This role differs significantly from providing therapy and requires specific knowledge, preparation, and ethical awareness to navigate effectively.

The role of an expert witness is to provide specialized knowledge that helps the court understand complex psychological or behavioral issues relevant to a case. According to California Evidence Code Section 720, *"a person is qualified to testify as an expert if he has special knowledge, skill, experience, training, or education sufficient to qualify him as an expert on the subject to which his testimony relates"*. For PCCs, this expertise typically relates to mental health conditions, treatment approaches, or behavioral patterns.

Expert witnesses have several key responsibilities. First, they must provide objective, unbiased opinions based on their professional knowledge rather than personal beliefs. The California Business and Professions Code Section 4999.90(d) prohibits *"gross negligence or incompetence in the performance of professional services,"* which includes providing expert testimony. Second, they must limit their testimony to areas within their scope of practice and competence, as defined in Business and Professions Code Section 4999.20. Third, they must communicate complex psychological concepts in clear, accessible language for the court.

Under California Government Code Section 68093, fact witnesses may receive compensation for their time and travel when subpoenaed to testify. In contrast, expert witnesses typically arrange a separate fee agreement with the attorney or party requesting their opinion. Counselors should clarify their role in advance, whether fact or expert, and communicate fee expectations before agreeing to testify.

A previously mentioned, a fundamental distinction exists between fact witnesses and expert witnesses. Fact witnesses testify about direct observations or experiences related to a case, such as a counselor describing a client's statements during therapy. In contrast, expert witnesses offer professional opinions and interpretations based on their specialized knowledge, even without direct involvement with the individuals in question. California Evidence Code Section 801 specifies that expert testimony must be:

1. Based on matter *"perceived by or personally known to the witness or made known to the witness at or before the hearing"*
2. Of a type that reasonably may be relied upon by an expert in forming an opinion on the subject
3. Helpful to the trier of fact (judge or jury)

Preparation for serving as an expert witness begins well before the court date. PCCs should thoroughly review all relevant materials, which might include medical records, psychological evaluations, deposition transcripts, and other case documents. They should also research current literature related to the specific issues in the case to ensure their opinions reflect up-to-date professional knowledge.

Documentation is particularly important. Counselors should keep detailed notes about their review process, including:

- Materials reviewed and when
- Key findings from each document
- Scientific literature consulted
- Process of forming opinions
- Alternative explanations considered

These notes not only help organize thoughts but also demonstrate thoroughness if the expert's methodology is questioned during cross-examination. When crafting expert witness statements, clarity and precision are essential. Effective expert testimony avoids technical jargon when possible and explains necessary technical terms. For example, rather than stating *"The subject exhibits symptomatology consistent with comorbid affective and anxiety spectrum disorders,"* a clearer statement would be: *"Based on my review of the records, Mr. Smith shows symptoms of both depression and anxiety disorders, which often occur together and can complicate treatment."*

Expert witnesses should also clearly distinguish between facts, professional consensus, and personal opinion. For instance:

- **Fact**: *"The treatment records indicate the client attended 12 therapy sessions between January and April 2024."*
- **Professional consensus:** *"Cognitive-behavioral therapy is widely recognized as an effective treatment for anxiety disorders according to multiple clinical guidelines."*
- **Personal opinion:** *"In my professional judgment, based on the information reviewed, the treatment approach used in this case did not adequately address the client's trauma history."*

Common challenges for counselors serving as expert witnesses include maintaining impartiality, handling aggressive cross-examination, and communicating effectively about complex psychological concepts. Cross-examination may attempt to portray the expert as biased or inconsistent. Preparation for difficult questions is essential, as is maintaining a calm, professional demeanor even when challenged.

Another challenge involves pressure to offer opinions beyond one's expertise. If asked questions outside their area of expertise, counselors could respond: *"That question relates to neuropsychological assessment, which is outside my scope of practice as an LPCC under California law. I would defer to a qualified neuropsychologist on that issue."*

Best practices for maintaining professional credibility while serving as an expert witness include:

1. Thorough preparation: Review all relevant materials multiple times and organize key points systematically.
2. Honesty about limitations: Acknowledge when you don't know something or when a question exceeds your expertise.
3. Consistent testimony: Ensure your opinions remain consistent throughout direct examination, cross-examination, and any written reports.

4. Clear communication: Use plain language whenever possible and provide concrete examples to illustrate abstract concepts.
5. Professional appearance and demeanor: Dress professionally and maintain a calm, respectful tone even during challenging questioning.
6. Balanced perspective: Consider and acknowledge alternative viewpoints or explanations, which demonstrates objectivity.
7. Current knowledge: Stay updated on research and best practices in your specialty area, as outdated information can undermine credibility.
8. Careful documentation: Maintain detailed records of your review process, opinion formation, and the basis for your conclusions.
9. Ethical boundaries: Decline cases that present conflicts of interest or require testimony beyond your expertise.
10. Consultation: When appropriate, consult with colleagues or legal counsel about complex ethical or professional issues.

Subject Index

Boundary violations 217–221

California Code of Regulations, Title 16 91, 155, 158, 161, 184, 187

Case law 146–148

Case notes 165–167

Child abuse reporting 102–115

Client confidentiality 83–86, 143–147

Client rights 93–95

Consultation (peer/professional) 161–163

Credential evaluation 6–8

Cultural competence 244–246

Danger to self 151–154

Documentation 165–169

Dual relationships 221–223

Duty to protect 146–150

Duty to warn 146–150

Emancipated minors 256

Health and Safety Code §123110 167–168

Health and Safety Code §123130 165–166

HIPAA 183–187

Informed consent 65–69

Intake 46–47

Law and ethics exam 13–15

Legal obligations 101–102

Malpractice 101, 152

Mandated reporting 102–115

Minor clients 98–100

Minor consent 98–100

Negligence 101, 108

Peer consultation 161–163

Practicum 95

Privilege (psychotherapist-patient) 133–136

Professional boundaries 220–221

Progress notes 165–167

Psychological testing 39–43

Psychotherapy notes 165–167

Record keeping 165–168

Referrals 43–44, 132, 134

Scope of competence 44–45

Scope of practice 35, 38–42

Standard of care 101–102

Subpoena 287–289

Supervision 84–85, 160–161

Tarasoff 146–147

Telehealth 266–272

Telehealth (informed consent) 267–268

Therapeutic relationship 60, 68

Treatment planning 44–46

Violations and discipline (BBS) 91, 108–110

Laws, Codes & Regulations References

Business and Professions Code
Business and Professions Code §11166
Business and Professions Code §2290.5
Business and Professions Code §2908
Business and Professions Code §4990.20
Business and Professions Code §4999
Business and Professions Code §4999.12
Business and Professions Code §4999.20
Business and Professions Code §4999.33
Business and Professions Code §4999.40
Business and Professions Code §4999.46
Business and Professions Code §4999.61
Business and Professions Code §4999.74
Business and Professions Code §4999.75
Business and Professions Code §4999.76
Business and Professions Code §4999.90
California Civil Code
Civil Code §43.92
Civil Code §56
Civil Code §56.10
Civil Code §56.11
Civil Code §1798.81.5
California Code of Regulations
California Code of Regulations Title 16, Section 1803
California Code of Regulations Title 16, Section 1815
California Code of Regulations Title 16, Section 1815.5
California Code of Regulations Title 16, Section 1821
California Code of Regulations Title 16, Section 1845
California Code of Regulations Title 16, Section 1881
California Evidence Code
Evidence Code §1015
California Health and Safety Code
Health and Safety Code §123100
Health and Safety Code §123110
Health and Safety Code §123130
Health and Safety Code §§123100–123149.5
California Penal Code
Penal Code §11165
Penal Code §11165.9
Penal Code §11166
Penal Code §11166.05
Penal Code §11167
Penal Code §632.7
Welfare and Institutions Code
Welfare and Institutions Code §5008
Welfare and Institutions Code §5150
Welfare and Institutions Code §5328
Welfare and Institutions Code §5585
Welfare and Institutions Code §15610
Welfare and Institutions Code §15630
Welfare and Institutions Code §15633
Welfare and Institutions Code §15634
Welfare and Institutions Code §§15600–15

www.ingramcontent.com/pod-product-compliance
Lightning Source LLC
Chambersburg PA
CBHW060451030426
42337CB00015B/1553